NEW

CAREERS

FOR

THE

POOR

NEW

CAREERS

FOR

THE

POOR

The Nonprofessional in Human Service

ARTHUR PEARL and FRANK RIESSMAN

THE FREE PRESS, NEW YORK

COLLIER-MACMILLAN LIMITED, LONDON

For the One Fifth

PREFACE

In a very real way, the use of indigenous nonprofessionals in staff positions is forced by the dearth of trained professionals. At the same time, however, the use of such persons grows out of concern for a tendency of professionals to "flee from the client," and for the difficulty of communication between persons of different backgrounds and outlooks. It is HARYOU's belief that the use of persons only "one step removed" from the client will improve the giving of service as well as provide useful and meaningful employment for Harlem's residents.*

THIS STATEMENT, taken from the HARYOU proposal, forms the basic thesis of this book. Hiring the poor to serve the poor, we argue, is a fundamental approach to poverty in an automated age. (Human service jobs are the least likely to be automated out of existence.) At the same time that it provides vastly improved service for those in need, this approach can also reduce the manpower crisis in the health, education, and welfare fields where there is a great and growing need for personnel despite widespread unemployment in the society as a whole.

The current trend in most of the human service areas, such as social work and psychiatry, is for an increasing ratio of time to be spent on consultation, supervision, teaching, and a decreasing proportion of time in direct service. Thus, there is considerable need for service-orientated people and we believe that the indigenous low-income nonprofessional

---

* Harlem Youth Opportunities Unlimited, Inc., *Youth in the Ghetto: A Study of the CONSEQUENCES OF Powerlessness and a Blueprint for Change.* New York, 1964, p. 607.

can fill this important vacuum. In this sense, the term "non-professional" is limited because it does not specify the nature of the tasks to be performed; the usefulness of the term, however, lies in calling attention to certain distinctions between a professional orientation and the performance of various tasks by people whose training is less inclusive than that of professionals, but who may have specific contributions to make in the performance of tasks related to the helping professions. This book is principally concerned with one type of nonprofessional, namely the indigenous nonprofessional working in economically disadvantaged communities.

The first part of the book critically evaluates various approaches directed toward overcoming poverty and attempts to provide a feasible alternative through a far-ranging development of new careers for the poor based on the creation of large numbers of nonprofessional positions in the human service areas. The particular importance of these new positions in the field of education is stressed and a specific proposal is outlined utilizing education as a model.

Chapters 5–7 are concerned with the employment of nonprofessionals in the mental health, research, and welfare spheres, and some illustrations of their functioning in these fields are provided. The reasons for their apparent effectiveness are discussed.

Chapter 8 is devoted to questions related to the training of the nonprofessional. Chapters 9–11 are a consideration of the various issues involved in utilizing this new type of personnel and the allies who are likely to support the new career movement. It is suggested that a strategy for new careers should include the civil rights forces, the "War on Poverty" groups, and the professionals.

The term 'Community Action Program' means a program. . . . which is developed, conducted, and administered with the maximum feasible participation of residents of the areas and members of the (low income) groups.

This important statement embodied in Title II, Section A, of the Economic Opportunity Act of 1964 provides a tremendous opening for the widespread employment of the poor themselves in programs for the poor. The implementation of this proposal forms the basis of this book.

ACKNOWLEDGEMENTS

WE SHOULD LIKE to acknowledge, in particular, the editorial assistance of Margaret Pearl. The following have contributed in many different ways to the formulations found in this book:

Martin Acker	David Hunter
Richard Boone	Raymond Jacobson
Lee Bounds	William Klein
Eli Bower	Sol Levine
George Brager	Raymond Lowe
Harry Bredemeier	Milton Luger
Edgar Cahn	Beryce Mac Lennan
Carolyn Chandler	S. M. Miller
Martin Deutsch	Harris Peck
Mary Dowery	Francis Purcell
Leonard Duhl	Robert Reiff
Jack Ewalt	Catherine Riessman
Jacob Fishman	Rachel Robinson
Hyman Frankel	Mel Roman
Marcia Freedman	Clarence Sherwood
Herbert Gans	Aaron Schmais
Emanuel Geltman	Harry Specht
Emanuel Hallowitz	Herman Stein
Norman Hill	Freeda Taran

The typing assistance of Helen McCarthy and Jean Rogers is gratefully acknowledged.

CONTENTS

CHAPTER *1*

POVERTY
AND NEW CAREERS
FOR NONPROFESSIONALS

THIS BOOK deals with a current and unforgiveable shame of the United States of America, the name of which is poverty. For too many years widespread and pervasive poverty has existed in this country and the public has been either unaware or unconcerned about the problem. Today there is awareness and concern, frenzied activity and legislation, demonstration programs, and volunteers in the field—all functioning with but one stated ambition—to help the poor. The concern is laudable although the activity might not be.

There should be no confusion on one point. *Poverty will not be easy to eradicate.* Poverty is not a superficial blemish on an otherwise healthy structure. It is not a passing phase of a society in flux. The causes of poverty are deep-seated. Short term stop-gap measures will not bring about a permanent solution to the problem. The need to reorganize and revitalize many of the structures and institutions central to society is the alternative to relegating large numbers of citizens to a spectator class—a permanent, stable "nonworking" class, whose children and grandchildren will also be unable to perform meaningful functions in our society. The prospect of many millions of Americans in such a nonproductive situation is not a science-fiction terror. The danger is real and upon us.

This presentation will include a description of the problem, an analysis of its causes and effects, an evaluation of suggested remedies, and a proposal for redress of the condition.

The complex of goals of the new career proposal includes the following:

1. A sufficient number of jobs for all persons without work.

2. The jobs to be so defined and distributed that placements exist for the unskilled and uneducated.

3. The jobs to be permanent and provide opportunity for life-long careers.

4. An opportunity for the motivated and talented poor to advance from low-skill entry jobs to any station available to the more favored members of society.

5. The work to contribute to the well-being of society.

To devise a program which will provide, in sufficient numbers, socially useful, compensated positions and which will also furnish equal chances for upward mobility, is no small task. If the poor and the currently unemployable are going to be brought into productive society there must be some determination of the capabilities of this group. What can the poor do? How can useful functions be developed that will meet the limitations of the population? What must be done to educate the uneducated in the labor force? What must be done to prevent future uneducated generations from developing? What responsibilities for providing the necessary jobs should be delegated to private industry? And, what is the public sector's responsibility? These are the basic questions confronting us.

It must be abundantly clear that in the solution of poverty every aspect of American life will undergo change. Organizational structures and institutions which have come to be accepted as basic and immutable must be transformed. Education in particular must be reappraised and adjustments must be made at every level. However, as will be stressed here, the modifications which take place must be keyed to the needs of the society. No good can come from a panic which demands change only for change's sake.

The methods of securing and changing employment in this country must also be overhauled. There is too much slippage between the referral office and the job. Too much of the job-securing mechanism concern is in satisfying the short-term needs of the employer. There is no articulated process for the job-seeker to obtain security. Too much of the risk in job preparation is absorbed by those least able to absorb risk—the poor. Civil service merit systems based primarily on an ability to perform written examinations may need to be updated to allow all persons, regardless of background, a more equal chance to obtain career placements.

The roles played by highly-skilled technicians and professionals need to be reviewed. Many functions currently performed exclusively by professionals must be delegated to persons with limited education, experience, and skill. Society insists that training take place prior to job placement. Such a system made sense (although it reinforced inequality) when only a small percentage of the population was engaged in highly skilled occupations, while most of the work force required little formal training. This condition no longer exists. Most of the needs of society can be satisfied only by the highly-skilled and the well-trained. In an era of rapid technological development even the skills of the professional rapidly become obsolete. Training cannot be considered a prerequisite for employment. While this is often understood for some functions it is not yet appreciated as a general proposition. There can be no end to poverty unless it is fully appreciated that, for the most part, training for the poor must take place *after* employment is secured. This may not be necessary in the future, when all of the population, rich and poor alike, are well-educated. But today, and certainly for the next decade, at least, many millions of persons will be seeking employment who have not had adequate education. This group, not only because of its plight, but also because it contains the parents of future generations, is the norm-setter. The poor job-seeker of the 1960's will develop and model the value systems, loyalties, and aspirations of those who are to benefit from new approaches to education. They must be permitted to play a useful, meaningful role in today's world. There can be no sacrifice of a population of today under the mantle of concern for tomorrow. Inability to deal with the poor of today will be transmitted to the poor of tomorrow.

Ours has been, and still is, a vigorous society. Growth has been rapid, and in the exciting, untrammeled course of that growth, much of the institutional structure has grown up unplanned. This lack of planning is often given accolades equal to those awarded the accomplishments. But the course of growth has necessitated interdependence and reliance upon government-sponsored activity. There is no denying the importance of the public sector, nor is there a path back from it. Education, welfare, recreation, and corrections are public responsibilities. A consequence of unimpeded and unplanned growth is lack of continuity and linkage between institutions, organizations, and agencies. This deficiency in connection is most strongly felt by the poor since they lack resources of their own. There is often no passageway for the poor from education to employment, from institutional commitment to living in free society, from economic calamity back to a sound economic footing. With limited resources, skill, and flexibility, the poor have little chance to recover from serious injury or prolonged illness. If there is to be a path from poverty, not only must there be change within structures, but there also must be integration between structures.

Changes of the nature outlined above can only come about when there is public consensus for their necessity. Therefore, many entrenched belief systems must be reconsidered and many myths exposed, with more adequate concepts offered in exchange.

One such fabrication places full responsibility on the poor. The details may vary, but there is a common theme; the poor are poor because of innate inferiority, a lack of desire—or the romantic variation—because they want to live the good, simple life. All of these are status-quo positions, implying that there is no cause for alarm and that the situation truly requires no change.

A variation of the theme is that the poor become poorer because they react violently, impulsively, and senselessly against middle-class values; or, conversely, the poor remain poor because the middle class can only maintain relative superiority by denying the poor equal access to opportunities.

This book will espouse an emphatic rejection of the desirability or inevitability of wholesale poverty. It is our thesis that no segment of our society stands to gain over the long run from the existence of a nonproductive class.

The poverty issue presents the United States with a totally new crisis, one that defies previously used solutions. It is a chronic crisis which does not lend itself to any partisan political position and would only worsen if atavistic procedures were employed as remedial measures. The crisis, on one hand involves the permanent poor, and on the other, involves an inability to provide, in sufficient numbers, persons to fill the most needed technological and professional roles. In over-simplified terms, there exist simultaneously large numbers of people without jobs and a great many jobs without people.

It is difficult to estimate accurately the number of jobs currently unfilled. There is a tendency for all operations to "make-do" with what is available. Administrators are often given credit for a "sound fiscal" operation when savings accrue from unfilled budgeted positions. However, there can be no doubt that were there thousands more fully accredited teachers, social workers, librarians, engineers, nurses, and doctors, the economy would absorb them.

The jobs which are needed are primarily in the public sector or are sustained by public financing. One reason that it is difficult to estimate job vacancies precisely is that definition of need is arbitrary. The public, through elected representatives, makes this determination. There are no established efficiency standards or guidelines to be applied to operations which are designed to provide helping services. Nor can there be any.

The value of an educated child, for example, cannot be reduced to a simple accounting of income obtained from tax investments. Adequate health, education, welfare, and recreation are available only to citizens of an affluent society. All societies need as much of these services as can be afforded.

The central thesis of this book is that in an affluent automated society the number of persons needed to perform such tasks equals the number of persons for whom there are no other jobs.[1]

The persons without jobs are not difficult to identify. They are the unskilled, the uneducated. In disproportionate numbers they are young; they are Negro. They are likely to remain poor and so are their children. There is almost nothing that they can do about it. Lack of control over destiny is a unique feature of today's poverty. The poor of the past, because of differences in structure and organization of society, had a much better chance to change status than do the poor of today. (The Negro poor of the past—the slave— was an exception. He was denied opportunity to improve himself and the consequences of enforced poverty have an important bearing on the existing scene. In subsequent chapters, the particular problems of the Negro poor are discussed in detail).

The distinguishing feature of the modern economic scene is that unskilled labor is ceasing to be a necessary component of functioning society. Traditionally, the poor have possessed one marketable commodity—unskilled labor. By means of their labor the poor could gain a toehold on the economic ladder, and many of the children of these poor could advance to higher stations through education or entrepreneurial enterprise. Technological advancement was on the side of the poor (in the long run, at least). Technological advance stimulated the economy and provided work opportunity. The history of the United States can almost be charted by immigration of impoverished people linked to specific technological changes.

Railroading was but one technological development of the 19th century, which, on a mass scale provided entrance to viable society for the poor immigrant. Many members of the establishment proudly refer to antecedents who, as poor immigrants, worked the mines, laid the track, or manned the foundries and mills. It was this profound influence of technological advance on the economy that encouraged immigration. If there had been nothing for the unskilled immigrant to do, the "dream" of America, the open society would not have been sustained. The promise of America continued because it was based on a hard core of truth.

The automotive industry further stimulated the economy and provided continued opportunity for the unskilled laborer. Technological advances in the 20's and 30's led to the assembly line which was specifically designed for the unskilled laborer. Complexity and variability of job performance was reduced to an absolute minimum. The essential feature of the assembly line was the reduction of job complexity to allow for interchangeability of workers regardless of skill. In a variety of settings increased affluence was accomplished at the expense of the skilled craftsman.

Technological advance in shoemaking resulted in modern assembly line production, new jobs for the unskilled, and the elimination of the highly-skilled craftsman. Job evolution, however, has come full circle. The unskilled workers' functions, to a large extent created by the machine, are now being replaced by the machine.

Automation must be recognized for what it is, a permanent fixture in American life which will enable private industry to produce efficiently, increase the gross national product, *and*—eliminate jobs. John I. Synder, President and Chairman of U.S. Industries, Inc., estimates that two million jobs are eradicated each year by automation.[2]

A magnificent year for the general economy was 1963. There was a healthy increase in gross national product; a new high was set for median income. In this same year, however, rising unemployment widened an even greater economic gap between the poor and nonpoor, and the Negro and non-Negro. Between 1957 and 1962, 500,000 fewer workers produced significantly more goods and one million jobs were eliminated in agriculture, although farm surpluses continued to accumulate.[3]

The future augers for more of the same; the unskilled worker is to be replaced by automated devices and the labor force augmented by the trained technicians. It is projected that approximately the same number of persons will be employed as laborers in 1975 as was employed in 1960—a period in which it is expected that 20 million more workers will enter the labor market. There will be in excess of a million and a half fewer workers in agricultural pursuits in 1975 than there were in 1960. These workers and their families will steadily flow to urban centers where they will lack resources, skills, and education—possessing only the qualities necessary to become part of the permanent poor.

To expect the private sector to absorb these additional workers while being confronted with decreasing need of currently employed, meagerly skilled workers is unrealistic.

Industry can engage in extensive job analyses and by re-definition create a considerable number of jobs which do not require extensive training or experience and industry should be encouraged along these lines by government subsidy. However, the greatest potential for new careers is in the public sector.

To offset the relative loss of employment in the private sector, there has been rapid growth in the public domain:

> Total government civilian employment rose from 5.5 million in 1947 to 9.2 million in 1962. . . . The addition of 3.7 million public employees accounted for one-third of the total increase in nonagricultural employment in the post war years.[4]

The bulk of the growth has been in education and health. In these areas the number of persons presently employed exceed by over 60 per cent the number employed 10 years ago.[5]

A GLANCE INTO THE FUTURE

The areas of health, education, and other services intended to help or uplift persons offer the greatest promise for employment opportunities in the future. Through extrapolation of populations, it is projected that between the years 1960 and 1975 there will be a sixty-five per cent increase in professional, technical, or kindred worker occupations.[6] During this interval the elementary school population will increase by fifteen per cent. There will be in excess of fifty per cent more youth of secondary school age, and at least a seventy per cent increase in youth of college-attending age.[7]

The increase in numbers of persons of school age cannot by itself be used as the sole gauge for estimating teacher need. Not only will students increase in number, but there will be a tendency for students to stay in school longer. Even without campaigns and public concern, the drop-out rate in this country has been declining steadily. Many more youth complete high-school now than was the case thirty years ago. A constantly increasing proportion of high school graduates go on to college. A higher percentage of those who enter college achieve graduation, and a higher percentage of those who complete college go on to attain higher degrees.

Between 1960 and 1970, 7.5 million youth will terminate an educational process without attaining a high school education, only if no remedial steps are instituted in this decade.[8] If youth could be attracted to education, and, most importantly, if education could be realistically perceived by youth to have value, many more students would be retained in high school than is currently estimated. The increased enrollment resulting from more effective programming would further increase demand for teaching personnel. Most projections of demand for teachers not only rely on a substantial loss of youth before high school graduation, but also assume that the teacher-pupil ratio will remain fairly constant.

The estimated pupil-teacher ratio for elementary, secondary, public and private schools combined for 1960 was 24.7 to 1. This rate is projected to decline to 24.3 to 1 by the middle of the decade and then remain stationary.[9]

Neither the assumed drop-out rate nor the assumed class size can be accepted without challenge. While no recommendation is made here that persons should be hired as teachers because our society can find nothing else for them to do, it is strongly urged that many more persons could play productive roles in the educational systems of the country than are currently being utilized. It is lamentable that research findings which give a factual base for the determination of optimal (or even tolerable) loads are almost totally lacking. To accurately appraise the maximum educational return for tax dollar investment it would be necessary to experimentally manipulate and compare outcomes in a variety of situations and contexts. Assessment would have to be made for teachers with differing skills and attributes, for youth of different ages, and for youth from diverse social backgrounds in schools and classrooms with different intellectual and emotional climates. There would have to be evaluation of the impact that the kind and level of course content had upon optimal classroom population, and also the influence of different techniques used to present material. In the absence of definite findings, any assumption that pupil-teacher ratio is relatively fixed is unnecessary and unwise.

The proposal to substantially increase the numbers of persons with teaching responsibilities carries with it a call for rigorous evaluation. If such an investment should not result in significantly improved educational outcomes for any substantial segment of the population, and if careful study of the process of utilization of "new careers" in teaching does not reveal faulty execution, then deployment of available manpower in such channels should be discontinued in favor of investments where "pay-off" could be demonstrated.

Central to this presentation is a very simple thesis—for the present and the foreseeable future our society can and should afford many improvements and additions to the services offered its citizens. As long as there are people without work and work which, most agree, should be done, then the role of a rational society is to provide the machinery and the procedures which make possible a connection between worker resource and manpower requirements. Improving education is one generally recognized need. The symptoms are clear. High incidence of school failure, premature school leaving, inability to generalize obtained education to work or life experience, are all obvious indices that what we possess is not the best of all education worlds. As will be elaborated later, advocating the addition of indigenous low-income people to the education system has both experimental and

theoretical justification. Such a proposal is intended to produce a better educational system as well as affording employment to millions of persons.

Education is not the only area where expansion of work
opportunities can be anticipated. In the next decade it is expected that more managers, officials, proprietors, clerks,
sales persons, craftsmen, foremen, and service workers will be
needed. Only for the unskilled laborer in the city or on the
farm are the prospects poor for increased employment opportunity.[10] Those developing job opportunities which do not
require substantial change in job definition are treated but
lightly in this book. There have been procedures established
which allow for the entrance of the disadvantaged into these
available job openings. The point being emphasized, however, is that the available opportunities are too limited.
There are not enough jobs being developed to accommodate
the numbers who need work. There is no assurance that the
work is permanent, and there is often no path to a better
station from the entry job.

Another area where potential for employment is great is
in the broad field of health services. Almost every aspect of
health service could be enlarged and improved. One segment
of the population whose health needs are likely to require
special attention are the elderly.

Between 1960 and 1975 the population over the age of
sixty-five will increase by almost one–third. There will not
only be more persons of retirement age, but they will live
longer, and they will be less reluctant to call for health
services. The number of persons needed, in a variety of roles,
to attend to the problems of the aging, even under current
definition, are already beyond the call of available resources.
With increased demands for service, the solution can come
only from increasing the numbers of persons involved in
health work. Therefore, in this field, as in education, there is
perceived to be a major opportunity for career development.

THE NEW CAREER CONCEPT

The new career concept has as a point of departure the creation of jobs normally allotted to highly-trained professionals or technicians, but which could be performed by the unskilled, inexperienced, and relatively untrained worker; or, the development of activities not currently performed by anyone, but for which there is a readily acknowledged need and which can also be satisfactorily accomplished by the unskilled worker.

Detailed descriptions of both reconstituted job endeavors and creation of new activities are to be found in later chapters. In both instances there is a common need for careful scrutiny of the job function for the purpose of defining duties which are structured at the level of the jobless.

Providing jobs which the poor can perform is only a first step along the path to a new career. The job must be made permanent and must be incorporated into the matrix of the industry or agency. If the position, for example, is in government, there must be legitimation of the activity by civil service certification and incorporation of the function into the agency table of organization. In the private sector, created positions must, by similar procedures, become securely fused into the organic operation.

Persons filling entry positions must have latitude for limited advancement without being required to undergo extensive additional training. This type of opportunity is generally available to governmental and private agency personnel assigned to clerical or non-professional services. Advancement within the "same line" provides an inducement to "life career" for the least capable and gifted. For the many who aspire to more, and are capable of it, such a narrow range of possible achievement would hardly suffice.

The chance for truly substantial advancement in job station is crucial to the new career concept. If significant rise to higher stations is to be a genuine possibility for the entering unskilled worker, then jobs which will require knowledge, experience and skill, and present more challenge than the entry positions, must be created. These jobs would have to be intermediate between the unskilled beginning duty and the terminal professional status. To be eligible for an intermediate position a worker would be required to perform notably at the less advanced position and participate in a training program offered partially on the job and partially in a sequence of college courses (or receive training which could be allowed college credit).

Establishing a continuum ranging from nonskilled entry positions, extending through intermediate sub-professional functions, and terminating in full professional status, changes the nature of the upward mobility in our society. No longer would professional status be attained *only* by first completing between five and eight years of college. The requiring of this training *prior* to entrance into a field of endeavor effectively eliminates almost all of the poor from eligibility. A sequence beginning with the unskilled aide and proceeding through an assistant (two years of college equivalence plus experience); an associate (four years of college equivalence plus experience); and terminating in an accreditation as professional is manageable and opens areas to which the poor can now hardly hope to aspire.

If such a program were accepted in the field of medicine, it would be possible for a person to enter the field as a hospital aide (menial worker, only); graduate to a medical assistant (engage in slightly more responsible work); move upward to a medical associate (engage in a more demanding relationship with patients under direct supervision of doctor); continue up a sequence of increasing challenge and responsibility until ultimately the status of medical doctor was reached.

The unique quality of the new career proposal might be best emphasized by consideration of the present inability of a registered nurse to obtain credit for training and skill toward becoming a medical doctor. It is proposed that ultimately such a course would be available. The nurse-to-doctor sequence, while probably more fraught with difficulty than most, would indicate the nature of resistance to be encountered and overcome before the new career concept can become a reality.

Probably only a small percentage of the persons who would enter a new career sequence as nonskilled aides would emerge as full-fledged professionals. Each advance based on merit would constitute a screening process which only the most sensitive, motivated, and capable would ford, but while all might not achieve the highest rung, the *opportunity* for attainment of a higher station would be available to all.

It is not recommended that there be only this arduous and circuitous route to professional status. The traditional path to the M.D., the Ph.D., the education or social work degree would be always an available alternative. However, there would be advantages to the aspiring professional in the development of a sequence of "landings" designed for subprofessionals. At the present time, if a student fails to attain full professional status there is no defined role for him. A person might invest almost a decade in education, only to be informed that he is not to be allowed to become a professional. There is no designated function for the "almost" doctor, lawyer, teacher, social worker, or psychologist. If a sequence of positions had been established, the person unable to attain full status might be eligible for an intermediate position.

DEFINING THE ENTRY JOBS

For *full* implementation of the new career concept there must be large-scale study of the activities performed by professionals in the fields mentioned above (and others) to delineate specific duties and functions which the unskilled can perform. Such studies must define precisely the relative challenge, complexity, and time expended on each function. The number of jobs required at each level and the number of levels necessary for a complete sequence can be *initially* estimated from the results obtained from such a study. Continued study would be needed for revision of job needs and duties arising from changing situations and technological development.

Inauguration of the new career concept should not, however, await the conclusions of an extensive job study. There is need for immediate test of the concept by demonstration and experimentation in a diversity of settings, with a broad range of persons, and in the performance of a variety of tasks.

There is sufficient experience for initial experimentation. An educated reckoning of job activities which the unskilled can perform can be continually refined after experimentation. Research, while needed, cannot be an excuse for inactivity. It is only through activity that data can be obtained for use in evaluation and further development.

On the other hand, the exigencies of the moment cannot justify unthinking exuberance. *Any* activity is not necessarily good activity. The plight of the poor is tragic and action is needed, but the action which is needed is long-term commitment to an ultimate solution, not a transient concern with superficialities.

THE TROUBLE WITH CRASH PROGRAMS IS THAT
OFTEN THEY DO JUST THAT

Poverty seems so ridiculously out of place in an affluent society, and so readily susceptible to remediation that enthusiasm and concern alone appear sufficient to produce change. The answer to poverty may seem to be found in a single word—"money." This is too sanguine a view. If care is not taken, money designed to aid the poor can be channeled in many useless directions. In the haste to meet the emergency, jobs which might, with careful preparation, be tailored for the poor could be filled by those in less dire need—e.g., middleclass housewives, students, or retired persons—or they might become second jobs for persons already employed.[11] A strategy which might satisfy both short-term concern for the jobless and long range interest in ultimate solutions might combine both types of programs. Investment in short run or symptom solution programs would be reduced as long range programs, attacking the significant causes of poverty gain a foundation of knowledge and experience.

WILL THE BEST NEW CAREERIST PLEASE STAND UP

Selecting persons to enter new career sequences presents a formidable problem. The sequences are projected in areas of considerable sensitivity and persons will be requested to play significant roles in education, in the socialization of children, and in the care and treatment of the sick. These are not positions which can be filled in a cavalier fashion. However, it should be clearly appreciated that if traditional measures are used to screen prospective workers, those who most need employment will in all probability be excluded.

If applicants are to be denied opportunity for employment in new career sequences on the basis of measured intelligence or aptitude, or delinquency record, or lack of school attainment, then the current jobless will, in disproportionately large numbers, remain jobless. There is a compelling reason to reject screening procedures which are based on test scores or prior records. These indices may reflect only the effect of an impoverished existence and would therefore not predict capabilities in a new context. Alien and defeated, the poor have had little incentive to excel in conventional academic activity.

One of the objectives of experimental demonstration with

new career programs should be determination of attributes of persons best suited to perform new roles. In the absence of criteria which have been subjected to rigorous validation, the fewer the prejudgments of potential ability the better.

Selecting new career candidates without discrimination is not as reckless a procedure as it might appear at first blush. All candidates would be subjected to short-term intensive training which would constitute a preliminary screen. To be eligible for placement, trainees would have to demonstrate an ability to perform the job and give some evidence of motivation and personal stability. (A more extensive description of training is found in Chapter 8 of this book.)

The new career assignment itself provides the greatest protection against abuse. In his initial assignment the new careerist is in a position of minimal sensitivity and responsibility. He is closely supervised by highly-trained professionals. He can attain more responsibility only by demonstrating capability. He is to be judged not on past record or tenuously related tests, but on actual performance.

Despite precautions and protections, there will be some risk in permitting persons with dubious backgrounds to perform in new career positions but it must also be recognized that there is risk in denying such persons an opportunity to participate in the program. The most obvious consequence will be that the program will fail to come to grips with one of the prime reasons for its existence. The result would be perpetuation of dynastic dependence—a vicious phenomenon of welfare recipient begetting welfare recipient.

Denial of opportunity to play a meaningful role in society may not only result in passive noncontribution, but could also trigger off violent reactions among the alienated and rejected. One likely course of action of any group denied access to status, dignity, and self-esteem by activity within the system would be the development of codes and behaviors affording status and leadership and an acceptable self-image. The recent violent outbursts by groups of slum youth in many cities in the country, resulting in wanton destruction of property and injury to persons, seem to have come about precisely because of the frustration of enforced exclusion from functioning society.[12]

Not all the risks would, however, take the form of affronts to society. Harm might come from failure to realize the specific talents of those persons who are excluded from jobs without trial. It may be precisely those persons who have exhibited leadership capacity in delinquent gangs who possess attributes to make unique contributions in new career roles.

A profound change must be made to occur in programs designed for slum youth. Schools must be revitalized, rehabilitation programs tailored to the needs of the community, health services altered—all of which will require enthusiastic workers, workers who can inspire the residents, and can offer trust and support, thus serving as ego models. It may well be that the very person who today is most troublesome to society can tomorrow become its most valuable contributor.

NOTES

1. Impoverished nations with relatively few persons in helping services are not without need for these services. They are simply unable to afford them.

2. Snyder, John I., The Myths of Automation, *American Child*, 1964, Vol. 46, No. 1.

3. United States Labor Department, *Manpower Report of the President and a Report on Manpower, Requirements, Resources, Utilization and Training*, U.S. Government Printing Office, Wash., 25, D.C., 1963.

4. *Ibid.*, p. 16.

5. *Ibid.*, p. 16.

6. *Ibid.*, page 100.

7. Source: U.S. Department of Commerce, Bureau of the Census.

8. Schreiber, Daniel (ed.): *The School Dropout*, National Education Association, Washington, D.C., 1964, page 2.

9. Manpower Report of the President, op. cit., page 126.

10. *Ibid.*, page 100.

11. There is no attempt being made in this book to arrange for employment of the poor at the expense of more affluent groups. The point being stressed is that persons with means and education have job opportunities available to them; this simply is not the case for the uneducated poor.

12. Although varying in specific details and emphasis, many social scientists explain organized juvenile delinquency as the result of denial of equal access to the benefits of society. See, for example:

Richard A. Cloward and Lloyd E. Ohlin, *Opportunity and Delinquency: A Theory of Delinquent Gangs,* Glencoe, Ill., The Free Press, 1960.

Albert K. Cohen, *Delinquent Boys: The Culture of the Gang,* Glencoe, Ill., The Free Press, 1955.

Louis Yablonsky, *The Violent Gang,* New York, The Macmillan Co., 1962.

CHAPTER *2*

ALTERNATE STRATEGIES
FOR ERADICATION
OF POVERTY—A CRITIQUE

THE NEW CAREER PROPOSAL is a call for wholesale change. It is likely that every institution of our society would be affected. Education, employment practices and recruitment, welfare, administration of health services—all would be greatly influenced if the new career program were instituted. Such traumatic transition can only be justified if less drastic measures are inadequate.

The essence of poverty (from the vantage point of the advocates of new careers), is the scarcity of unskilled jobs. Seen from this perspective, antipoverty measures must begin with the creation of job opportunities for *those without jobs and for those who are not even in the labor market*. These opportunities exist now, and for the foreseeable future, primarily in areas currently restricted to affluent, well-educated applicants. In order to open the system to the poor, jobs must be redefined to enable the unskilled, inexperienced, and uneducated to be eligible for employment in these areas, and, once employed, machinery must be introduced so that advancement to higher-paid, more responsible jobs, is possible. Therefore, rather than employ, for example, more welfare workers with advanced degrees to administer aid to the poor, it is suggested that new jobs be defined in welfare administration which could be performed by the recipients of aid. Reduced to the simplicity of a slogan, new careers are a means to: *obtain service from the poor in the place of providing service to the poor.*

The solution to poverty has intrigued a great number of persons and a variety of programs have been proposed to reduce or eliminate poverty. To appraise the merit of these schemes, some standards for evaluation must be established. We suggest that such programs should provide positive answers to the following questions:

1. Does the program either directly provide jobs for the poor or is it reasonable to assume that jobs will be forthcoming if the program is adopted?

2. Do these jobs have some degree of permanence?

3. Is there opportunity for upward mobility? What range of advancement is conceivable?

4. Is implementation of the program feasible?

5. What period of time would be required before influence of the program could be felt, and is this the shortest time in which it is reasonable to expect resolution of the problem?

6. What are the long-range implications of the program? Is there danger that concern with immediate issues disregards possible negative future consequences?

How, then, do the profusion of poverty cures measure up against these standards?

THE OPTIMISTIC SOLUTION—
WHAT HELPS THE ECONOMY
HELPS POOR PEOPLE

There are a variety of programatic statements sharing the common theme that poverty needs no *special* attention. Some of these are well-formulated while others are merely a vague pronouncement of an ideology or hope. Poverty, as seen by persons holding the optimistic view, will disappear if it is merely left alone. There is a delightful appeal to parsimony in programs which promise resolution of social problems with a minimal expenditure of effort and money.

The essence of the economic stimulation position is eloquent in its simplicity. All that is truly necessary for the eradication of poverty is a continually growing economy. The economy can maintain growth if properly stimulated, and stimulation can be facilitated by tax reduction, interest manipulation, and, in extreme situations, by government subsidy.

Advocates of poverty cure through economic expansion see nothing particularly new in the current technological change. It is their opinion that machines will create, not eliminate, jobs. Pointing to a history of job growth through technological advance, champions of the healthy economy viewpoint perceive no threat to employment in automation. Their position reduces to a conviction that ours is a society which has flourished because of increasing per capita production, the benefits of increased production ultimately being passed on to all segments of the society. It is their opinion that jobs can be created primarily in the private sector and, further, that the heavy burden of government employment tends to inhibit private development.

If the position that general economic growth reduces poverty has validity, there should be correlation between economic health and reduction of joblessness. During the post-World War II years the economy has thrived, yet despite this robust development, unemployment has also grown. In 1947, the Gross National Product of the United States was 282.3 billion dollars (1954 prices). By 1963, GNP had increased to 493.0 billion dollars (1954 prices) or an average annual increase of over 12 billion dollars.[1] In the same interval *unemployment* increased from 2.4 million persons to 4.2 million persons, or an average of over 150,000 more jobless persons every year.[2] The years 1947 and 1963 were not unusual. The growth rate of our GNP has been fairly constant during this period, and economic growth has been particularly consistent during the past five years, expanding from 428.6 billion dollars in 1959 to the 1963 standard of 493.0 billion. While unemployment growth has not been consistent, varying considerably from year to year, there has been absolutely no indication at any time during this five-year period, that economic vigor alone could reduce unemployment.

Although economic health is a necessary precondition for easing poverty, when the optimistic solution is put to the test developed to assess antipoverty measures, it fails totally. There is no evidence that such a program will create jobs in sufficient numbers to remove the basic roots of poverty, and in the absence of jobs, consideration of upward mobility and feasibility of implementation is irrelevant.

The long range implication of a "prosperity is contagious" position should, however, be considered. Although cast in the light of sound fiscal policy, there is an undeclared false note in the economics. Failing to spend money to create jobs does not relieve a society of responsibility to its poor. Poverty, while expensive to overcome, is also expensive to maintain. Persons without jobs or hope of jobs are not merely going to quietly pass out of existence. Having no stake in the system, there can be little doubt that antisystem activity will be encouraged. At the very least there will be a continued drain in welfare and institutionalization of criminals. The costs of warehousing people are extensive. Building a single cell in a maximum security prison costs taxpayers $10,000, and sustaining one delinquent youngster in a California Youth Authority facility comes at the expense of $4,000 per year. For the same amount of money many productive jobs could be established.

There are other consequences of a program not specifically designed to uplift those caught up in a network of poverty, one of which is the lack of stimulation of GNP which occurs when a large proportion of the population produces nothing and consumes little.

Oscar Ornati, citing the results of his Twentieth Century Fund Study, neatly summarizes the potential of economic growth alone as a cure of poverty:

What is crucially different about our high-income economy is the fact that high rates of economic growth do not do away with poverty. Similarly it is by now clear that significant rates of economic growth can be achieved without proportionate increase in the employment of human beings. We also know that even greater than historical rates of expansion in employment does not necessarily mean decreases in poverty.[3]

There is a substantial issue too often ignored in programs in which the emphasis is upon economic growth: that even if jobs were created, it does not necessarily follow that those in greatest need would get the new positions. In fact, there is good reason to believe that new jobs will carry with them requirements and qualifications beyond the current capabilities of the poor.

The optimistic position is less a program designed to eradicate poverty than it is a declaration of faith. Unfortunately, the position lacks both theoretical foundation and factual support. The issue of poverty is too critical and the sufferings of too many people too real to give credence to programs consisting, at heart, of mere empty slogans, entirely devoid of substance.

THE PESSIMISTIC SOLUTION—
THE LEISURE DOLE

Opposed to the idea that a healthy economy is a positive guarantee against poverty is the thought that an automated society cannot provide jobs for all its citizens. There is, in the minds of some, an almost obsessional notion that modern technology is inherently a job destroyer, and that given this fact the only course is to provide a guarantee of income for those without marketable skills. Proponents of this position argue against

... the possibility of *ever* reaching full employment in the face of automation's increasing ability to replace human muscle and skills with machines.[4]

The guaranteed income *could* eliminate poverty by providing the poor with economic resources, but is such a step necessary?[5]

We are hardly a perfect society. Some persons need an education; others have unmet health needs. There are diseases whose cures are yet to be discovered. More recreation facilities need to be built and staffed. There are slums to be cleared and highways to be built. Natural resources need to be conserved and water and air must be purified. After these goals are accomplished in America, there are the other less fortunate nations. With this variety of national and international needs, it is premature to consider retiring the able to remunerated indolence.

The advocates of the 'Leisure Dole' do not seem to fully appreciate that the poor are often without jobs, not because there is no work, but because of arbitrary requirements, qualifications, and certification procedures which bar the poor from available and potential employment. There is a tendency to minimize the extent to which organization, structure, and operational restrictions contribute to the problem of poverty. Poverty results from such factors as bureaucratic intransigence, frantic defense of status by new professional groups, and a gross underestimation of the potentialities of the poor. Poverty, to a large extent, is the by-product of resistance to change and unwillingness to place reason above ritual

Poverty is more than a state of money. To be poor means, in addition, to be without material goods, to be denied a sense of worth. And, although a guarantee of income is preferable to the humiliation that a welfare recipient is forced to suffer, it does not allow the beneficiary to make a contribution to society.

There may come a time when recompensed leisure would be a defensible policy. But for the present the challenge is to provide work (for those who need work) which could be performed to the benefit of all society.

COUNSELING AS SOLUTION— OR POVERTY IS A STATE OF MIND

There is a recurrent view that somehow the poor would, if only they applied themselves better, be poor no longer. It is postulated that the poor, through lack of diligence and maladaptive life styles, squander job opportunities. The solution thus lies in counseling them to do better.

There are very few things which are crystal clear in the poverty picture, but the aspect of the problem which comes closest to being self-evident is that there are simply not enough jobs, as jobs are currently defined, for the poor. No amount of counseling will alter this situation. And, no amount of counseling will, given the current prerequisites for employment, create jobs for the poor.

There is no doubt that some of the poor are in need of counseling services. However, counseling low-income persons is no mean feat in itself. The poor are difficult clients for the middle-class practitioner. There is a clash of styles and values, and a difference in goals between the client and the counsellor. The techniques used by the counsellor are often inappropriate, sometimes, indeed unintelligible. The counsellor cannot fully understand or empathize with the client, nor can he control his prejudices or conceal his disapprobation of the clients' customs and mannerisms.[6]

If counseling is to be in any way an effective intervention with the poor, then there must be significant change in the process. Either the middle-class practitioner should be trained and sensitized to the problems of the poor, or some of the poor must be taught a modicum of counseling skills, or counseling could be a team activity employing the skills of sensitized middle-class professionals *and* especially trained low-income aides. Any increase in counseling service to the poor must create new jobs. If only middle-class professionals and subprofessionals are used, it is likely that the counseling activity will come to naught, but, if the poor are brought into the process, there is reason to expect a double dividend on the investment—one, a better counseling service and two, jobs for low-income persons now employed within the program.

Counseling can only be thought of as an adjunct to a poverty cure, but it can be an important adjunct if jobs for the poor are created in the process.

SPECIFIC JOB TRAINING AS SOLUTION

Programs with less ambitious claims than being a *cure* for poverty involve training unemployed persons for available job openings. Much of this endeavor has come under the auspices of the Manpower Development and Training Act of 1962. Under the provisions of this act many thousands of the jobless have been trained. The purpose of such programs is refreshingly clear, i.e., to provide qualified persons in those areas where there is demonstrable worker shortage. The aims of job training are extremely confined. There is no pronounced effort to redefine jobs. The programs attempt only to fill vacancies according to current definition. The number of such openings is limited, and, all too often, those most sorely in need do not qualify for training. One additional problem is that of placing the newly-trained personnel.

There should be no question that job training and short-term skill development are essential parts of an antipoverty campaign, but it must also be fully understood that training by itself is insufficient to eliminate poverty. As has been repeatedly emphasized here, training does not create jobs for the poor nor does training stimulate change in job requirements to permit the poor to gain entrance into the fastest-growing employment categories—that is, those activities which are now exclusively performed by highly-skilled technicians and professionals. Training which is restricted to current job openings is static and does not allow for the dynamics of an economic world in technological flux. Such training can, at best, provide temporary relief. There needs to be more creative use of funds designed for job training which will initiate new jobs in areas where the poor rarely gain admittance.

In one sense, however, MDTA funds *do* create jobs. These new jobs are for the college-educated and highly-skilled who comprise the training staff. Funds provided for training *can* offer a true potential for employment of the poor which at present is unexploited. Using MDTA mandated funds to create jobs requires extensive and imaginative planning. This planning needs to envision a training team encompassing a wide spectrum of functions, some of which demand extensive skill and training, and others which require little experience or knowledge. Initially, a training project staff might include only highly-qualified persons, but it should be possible to incorporate individuals with lesser skill as the program con-

tinues. Persons to fill entry jobs could be recruited from
those who have successfully completed the training program.
If persons offered entry positions on a training team were
provided with an opportunity to advance to higher positions
on the team, through the provision of further education and
training, then for a limited but increasingly significant proportion of the poor the funds allocated for training would
provide a real avenue to a changed status.

One point that should not be ignored is that unless a
training team includes some entry positions, staff increases
will consist solely of professionals and highly-trained technicians. Highly-qualified personnel are both scarce and expensive commodities. At least two nonprofessionals can be
hired in place of each professional. If persons with lesser
experience can be retained in training without diminution of
service, failure to utilize them would not only deprive the
needy of chances for jobs and advancement, but would constitute a profligate use of tax funds.

PUBLIC WORKS AS SOLUTION

A proposal which would directly create jobs for the poor
is to be found in the demand for a massive program of public
works. A call for public works projects might truly benefit all
society by producing much needed schools, roads, parks, and
renewed urban centers, and would, at least temporarily, provide jobs for the poor. However, since poverty is not an
acute phenomenon but a chronic problem, it is unlikely that
temporary solutions will suffice.

Jobs to be offered in public works programs would fall
primarily in the category of construction, and the future for
the unskilled worker in this field is dubious. Technological
advance has taken its toll here, for despite a substantial increase in construction activity, there were 400,000 fewer
persons working in this field in 1962 than in 1957.[7] The trend

for the future will be toward further reduction in the numbers of unskilled workers needed in construction.

A sceptical view of public works as the solution to poverty is occasioned by more compelling reasons than the inability of such projects to generate permanent jobs. Creating jobs is but one dimension in the eradication of poverty, for the jobs must be permanent and provide opportunities for upward mobility. It is difficult to conceive of public works projects meeting these latter requirements of an effective anti-poverty program.

Poverty is relative. The poor in this country while living in depressed circumstances, are immeasurably better off than the poor of Asia. Equal opportunity to advance, however, must be ultimately achieved, and public works projects tend to reinforce denial of equal opportunity. The poor will do the ditch-digging and the hod-carrying, while the beneficiaries of affluence and education will be given the supervisory and engineering assignments. The opportunities for advancement from low-level jobs to higher positions will be virtually nonexistent. Therein lies the essential difference between mere job creation and the new career concept. Entrance to a new career sequence will begin with low-level, low-paid, low-status functions, but, unlike the construction worker, opportunity for advancement will be provided, which, if carried to its ultimate, will be unlimited.

REDUCED WORK WEEK
AS SOLUTION

Throughout the years man has accommodated technological advance by reducing the hours he worked. Some have expressed a belief that the current poverty problem could be eased by a further decrease in the work week. However, it is hardly certain that a reduction in hours worked would ameliorate the present situation. The jobs which the poor are *permitted* to perform are the hardest hit by automation. One result of a diminution of hours worked (at no loss in pay) would probably be to stimulate further acceleration of the automation process. The jobs likely to be created are those currently closed to the poor.

The call for a reduced work week points up problems of social engineering which could plague any effort to erase poverty. There is always the possibility that the program in practice would not resemble what is advocated in theory. The slogan of a shorter work week may be a euphemism for a pay increase. As has happened in the past, the jobholder may continue to work the same number of hours but will receive overtime pay for more of the hours worked.

Although the number of jobs which will be created in product-producing industries through reducing hours of work are likely to be small, indirectly a substantial number of jobs could be generated by a true reduction in the work week, work year, or work life. (Reduced work year would provide more paid holidays and longer vacations; reduced work life would follow from earlier retirement.) Jobs would be created in the industries and the services which cater to recreation and leisure time activities. The current jobless would qualify for some of the new jobs, but the central issue is likely to be begged, particularly if the insistence on increasing educational requirements for jobs continues to deprive the poor of an opportunity to obtain employment.

PASSING A LAW
AGAINST POVERTY

Many of the proposed solutions to poverty are encompassed in the omnibus Economic Opportunity Act of 1964.[3] This bill, which authorizes almost one billion dollars to be spent in antipoverty programs, covers a wide enough range of possibilities to enliven the hopes of its supporters and foster the denigration of its detractors.

The law has the potential to make an impact upon poverty, but there is no guarantee that such progress will take place. The success or failure of the legislation will not be in its mandate but in its implementation. The danger is that few *permanent* new careers will be created and that the paid work experience will be extraneous to the permanent entrenched agencies.

Although the bill encourages employment of the poor, and many agencies will eagerly accept grants for this purpose, hiring persons with federal funds does not guarantee creation of permanent staff positions. No agency is required to provide permanent positions in order to be eligible for sponsorship of programs in any title of the poverty measure. The major difficulty confronting administrators of the antipoverty act will be the achievement of a lasting contribution —and while this clearly is their intention, they can attain such a goal only if abetted by an enlightened citizenry.

It must be stressed repeatedly that the structures for employment (where opportunities are available now and are likely to increase in the future) are in the school systems, the health departments, the welfare departments, and the various university and nonuniversity based research organizations. There is no assurance that activities promoted under the auspices of the antipoverty legislation will generate permanent career phased employment for the poor in these systems.

There is no single direction in the Economic Opportunity Act. The bill encourages the further utilization of teachers, social workers, counsellors, etc., to administer to the needs of the poverty-stricken. The poor do require the help of trained professionals, but they also can, if given training, help themselves (and, in part, the implementors of the legislation recognize this).

If authorized funds are expended primarily to pay the salaries of professionals and near-professionals, then much of the opportunity for significant change will be lost. Moreover, there will not have been the most efficient use of the tax dollar. If, for example, $500,000,000 of the antipoverty funds are used to retain staff for the various programs, and only qualified persons are retained, then these funds could generate 25,000 to 50,000 new jobs (in the annual salary range of from $8,000 to $15,000). However, if this money were utilized for hiring the poor as counselor aides, teacher aides, aides to work supervisors, and research aides, then as many as 100,000 jobs could be created (annual salary averaging $4,000). Failure to fully exploit the potential of the poor puts an even greater strain upon the meager supply of trained professionals. To attempt, in short order, to employ additional thousands of scarce professionals, will lead only to pirating staff from competing agencies, which, in essence, is creating service at the expense of service.

The poverty bill funds will be minimally effective if the purpose is merely to add appendages to what currently exists. There is the need for rational change and updating of administrative apparatus. If, for example, the conservation camps are used solely for short-term training, after which youth are returned to an essentially unchanged environment, then a moratorium rather than a change will have been wrought. However, conservation constitutes a basic long term need, and thus the camps can have the function of training for *life careers* in conservation service (or rural recreation). Youth could be encouraged to venture forth, in the best tradition of our nation, to a modern pioneering effort. If this strategy were adopted, then one of the camps could be singled out as an academy for advanced training to allow the more gifted and persevering workers to progress to professional status.

If the camps assume a training function to provide vitally important workers, then their existence as permanent establishments is justifiable. Staff recruited to form the table of organization of a camp could view the assignment as a life career, thus providing still more opportunity for those currently without job or hope.

The poverty bill is an important first step, but it would be unrealistic to expect wondrous results of the initial efforts conducted under its auspices. Some ventures will be spectacular failures, others modest successes. If all activity is subjected to rigorous evaluation, then sound programs can emerge out of failure, and success can be built upon success. The value of the programs must be scientifically adjudicated and not subject to the whim of unsubstantiated opinion, no matter how well motivated.

EDUCATION—THE COMPLICATED, THE ULTIMATE, AND THE ENIGMATICAL SOLUTION

The most enticing, the all-encompassing, and the most opaque of all proposals for the reduction of poverty is education. Out of a morass of comment and argument education emerges most constantly as the panacea for the poor. The reasoning is pristinely simple—the poor remain poor because they lack the skills necessary to function in a society driven by advanced technology, and education would provide the poor with the skills they so desperately need.

There is no challenging that the poor are in need of better education. In disproportionately large numbers, economically disadvanatged youngsters fail to complete high school, and those who complete high school have not achieved as much, on the average, as their more favored counterparts. There is no contesting that were the poor better educated some of the opportunities currently denied them would no longer be closed.

Improving education for the poor, however, is really an intervening process which can hopefully lead at some future date to productive employment. Education in itself cannot immediately produce jobs for the poor. In most instances years would elapse before it could be ascertained if there were a return from the investment, and *unless a parallel development of increasing educational prerequisites for entrance to jobs were halted,* there could be no assurance that uplifting education could even keep pace with the employer's demand for higher qualifications.

Moreover, improving education is much easier said than done. There is no clear definition of a good school, an able teacher, an optimal classroom size, or a sound grouping policy. No minor changes will alter the situation. Teachers who are not adequate at $5,000 a year will not improve if paid $10,000. New physical plants will not produce a climate for education. Integration is a necessary precondition, not the end result of a healthy educational process.

Some argue that improving education for the slum youngster is not enough. There must be compensation for the environmental deficits accrued during their early, formative years. Slum youngsters, in order to compete equally with more advantaged youth must be given intensive preparation and training during preschool years in order to receive the advantage of a full academic program. Whether such a proposal would lead to more jobs for the poor who receive the aid could only be ascertained in the next decade; however, the day-care centers established to provide the recommended services can either limit their employment opportunities to the skilled and advantaged (i.e., the professional teachers) or be so conceived that they open up new jobs and training for the uneducated poor. If the latter course is pursued then not only will jobs be made available to the poor (at less expense to the taxpayer than if only professionals were hired) but also, for reasons explained in a later chapter, a more exciting, vibrant, meaningful preschool center would emerge.

The poor are not poor solely because they are uneducated. Inadequate education is both a cause and effect of poverty. When inadequate education is considered as the consequence of poverty, the problems of student motivation, of parental inadequacy to aid in the schooling process, and the lack of stimulation from peers become central. To expect low income persons to undergo extensive education experience *before* employment is offered doesn't really reckon with reality. There is an alternative, however, and that is to *provide employment first and offer an opportunity for learning while, or after there is earning.*

Furthermore, the field of education, itself, offers an opportunity to provide meaningful experience to alienated, disadvantaged youngsters. The employment of the poor in the schools may provide the decisive bridge between the school and the "slum" child.

In the chapters which follow, the use of the poor to help educate the poor is elaborated. This is the keystone of the new career concept—hiring the poor not to provide charity but for the value which will be received.

NOTES

1. U.S. Department of Labor: *Manpower Report to the President and a Report on Manpower Requirements, Resources, Utilization, and Training;* U.S. Government Printing Office, March, 1964, p. 195.

2. *Ibid.,* p. 9.

3. Oscar Ornati: *The Strategy and Political Economy of the War Against Poverty;* paper given at Georgetown University, Poverty in Plenty Seminar, January 23, 1964.

4. Michael D. Regan, For a Guaranteed Income, *New York Times Magazine,* June 7, 1964; p. 20.

5. The position for guaranteed income is not as boldly stated as it is presented here. Those who hold this view place it in a context with other program components. However, the view of solving poverty through a wholesale dole is by itself worthy of appraisal.

6. For a review and critique of the general problem of mental health services for the poor see: Frank Riessman, Jerome Cohen and Arthur Pearl, *Mental Health of the Poor;* New York Free Press, 1964.

7. *Manpower Report of the President,* 1963, op. cit.

8. The major provisions of the law include the following: (1) a job corps consisting of camps in which 16 to 21 year-old youth will be provided education and vocational training; (2) work-training programs in which unemployed youth will engage in useful paid experience; (3) work-study programs to provide part-time work for students; (4) Community Action Programs which broadly extend support to communities mobilized to combat poverty; and (5) grants and loans to the rural poor.

CHAPTER *3*

THE POOR
AND
THE SCHOOLS

Henry Saltzman
Program Associate, Public Affairs Program, Ford Foundation

INTRODUCTION

THE USE OF THE POOR within the educational establishment
in America is under serious examination by scholars, social
scientists from a variety of disciplines, and educators and
government officials concerned with the alleviation of poverty through the expansion of employment opportunities. The
shrinkage of unskilled work, the continuing loss of entry jobs
through automation, the down-grading of manual work in an
increasingly "white collar" society, and the inability of industry to produce new jobs which can be filled by under-
educated people have turned the search for work to the public sectors, to the design of new careers in human services.

The largest of these services is education, and the size of
America's educational plant is being increased at a rapid
pace. It is logical and appropriate, therefore, to examine this
field with a view to identifying within it work opportunities

for the workless Americans and for those vulnerable to work-lessness. In the main these are the Negro, the Mexican-Americans, the Puerto Ricans, the rural whites of poor educational backgrounds, the Indians—in short, all those who are over-represented in the unemployed and under educated population of America.

Educators may tend to reject responsibility for the recruitment, training, employment, and supervision of unskilled people working in the schools unless they are convinced that the work to be done by nonprofessionals is (1) necessary, (2) aimed at the improvement of the functioning of the schools; (3) outside of the professional's area of competence and/or interest and; (4) in the realm of a perceived role which the school has assumed or is willing or able to assume. Hence, if large numbers of the poor are to become employed in school systems, a rationale for their employment must be developed in terms which are understandable and meaningful to educators. In turn, the educator must begin to view the poor as a manpower pool from which to draw personnel who can do more than simply relieve teachers of non-teaching duties. The educator must begin to see that members of the slum community can bring to the school skills and perceptions *essential* to the improvement of the school's program.

This chapter, therefore, will attempt to outline one area of development in current American educational theory and practice—compensatory education—and to suggest how it offers new opportunities for the useful employment of the poor in the schools.

EDUCATIONAL PROGRAMING

In the decade following World War II, American education, like the American consumer, seemed hell-bent to satisfy all the wants it had accumulated during the war years.

Schools had to be built, new teachers in large numbers had to be trained, salaries had to be raised, the new technologies of television, computers, and programed instruction had to be introduced, giving schools that modern look, "new" ideas had to be introduced such as ungraded programs, team teaching, etc. Educators joined in the general orgy of consumption, and joyously competed in the race to soak up backed-up demand by appealing to the taste for the new and the splashy.

During this decade, the schools appeared to be following Aphra Behn's injunction to "Come away, poverty's catching." There was little discussion of the poor, the deprived, the migrating Negroes and Puerto Ricans. The slum school and neighborhood were lost sight of in an actual and metaphorical rush to *Suburbia*. More money was spent on the schools in affluent neighborhoods, larger per pupil expenditures were permitted in the better areas of the city,[1] and the older schools and their older neighborhoods were left to struggle along with the raw recruits to the teaching force, the hand-me-down buildings, textbooks, and equipment. Nobody seemed to care very much.

Beginning in the mid-fifties, the dimensions of this migration of the poor to the central cities reached such proportions that it could no longer be ignored. Astute mayors and school superintendents began recognizing that a new bloc of voters was on the scene, with the capacity, if not yet the organization, to veto their plans for urban and educational renewal. If bond issues were to be approved, construction programs to proceed on schedule, relocation of slum dwellers carried out, and new school programs effectively introduced, the demands of the "new poor" would have to be measured and met. The balance of power in American cities was slowly shifting.

In the mid-fifties, school system after school system began to program for those they chose to call the "culturally-deprived." New York City's Higher Horizons program set a

style and a pace. The National Scholarship Service for Negro
Students helped spread the word. The Council of Superintendents of the fourteen Great Cities, with Ford Foundation
help, promoted demonstration projects under the Great
Cities School Improvement Program. James Conant in *Slums
and Suburbs* alarmed many with his angry sketch of the
central cities' school problem. The school drop-out became a
matter of concern and the object of countless "drop-out prevention" programs. Through the President's Committee on
Juvenile Delinquency and Youth Crime, Federal money, in
relatively small but conspicuous fashion, began going directly to cities willing to work broadly on reducing juvenile
delinquency. New York's Mobilization for Youth set a model
for comprehensive community action. The Ford Foundation,
contributed to the effort to develop major community social
action programs by supporting "Gray Area" projects in Boston, New Haven, Oakland, Philadelphia, Washington, D.C.
and on a state-wide basis in North Carolina. With other
grants, the Ford Foundation and other foundations also encouraged work-study, youth employment and training, and
preschool education programs.

The need for making special efforts on behalf of the poor
was given heightened urgency by the revolution in civil
rights. The Negroes' dramatic stand for equality and freedom
focused sharply on educational inequities, spurred programming for the poor and the deprived, and continues to spur
all the bureaucracies to deal with the "slums" and their
people in more honest fashion. For the educator, this special
effort has come to be called "compensatory education."

These educational programs are guided by four underlying principles:

1. The human potential for learning, although sharply
curtailed by poverty, is greater than that measured by any
tests so far devised. Compensatory education represents a
reaffirmation of the belief in the power of an individual to
expand his capacity to learn—a simple statement that schools

do not know the limits which environment puts on ability and should not compromise in any effort to determine the limits of the slum child's potential;

2. There are specific, identifiable factors in the social, physical, and cultural environments of the poor which retard intellectual development. These factors exist because of the nature of poverty and the response of the poor to these factors must not be casually related to inherent inferiority, inherent anti-intellectualism, or inherent insensitivity;

3. It is the responsibility of educators to engage in a process of analysis of these factors and in an unending process of adjustment of the school program to overcome these blockages to successful learning;

4. The act of compensating for the deficits imposed upon the child by the slum environment is a political as well as educational response on the part of school systems, and must be planned for as an act of policy as well as an act of administration. Based upon school systems' experiences over the past decade, compensatory education programs require considerably higher per capita expenditures for the pupil in the "slum" schools—not simply to bring them up to the "middle class" schools' standards, but to bring them to whatever level of performance is required to insure school success for most, if not all, of the student population.[2] It is clear that achievement of the type of program which will enable "slum" children to acquire secondary and posthigh school training in larger numbers will involve more cost than those programs presently achieving this purpose for the children of the middle classes. With limited amounts of money, boards of education will have to face the painful task of diverting scarce funds from the potent middle-class population to the increasingly vocal poor, i.e., Negroes, Puerto Ricans, Mexican-Americans, etc.

In almost every major urban area of the country, some form of compensatory education programming is underway. An overview of the nature of these programs can be sketched using a stimulus and response model—the stimulus in this case being those aspects of the poverty environment which, in the judgment of educators and/or social scientists collaborating with educators, are retarding the growth of the child.

I. IN-MIGRATION

The familiar patterns of rural life are broken in the move to the city, and the often bewildering urban style of living usually creates new problems of adjustment for the family.

One form of school response has been the orientation class—an ungraded "reception center" which aims to:

1. Acquaint newly-arrived children with the city and its services and facilities;

2. Evaluate the true level of academic preparation and intellectual potential of the child;

3. Prepare the child through counselling, remedial services, and cultural enrichment for entrance into the normal school programs;

4. Provide an orientation to the school system and its requirements and mode of operation;

5. Provide in-migrant parents with similar orientation to the school and community;

6. Work to bring necessary social and economic supports to the family during its period of adjustment to the city.

II. HOUSING

The crowded, inadequate housing in the "slums" makes home study difficult. Noise, one of the hallmarks of "slums," may not only contribute to the development of poor study habits, but also could lead to nervousness, a high level of irritability, and exhaustion due to lack of sleep.

Consequently, the schoolhouse is being viewed as a refuge from crowdedness and noise, as a place for quiet study, for recreation and enrichment, for the provisions of the reference materials and tutorial services which are provided quite normally in more affluent homes. Increasingly, urban

schools are being kept open after the normal school day is
over and staffed for tutoring and various enrichment programs. The "community school" is an outgrowth of this response.

III. LACK OF MONEY

Simple poverty curtails the range of enriching experiences children are provided. Without trips, vacations, toys
and books, poor children often fail to acquire concepts about
the society which the school takes for granted and upon
which much of the curriculum is built. This narrow base of
experience, in turn, prevents the "slum" child from developing much enthusiasm for learning, because the materials presented by the schools are so foreign to what he has experienced.

School systems have taken the "higher horizons" approach to this problem—structuring into "slum" schools special personnel to work with parent, child and teacher in organizing a wide variety of cultural experiences which will
take the child and his family out of the "slum" milieu and
into contact with the worlds of art, music, drama, college
life, and a variety of occupations both professional and semiprofessional.

IV. PRESCHOOL DEFICIENCIES

The poor home may do its greatest damage to a child's
intellectual capacity before he ever reaches school. In the
preschool years, habits of thinking are set, language patterns
are molded, the values and attitudes of the parent are impressed upon the child. These habits, patterns, values, and
attitudes can add up to a style of thinking and learning
which is poorly adapted to the academic style of the school.

Therefore, school systems such as those in New York
City, Boston, New Haven, Philadelphia, Oakland, Ypsilanti,
and Baltimore have begun developing preschool enrichment
programs whose purpose is to bring the deprived child into

an enriched learning environment at the age of three or four and to develop a curriculum which will enable him to cope more effectively with the learning tasks which the school will present to him in the early and middle grades. Usually, these preschool programs lead the child into an ungraded primary program in the early grades which provides the "slum" child with an additional uninterrupted three-year period in which to develop his basic learning skills.

V. NEGATIVE ATTITUDES TOWARD AUTHORITY

No one particularly likes authoritarian institutions. But most middle-class people develop the skills to negotiate with authority and, indeed, learn how to make authority work for them. Unfortunately, this is not so of the poor. Authority, they find, usually works against them and they learn to shun it or oppose it when possible.

The school is often seen as an authoritarian institution, walled off from the slum community, incommunicative except when it chooses not to be, and aloof from the lives of people to the point where its attitude is often interpreted as unsympathetic and disapproving of slum people. A school which does not secure the trust and confidence of its community has failed. Therefore, many school systems have undertaken much more aggressive school-community relations programs in an effort to narrow the social distance which exists between the educated work-secure faculties and their less educated insecure communities. Often these programs take the form of community school programs, and the hiring of special personnel—as "bridge" people who work between the school and the neighborhood, interpreting the school to the community and the community to the school.[3]

VI. ABSENCE OF MODELS OF
LEGITIMATE ACHIEVEMENT

People who achieve even a modicum of financial success don't usually remain in slum areas. Often the slum child will have no one in the family or in the neighborhood who can offer him a model of legitimate success toward which he can aspire. If the child is nonwhite, this situation is aggravated by the absence of representation of his group in textbooks and the mass media, including television.

Schools have been attempting to compensate for this by: 1. revising social studies curricula to include more information and materials dealing with the contributions of nonwhite, and other minorities to America's development;[4] 2. developing or urging publishers to develop "integrated" reading and audio-visual materials;[5] 3. sponsoring "career guidance" programs which take slum children to the places of work of successful "graduates" of the slums; and 4. providing for school visits of such "models" for purposes of large and small group discussions of what it takes to break out of the slum.

VII. GENERAL ISOLATION FROM SOURCES OF INFORMATION

The problems slum people have with the authorities, their different patterns of speech and restricted vocabularies, their social and physical isolation from the rest of the community, work against them by severely restricting their knowledge of and receptivity to necessary information. The flow of information reaching the slum resident is inadequate and his ability to process and utilize this information is not well-developed.

School responses to this have been varied: elementary school counseling programs have been expanded, theoretically at least, to bring more information to children and parents about the lines of choice available within the school system, career information, and the relationship of changes in the economy to the education of the child, as well as the more usual guidance activities which center on school adjustment. Larger stocks of books, periodicals and audio-visual materials have been provided for classrooms and school libraries; parent education programs—formal, as well as informal—have been expanded; administrative encouragement is given to home visitation by teachers; the style of written communication between home and school has been improved by reducing complex sentence structure, by the use of native languages as well as English, and by more use of visual techniques. More important than specific techniques is the recognition by school people that it is difficult for people to change if they don't know how or why they should change and that the school has an appropriate role in (1) bridging the gap between the slum resident child and adult and (2) in expanding as much as possible the supply of useful information to the slum family, particularly in regard to vocational planning.

Along with these examples of education's response to the needs of slum children should be listed the effort being made to improve slum schools generally. Accelerated school construction programs, reductions in class size, increases in specialized personnel—guidance, remedial, and administrative—utilization of team teaching and ungraded systems, upgrading of curricula and learning materials, represent a general effort by school systems to give particular attention to schools in poorer neighborhoods.

Unfortunately, too much of the compensatory programming visible in American school systems is still on a "pilot project" or "demonstration" basis. The massive job of instituting improved practices in all of the schools requiring these has but barely begun. Nevertheless, from these programs the outline of a coherent rationale can be discerned. The American school which serves a poor community must be a different school from that in a more affluent area. And, as stated above, to achieve this differentness it must become sensitively aware of the needs, assets, handicaps, and hopes of its community.

Within the framework of compensation, *the employment of the poor in the slum school becomes appropriate,*

logical and important, perhaps crucial.[6] For, while members
of the slum community may lack much formal education,
they may have the wisdom dearly bought from the experience of surviving the rigors of their environment; while
they may lack an understanding of the organization of the
school, they may know intimately the organization of the
community; while they may be unschooled in the nuances
of middle-class mores and customs, they may know full well
what will or will not "go" in the slum community; while
they may lack a grasp of educational philosophy and theory,
they may be fully conversant with what is or is not perceived as important, honest and useful by the school's con-
stituency.

In the design of compensatory programs, in their implementation and in their translation to the slum community, the involvement of knowledgeable slum residents
should be seen as harmonious with the basic commitment
of the school. Employees selected from the slum can assume
significant roles in helping the school frame and execute
programs to deal with each of the barriers to school success outlined above:

1. "Family helpers" could work with in-migrant parents
in the adjustment process.

2. "Library aides" could help keep school libraries open
after hours or help move books out into homes.

3. "School guides" could arrange and manage cultural
enrichment tours.

4. "Nursery mothers" could help strengthen preschool
programs.

5. "School-community agents" or "co-ordinates" could
shuttle effectively between the school and the community
helping each to know more about the other.

6. "Talent searchers" could work to bring to the school
the successful graduates of the slum and in reverse, the children of the slums to the working places of these graduates.

7. "Home visitors" could assist in reaching the "hard-to-

reach" in a manner which might reduce their isolation and lack of knowledge of sources of help and opportunity.

This is no exhaustive list. It need not be because if educators recognize the potential contribution which the slum residents themselves can make to the improvement of the school, then many work roles, each with is own rationale, will be designed.

Indeed, there are already a number of excellent examples of how the intelligent and careful use of nonprofessional employees drawn from the slum community can be crucial to compensatory education programs.

When the Philadelphia Board of Education developed its Great Cities School Improvement Project,[7] it established as a major goal the improvement of school-community relations. It proposed to accomplish this through the use of school-community coordinators who were to be selected from the community served by each of the project schools. The project director asked each school principal to recommend local residents who could function as liaison personnel between the school and the community. No formal education requirements were established. The crucial criteria for selection were the candidate's maturity, ability to relate to school personnel and to area residents, and the possession of some recognized status in the community. Those selected were employed as noncertificated personnel on an 11 month work year basis. The salary level was set at approximately $400 per month.

The five coordinators hired in 1960 to serve four schools (one school was double teamed to provide a Spanish-speaking coordinator) have now been expanded to nine coordinators for seven schools. Board of Education staff responsible for the program state that only the shortage of funds is limiting the expansion of the number of coordinators because the merits of this approach have been amply proved by improved school-community relationships and vastly expanded participation of parents in school activities. Perhaps an even more significant result of the program is the expanded participation of school personnel in community activities.

In Philadelphia's program, the coordinators are responsible to the principal but they work most closely with the school guidance counselor. Most of their time is spent in the community—in the homes of pupils talking to parents about their children's strengths and their needs, in helping parents learn how to help their children, in interpreting school programs and activities and in being helpful to community organizations. The coordinators attend faculty meetings and also sit in on case conferences of counselor and teachers.

No preservice training for coordinators has been developed as yet, but the project director holds regular briefings with all the coordinators, to discuss their work, and the Director of Pupil Personnel instructs them in interviewing and counseling techniques, and aspects of child development.

That these nonprofessionals have functioned well is attested to by the fact that, over the past four years, principals and guidance counselors have reported no significant problems in the coordinators' handling of their role—on the contrary, most reports focus on the significance which the coordinators' work has assumed. Except for the loss of one coordinator who moved out of the state, there has been *no* turn-over.

A similarly positive experience in the use of nonprofessionals has been that of the Pittsburgh Board of Education in its Team Teaching Project.[8] In 1960, twenty "team mothers" were recruited from the neighborhoods to be served by the newly organized teaching teams in Pittsburgh's Hill district—a predominantly low-income Negro area. Primarily, the team mother's role was to perform those nonprofessional duties essential to the smooth operation of a team teaching program—the duplication of teacher-prepared materials, the operation of audio-visual equipment required in large group instruction, the preparation of displays, bulletin boards, etc.

The team mothers work the same hours as a classroom teacher and are paid approximately $235 per month for a ten month work year. They are supervised by the leader of the teaching team and they participate with teachers in planning workshops and attend faculty meetings. In their recruitment, preference was given to mothers known to principals and more than half of those selected had children in the school.

Consistently, the reports of the team leaders and the principals indicate that the team teaching-program could never have functioned as effectively as it has without these nonprofessionals. In old schools, designed for self-contained classroom instruction, the physical plant works against a team teaching-strategy. The use of nonprofessional assistants was a crucial factor in making it possible for the program to get off the ground, take hold and become an accepted part of the program of the Pittsburgh schools.

A major dividend accruing from the employment of these local people is the continuous, albeit informal, community liaison which they provide. These mothers (some are grandmothers) know many families and their range of acquaintances spans the whole of the Hill district. Through them can come important insights which teachers cannot obtain in any other way. Also, daily they take away from the school to the community an insider's knowledge of what is being attempted and why. On the street, in the shops, in homes, these women informally disseminate important understandings and facts about the school program which are listened to with respect. One of the early worries of the designers of the program centered on how responsibly these women would handle the knowledge they were bound to obtain about the children. This worry has been long laid to rest by four years of positive experience.

Perhaps the best evidence of success is the fact that the

Board of Education has doubled the number of team
mothers. In four years only one has been discharged; she
was living outside of the school's area. Another two or three
have moved from the community. Aside from these, there
have been *no* resignations, *no* discharges—as in Philadelphia, almost total holding power! In addition to the welcome income, the team mothers have received training from
the Audio-Visual section of the Bureau of Curriculum, the
Art Department, and from the clerical staff. Thus all parties
involved—the professional staff, the mothers, the children
and the community—have benefitted.

In advocating large scale employment of the poor in
the schools, one must be conscious of three pitfalls:

1. There is a tendency to strengthen the argument by
exaggerating somewhat both the potential and the strengths
of the slum resident. A "new romanticism" has been creep-
ing into current literature on poverty which is somewhat
reminiscent of the proletarian literature of the Thirties.
Slum life leaves its scars—and these are not eradicated
overnight by a job. Great care and thought will have to be
given to the screening of potential employees. In the projects described above small numbers are involved. If education is to become a major employer of the poor, more systematic recruitment processes must be developed as well
as more experimentation in the use of nonprofessionals.

2. The argument of economy is seductive. If hiring a
slum resident costs half or a third as much as hiring a
teacher, the argument goes, school administrators should
be delighted by such a plan. However, in the education of
a child, no economy for economy's sake can be tolerated if
the development of the child may be hindered in any
manner. While it is possible to demonstrate that school
districts can greatly expand their work force with little
net additions to their budget, this argument cannot stand
separate and apart from the issue of the quality of the
educational program which may result. The place of each

subprofessional needs to be carefully designed—as in Philadelphia and Pittsburgh—to insure that he fills an appropriate, useful role which is geared to fit in with the over-all program of the school.

3. In the exuberant embrace of this approach to the expansion of employment opportunities for the poor, there may be a too-rapid glossing over the problem which can develop between professional school personnel and their new nonprofessional helpers. The responsibility for training and supervising these new employees cannot be lightly deposited on the doorsteps of already burdened and harassed school principals and classroom teachers. The orientation of professional staff to the work of the new workers, the advanced planning and definition of work roles, the structure for mediating between professionals and nonprofessionals, the working out of procedures for up-grading the new workers, etc. are nowhere clearly defined. A great deal of work will have to be done.

While recognizing that these are serious considerations, the Philadelphia and Pittsburgh experiences stand as promising examples of the rich rewards to be harvested from the use of slum residents in the schools. The key point in arguing for the use of these people is the fact that they can bring to the school experience and knowledge of the slum community which professionals too often lack and have little time to acquire, and which can improve the schools' program. Also, when the schools turn seriously to the development of compensatory educational programs, these workers can provide *essential* skills which complement those of the professional staff. The total program of the school can be improved by the judicious and carefully planned employment of slum residents.

Therefore, no simple WPA type project is herein being advocated for the schools. Rather it is our argument that school administrators seriously planning compensatory educational programs, consider how their programs may be

strengthened and made more effective by the recruitment of
lay people from the slum areas themselves.

NOTES

1. Sexton, Patricia Cayo, *Education and Income: Inequalities of Opportunity in our Public Schools,* N.Y. Viking Press, 1961.
2. See, for example, report from the Great Cities School Improvement
Projects, available from the Boards of Education in Cleveland, Detroit,
Milwaukee, Philadelphia, Pittsburgh, St. Louis, San Francisco, and Washington, D.C. Also, New York City's *Higher Horizons Program* reports
and the *Special Service Schools Program.*
3. Of particular interest in this regard are the community school
programs in New Haven, Flint, Detroit and the All-Day Neighborhood
School Program of the New York City Board of Education.
4. As an example, see the Oakland Public Schools new fifth grade
curriculum which highlights the contribution of the Negro in America.
5. The Chandler, Follett and Macmillan Publishing Companies have
already produced materials of this type.
6. While this discussion of the use of the poor emphasizes the slum
school—it is *not* to be concluded that such a practice is advocated for
such schools only. Similar work opportunities for low-income nonprofessionals in the growing number of integrated schools would be most desirable
in terms of providing middle-class children contacts with adults of different
social backgrounds in an educational setting. Similarly, the employment of
poor people in schools regardless of socio-economic composition of the
student body and neighborhood should also be considered seriously by
educators.
        The chapter stresses the slum school in an effort to show that the
use of lay people can be educationally sound within one type of public
school setting.
7. Philadelphia Board of Education, *Great Cities School-Community
Improvement Project,* Annual Reports for 1962–1963.
8. Pittsburgh Board of Education, various reports on the "Team Teaching Projects."

CHAPTER *4*

EDUCATION
AS A MODEL
FOR NEW
CAREERS

EDUCATION must ultimately become the United States' largest enterprise. There are many reasons for this—population growth alone requires expansion in education. By 1975, half of the population in the United States will be less than twenty-five years of age.[1] Most of these young people will be undergoing some sort of training (as likely will be many thousands over the age of 25). Technological advance is another stimulus to education. The gain in productivity obtained from machines not only produces the wealth that makes a greater investment in education possible, but also establishes the need for more highly-trained personnel and obviates the need for the uneducated. When there is such increasing emphasis on education, a society is in trouble if it cannot establish the means to incorporate the poor as paid employees in its fastest growing and most important industry.

There is an undersupply of teachers today, and qualified teachers will continue to be hard to find unless there is significant and fundamental change in the structure of education. A proposal for such a change will be detailed here; however, the need for this departure should be fully understood, and figures tell part of the story:

> To take care of the growth in enrollment expected during the 1960's, the number of classroom teachers will have to increase by at least a fourth—from 1.7 million in 1960 to nearly 2.2 million in 1970. In addition, about 1½ million new teachers will be required during the decade to replace those that retire or leave the profession for other reasons.[2]

Education is not alone in the search for available talent; other fields are on the prowl as well. A danger voiced by one renowned scholar is that, in the competition for the college graduate, education will be the refuge of the leftovers, with a negative effect for the quality of education:

> . . . at all events, the attraction of the learned professions of law, medicine, and college teaching, as well as business, engineering, theology, and other vocations will lead many of the most able men and some of the women into other careers than teaching school.[3]

A way out of the dilemma is through development of new careers in education.

NEW CAREERS IN EDUCATION

Currently in the classroom there is but one designated role—teacher. Incorporated in that role are a great number of diverse functions—the teacher is an educator, but he is also a clerk, a custodian, an operator of audio-visual equipment, and an audio-version of a printed book. In many slum schools the impression gained is that the teacher is part lion tamer and part warehouseman. The latter roles must be eliminated and many of the others can be assumed by less qualified personnel. In some situations volunteers and older students have been used to assist the teacher, but this has not been done consistently or systematically, and the new functions have not been integrated into the fabric of the system. These informal operations are insufficient. There must be redefinition and structural change in education if we are to meet the obligations of educating our population and eradicating poverty.

What is needed is redefinition of the teaching role. The teacher encompasses too many activities, and it is proposed here that five different functions can be abstracted from the one omnifarious duty now performed. These roles are (*1*) a teacher aide; (*2*) a teacher assistant; (*3*) a teacher associate; (*4*) a teacher; and (*5*) a supervising teacher. These five teaching roles would exist along a continuum in which advancement from entry position to full-fledged professional could be negotiable on the basis of talent and motivation, rather than economic means.

The base line or entry position, teacher aide, would be open to all regardless of schooling attained (or delinquency record) and would require only that a short training experience be successfully completed.[4] If capable and motivated, the aide would be encouraged to continue his education. With an A.A. Degree (two years of college or equivalent) he would become eligible for an intermediate role—the teacher assistant. With further education and a B.A. Degree, eligibility for teacher associate would be obtained. Thus, by systematic steps and intervals a series of positions are created which narrow the present gulf between the disadvantaged and professional standing. Each level attained can constitute a career. For those aspiring to higher stations, however, opportunity for advancement has been established. A teacher could attain the higher status, supervising teacher, in the same manner that a teacher now advances into counselling or administration. It is not supposed that the use of aides would be appropriate in every instance, but the situations in which benefit could be obtained from the new roles can only be ascertained by rigorous experimentation.

THE ENTRY POSITION—THE AIDE

A number of different functions could be performed by persons at the aide level. These functions range from supervision of recess and lunch time activities to operating audiovisual equipment. They include assisting children at home with homework, assuming the teacher's clerical functions, maintaining supplies and special equipment, and exercising control over a class while the teacher gives instruction to a particular child in need of special attention. The aide would be directly responsible to a supervising teacher, and twenty aides would constitute a case-load for the supervisor. Aides would be expected to meet after school hours to discuss difficulties and to expand their skills in sessions of instruction.

The aide could be judiciously employed in a number of situations. For example, teaching reading to a second or third grade class poses considerable difficulty. Not all children are able to learn at the same rate, nor do they experience the same kinds of difficulty. Classes are often divided into three groups—the slow, the intermediate, and the quick readers. While the teacher is giving attention to one group, the other two are left to their own devices. The group which is slowest in learning is in need of greatest attention, but often can only be spared scant instruction. If two aides were enlisted to help the teacher, there could be constant supervision of all groups. Or if a number of pupils were experiencing difficulty, the aides could read to the assembled class or supervise group activities while the teacher helped those requiring the particular attention of a trained professional. In this way the needs of the individual could be served without reneging a responsibility to the entire class.

If an issue arises in which the aide behaves irresponsibly or inadequately, the supervisor can be notified immediately and procedures instituted to correct the difficulty. In some instances aides will have to be discharged. The new career concept is not intended to be a panacea for all of society's ills. The proposal is intended to deal with the larger problem of poverty, and not offer solutions to all individual maladjustment (although permitting the poor a say in their own destiny should exercise a positive effect in reducing incidences of aberration).

THE INTERMEDIATE ROLES—
THE ASSISTANT AND
THE ASSOCIATE

Some aides will demonstrate ability worthy of greater responsibility. Opportunity for promising aides to realize their potential must be created. A system of credit for on-the-job activity plus college courses can be developed to allow for advancement. Using a system similar to that employed in the field placement of a social work student or to the practice teaching of the aspirant to education, college credits could accrue to the aide for his experience in the classroom. If, in addition, the aide were encouraged to extend his education (community colleges and junior colleges could be utilized for this purpose), to take some courses specifically designed for the job role, and to broaden his range of competence and knowledge as well, he could advance to eligibility for assistant teacher. The two years of college credit necessary for eligibility could be achieved in three years.[5] (An alternative route to the position of teaching assistant could be developed for the full-time student in which part of the training would be field experience. The full-time student should be able to attain the position in two years.)

The assistant's functions would include preparation of material used in teaching and demonstrations, correction of homework, and assisting students at home in subjects which require special knowledge and competence. The teaching assistant could, on the basis of his education, assist in teaching algebra, botany, history, etc., and could perform a role analogous to that filled by a teaching assistant in a university or college.

Advancement to the level of associate teacher would follow a similar course of two additional years of work and academic training (university and college substituting for junior college). The functions of the associate would be similar to those performed by the classroom teacher; however, the associate would be subject to the direction of a supervising teacher.

It is important to stress the difference between the establishment of an associate in education and the current common occurrence in which persons who are not certified are performing teacher roles. In the present situation the nonprofessional is asked to perform the same duties as the professional. He is not provided with special supervision or consultation. The role he performs is not legitimated by tenure or official status. Many of the persons now working as noncertified teachers could more appropriately be retained as associates.

The associate could advance to the position of certified teacher in two more years of combined teaching and course work (2 years field placement equals 8 units; one course per semester for two years equals 12 units; and one summer school course, 4–6 units, or a total of 24–26 units).

If the new career concept were adopted, a poor youth who had not completed a high school education could revitalize an entire existence and in less than ten years emerge as a fully-certified professional (1–2 years to attain high school diploma or certificate, 3 years to become assistant, 3 years to become associate; and 2 years to become certified teacher). During this entire period he would be socially useful.

The teacher, no longer burdened with menial tasks (now the responsibility of aide, assistant, and associate), would be liberated to act as a true professional. The creation of new roles in education will necessitate redefinition of the teacher function. The teacher must be able to utilize assistants maximally. The teacher must be given training in administration to insure that functions which require less than professional training are delegated to the nonprofessional.

The assumption of a professional role contains both challenge and threat. There must be training to help the teacher perform the new role successfully, and there must be recognition that some teachers will react negatively to change and others will have taken refuge in the less challenging aspects of the teacher role. To naively expect unanimous welcome of the concept by all teachers would be as unrealistic as assuming that instituting new careers in education is impossible.

The supervising teacher is cardinal in the new career sequence. The nonprofessional placed in a teaching role would possess minimal skill, training, and experience, and thus could only function adequately if given constant and imaginative supervision, counselling, and training. Those vested with the responsibility for supervision must, therefore, have a high degree of competence. They must be drawn from teachers with histories of outstanding achievement and they must, in addition, be given special instruction in supervision. They must be thoroughly familiarized with all aspects of the duties of the aide, the assistant, and the associate. They must be trained to be incisively perceptive, to evaluate accurately the limitations of each person they supervise, and to be prepared to offer individual attention when needed.

If the sequence of aide to teacher is truly to become operational, then it is mandatory that the supervisor become a formal affiliate of the higher education process. The award of college credit to the nonprofessional for work performed can only be justified if the supervisor has some college faculty status. While it will take considerable working through before such appointments can be developed, this should be the ultimate goal in the establishment of the new career sequence.

The supervising teacher provides another avenue for advancement (other than counselling and administration) for gifted teachers and should, therefore, sustain incentive for those desiring to devote their lives to education.

STRATEGY FOR IMPLEMENTATION

The process of determining qualifications and integrating new careers will take time. The need will arise for educators to study the proposition carefully and introduce limited numbers of the new career educators into the table of organization. Schools of higher learning must provide appropriate curriculum, and this, too, will take time. However, there is a need for immediate action, particularly in the schooling of the economically disadvantaged.

What is needed is interim demonstration while principle and procedure for large-scale implementation are being decided. An immediate possibility is the employment of aides to assist children at home. Such assistance, while supplementing education, would disturb neither the structure nor function of the school program. It would provide a necessary facet of learning which is sorely needed by children who do not have sufficient educational support at home.

The qualifications for the aide position should be minimal. The aide should have basic skill in language arts, and arithmetic of at least sixth grade level. He could not be currently involved in antisocial behavior, or be subject to pending legal proceedings. If deficient in basic skills, applicants could be referred to remedial programs[6] to attain the necessary standard for entrance positions. Aides could be recruited from employment centers, private agencies, the schools and youth welfare and correctional facilities. They would be required to participate in a short-term training program which would consist primarily of orientation, job experience, and discussion of job performance. The training should be a group experience in which learning is facilitated by group influence.[7] (See Chapter VIII for further amplification of the training experince.)

In the initial phases, it would be preferable that the aides be lodged in a demonstration program of short-term duration. The chief virtue of using a demonstration as the base for the program is that bureaucratic structure can be avoided. However, it should be explicit that the ultimate goal is incorporation of the function within the existing structure. The funds provided in the Economic Opportunity Act of 1964 could be used for the demonstration.

INITIAL AND ULTIMATE EXPENSE
—A ZERO SUM STRATEGY

One approach to the use of the new career positions would be to assume that money for education were fixed and that the ultimate strategy would be to employ the maximum number of persons (at the same time maintaining a high level of educational services).

Full-scale implementation of nonprofessional roles in an educational system could result in the employment of more persons at no increase in public expense. The following example illustrates how such an event could be accomplished.

In a great many cities simultaneous demonstration programs would be initiated in selected urban areas where educational improvement is drastically needed. If, for example, a finite number of schools in a slum area were selected for pilot efforts where normally 300 teachers were currently employed, over a period of ten years, with the use of new career nonprofessionals and subprofessionals, almost 20 per cent more new employees could be absorbed into the system at the same cost that would be necessary to employ only fully-certified teachers.

To illustrate this, assume that in 1965 a program were started with 50 aides and 4 supervisors retained to perform homework-helper and remedial functions. The cost of this service would be approximately $240,000 for the first year, which would be borne by outside funds.[8] During the first three years, persons hired for the demonstration would be systematically absorbed by the school system.

To understand how nonprofessionals could be absorbed into the educational system at reduced costs, certain assumptions must be articulated. One assumption is that if nonprofessionals were not incorporated into an educational system, most functions would still be performed by teachers. The second assumption is that teacher-pupil ratios would remain relatively constant and that 60 per cent more teachers would be needed in the next decade. Assuming that this growth is constant and applicable to the study area, the following table contrasts the annual cost in salaries three years after initiation of the program of two alternative strategies—one, in which all functions are performed by teachers, the other incorporating nonprofessionals within the system. (In the latter it is assumed that negotiations with the various control agencies have been completed and associate and assistant roles have been defined and legitimatized.)

In three years the inclusion of nonprofessionals in teaching roles would amount to the following:

65 more personnel at an annual increase of salary expenditures of $135,000.

During the first three years of operation some of the aides

Table 1—Two Systems for Meeting Education Need Cost Three Years After Inauguration of Program[a]

System	Teacher Category	Number	Salary	Cost[b]
Certified teacher only	Teacher	360	$7,000	$2,520,000
Certified teacher and non-professional	Supervisor	10	8,500	85,000
	Teacher	310	7,000	2,170,000
	Associate	5	6,000	30,000
	Assistant	20	4,500	90,000
	Aide	80	3,500	280,000
		425		$2,655,000

a. In this example it is assumed that salary rates will remain constant during the ten-year period. Actual increases in salary rates would only serve to further emphasize the value of the proposal, since salary increases are most often based on percentage increase of current rate.

b. Excluding fringe benefits and overhead.

would be able to attain the prerequisites for the assistant position. It is conceivable that all 20 of the assistants would be recruited from the original complement of aides. Some of the aides would be paid at the starting wage (in this instance a $3300 yearly wage is projected), others would have earned increments of approximately $200 for each year of service. The average aide salary at the end of three years of the program is estimated to be $3500 per year.

In three more years of program operation more personnel would be needed. At this point it would be possible for all the additional assistants and associates needed to be drawn from the original group of aides. Table 2 indicates that after

Table 2—Two Systems for Meeting Education Need Cost Six Years After Inauguration of Program

System	Teacher Category	Number	Salary	Cost
Certified teacher only	Teacher	420	$7,000	$2,940,000
Certified teacher and non-professional	Supervisor	15	8,500	127,000
	Teacher	320	7,000	2,240,000
	Associate	10	6,000	60,000
	Assistant	40	4,500	180,000
	Aide	110	3,500	385,000
		495		$2,992,000

Result: 75 more personnel at an expense of $52,000 per year.

six years of operation more persons are being included in the system but at reduced cost.

At the end of the decade, the strategy of nonprofessional *plus* certified teacher would call for more certified teachers in the system than there were at the start of the program (330 in place of the original 300). In addition there would be almost 20 per cent more persons employed in all categories of teaching function than would be the case if only certified teachers had been used. Table 3, which follows, presents in detail the differences in cost of the two strategies at the end of ten years.

Table 3—Two Systems for Meeting Education Need Cost Ten Years After Inauguration of Program

System	Teacher Category	Number	Salary	Cost
Certified teacher only	Teacher	480	$7,000	$3,360,000
Certified teacher and non- professional	Supervisor	20	8,500	170,000
	Teacher	330	7,000	2,310,000
	Associate	20	6,000	120,000
	Assistant	60	4,500	270,000
	Aide	140	3,500	490,000
		570		$3,360,000

Result: 90 more teaching personnel at no increased cost.

To summarize, a strategy has been projected which results in an increase of almost 20 per cent more teaching personnel than would occur if standard procedures were used. At the end of a decade the strategy with more personnel would cost no more than the standard practice. At the beginning of the program each additional person would cost approximately $4,000 a year; within three years this could be reduced to $2,100 per new person per year; in six years the cost would have diminished to $700 per new person per year.

If such a program were universally adopted then it would be possible to expand the projected 2.5 million teachers to almost 3 million persons in teaching positions by 1975 at no additional expense to the taxpayer.

The changing of the staffing pattern in the classroom presents the school with formidable obstacles. The absorption of additional teaching staff (comprising a wide range of training and competence) will not be a simple proposition. The most obvious deployment strategy would be team teaching or some modification of this approach through variation of classroom size; however, the possible variations are multifold.

The problem of effective utilization of manpower is not unique to education nor would the problem be obviated if, by some miraculous process, a sufficient number of fully-trained teachers should suddenly become available to meet the need. It is clear that even where teachers exist in sufficient numbers there are serious deficiencies in the present educational system.

Educational problems can only be solved by systematic experimentation in which each study is reviewed, with such reviews providing the inspiration for further research. In the absence of knowledge about the capacities of the nonprofessional, the abilities of teachers to assume new roles, and pupil response to the use of nonprofessionals in the classroom, a more definitive statement regarding effective or ineffective classroom organization would be inappropriate.

The confluence of the factors of present and projected teacher shortages, the need to develop new employment opportunities for the poor, and the failure to provide adequate education for large segments of the population is sufficient justification for experimentation with new manpower and new techniques in the schools.[9] Education is at least as important to our society as space exploration. Progress in the latter comes only after systematic study of failure and minimal successes. If commensurate investment in the study of the educational process were embraced, it would be reasonable to expect corresponding advances.

NON ZERO SUM STRATEGIES—
PAYING MORE FOR THOSE
WHO NEED MORE

Getting the most education for the least cost is a laudable aim, but expense is not the only consideration in evaluating education. Over-riding everything else must be the quality of the product—the state of competence of persons who have undergone the experience. There can be no disputing that many people are growing up inadequately educated; some, despite years of schooling, are functionally illiterate. For this group, no matter what the cost, society failed to get its money's worth. As has been repeatedly stressed in this book, the uneducated may at one time have been a luxury our society could afford. The uneducated today are a liability that could be our undoing. Therefore, as others have stressed (see Chapter II), one possible way out of poverty is through education of this group.

In the preceding paragraphs a system of education was described the features of which were creation of jobs for the poor, an increase in the number of persons in teaching roles and greater professionalization of certified teachers, all with no increase in cost to the taxpayer. If adopted, the new career concept would, through the increase in teaching personnel, result in a reduction of pupil-teacher ratio to approximately 20 to 1. For the disadvantaged, a 20 per cent increase in teachers might not be enough. It is conceivable that for this population, to compensate for the lack of help at home and the need for greater assistance at school, a ratio of one person in a teacher role for every seven pupils would be necessary if the desired level of achievement is to be obtained.

The exact number of youth who would need this enriched educational program is not presently known (nor is the ideal pupil-teacher ratio), but assuming that a third of the approximately 60 million youth who will be attending school in 1975 could benefit from more intensive instruction, and that 7 to 1 pupil-teacher ratio is a reasonable first estimate[10] of what is needed for this group, then 1.85 million more persons would be needed in teaching roles at that time (assuming that the 20 per cent increase suggested previously had been put into effect). Employing the new career strategy the additional positions could be obtained at an annual cost in salaries of 9.4 billion dollars. If, however, it were decided that such investment should be made using only certified teachers, the yearly cost would be in excess of 12.5 billion dollars for teacher salaries.

The 10 billion dollars required to provide this service is undeniably a lot of money, but such a sum would be less than 5 per cent of the projected Gross National Product for 1975. The alternative to this expense might be the unassessable cost of 2 million persons relegated to permanent inactivity. It may be that governmental powers are *unwilling* to make that substantial an investment in education, but unwillingness should never be confused with *inability* to afford the investment. Unwillingness and/or inability to afford, however, are not the fundamental issue—which is whether such an approach can lead to improved education and, if this is true, whether this is the most efficient way to produce the desired result. The answer to these questions can come only from carefully controlled and systematic research.

Whenever essential knowledge is lacking, decision-making should be based on enlightened guesswork. The estimate that one third of the school population will need special attention is based on the proportion of youth who fail to complete high school. The practice of sorting students into slow, medium, and quick groups suggests that three persons would be more appropriate to teach than one (although, perhaps, a more logical defense of increase of staff would be in redefinition of function, the generalist teacher to be replaced by one person assigned to home help, another to give individual attention in the class and, still another, to present material to the assembled class).

Putting the new career concept to work in an intensive education program for the disadvantaged would require a different distribution of professional to nonprofessional than was suggested in the previous section. In the model described earlier, after a decade of program performance slightly more than one-third of the teaching staff would be nonprofessionals (see Table 3, page 66). If the staff were to be substantially increased, the proportion of nonprofessionals would, almost by necessity, have to increase.[11]

In Table 4 a model is projected which calls for 80 per cent of the staff to be nonprofessional. This model provides for optimal utilization of the poor to help the poor.

Table 4—Distribution and Cost of Staff in an Intensive Education Project for the Disadvantaged

Teacher Category	Number	Salary	Cost
Supervisor	75,000	$8,500	$ 635,000,000
Teacher	285,000	7,000	1,995,000,000
Associate	300,000	6,000	1,800,000,000
Assistant	400,000	4,500	2,200,000,000
Aide	800,000	3,500	2,800,000,000
	1,860,000		$9,430,000,000

THE NEED FOR A CHANGE IN
EDUCATION OF THE POOR

Throughout this book there are a number of recurring themes—one repetitious lament is that more could be done, if only more were known. Ignorance is never a defensible excuse for inactivity. Ignorance does place a heavy burden on the advocate of change—in the absence of proof, defensible logic must prevail. The use of the poor for the instruction of the poor is predicated on the argument that education is currently beset with unanswered problems and that the poor could, as teachers, make a unique contribution to change in education output by helping to create a better climate for education and inspiring the student to greater effort.

The idea that the poor are not given a "fair shake" in education is not new. Although there is no consensus, many social scientists have postulated that inequities persist in the schooling process.[12] They have advanced the thesis that the school, being a middle-class institution, tends to cater to those with particular value systems and styles of life.

Edgar Friedenberg makes a more general attack on American education in his book *The Vanishing Adolescent*.[13] He charges that the school tends to destroy self-esteem in all youth but that the poor are most adversely affected:

These youngsters are handy with their fists and worse, but they are helpless in the meshes of middle-class administrative procedures and are rapidly neutralized and eliminated by it . . .[14]

The most tragic thing that happens to lower status youngsters in school is that they learn to accept the prevailing judgment of their worth.[15]

Some students of society place blame for poor educational achievement on the poor. They place great significance on differences in social class perspectives of the future. The middle-class youngster is described as 'reality oriented,' willing to make the day-to-day sacrifice which schooling demands, in the interest of some future pay-off; whereas, the low income youngster, governed by a 'pleasure principle,' lives only for the delights of the present. As enticing as this "ant versus grasshopper" distinction might be, it fails to recognize a signal fact. There *is* a future in schooling for middle-class youth; this just isn't true for the great majority of the poor. Schooling is, by and large, a rewarding experience for the affluent; for the poor it is largely a misery to be borne.

The middle-class student has a virtual monopoly on the rewards of the system. He gets the good grades, the teacher expresses pleasure at his performance at school and his parents express pleasure at home. School affords him dignity, enhances his concept of self, and allows him to feel adequate.

In attaining success, the affluent youngster is required to make very few sacrifices and he attains one of life's most precious gratifications—he is allowed to have a feeling of competence. In addition, he participates fully in extra-curricular activities and is given the greatest measure of self-determination that the system allows.

Contrast the middle-class experience with the schooling of the poor. The disadvantaged youngster receives few rewards because he has none of the attributes to attain rewards. His parents cannot help him. He has few books at home, little space to study, and little stimulation from his peers. He has a language style and a behavior pattern that do not fit easily into the standard classroom situation. He is taught by persons who neither fully understand nor empathize with him. He is truly impotent. Most choices available to him are unattractive, and if he chooses not to come to school at all—then he is in trouble with the law. In the course of this experience he is stigmatized as stupid, robbed of dignity, humiliated, and afforded no sense of competence. When seen in a larger context, the school is but another agency in the anatomy of the establishment overwhelming the poor.

NEW CAREERS—A MEANS TO REDUCE COLONIALISM
IN THE SCHOOLS

Schools constitute a colonial imposition because nothing about the system belongs to the poor. Introducing the indigenous poor into meaningful teaching roles could be an important initial step toward producing a fundamental change in the character of the school. However, the step taken would have to be real and not mere window dressing. The poor must become truly a part of the teaching organization. They must be allowed to help in the determination of policy and program, and they must be given opportunity for meaningful advancement. The school then can take on a different complexion; persons known to be friends and neighbors could also be known as teachers. The school would no longer have to be forbidding and awesome to parents. Within the school there would be persons who could be talked to, and the conversation need not be strained or hampered by suspicion. If the parent were unable to converse with the teacher at the convenience of the school then it might be possible for the parent to visit the teacher aide at home to discuss the education of the child.

The student would recognize transformation in the school. If it were possible for the teaching staff to become accessible and comprehensible to the public, then learning no longer need be corrupted by patronage or prejudice.

NEW CAREERS—A MEANS TO GENERATE PUPIL INCENTIVE

The new career concept is designed to put meaning into education. The meaning would come from making possible exciting employment for the high school graduate, and making attainable the heretofore unreachable college education. Students would be aware of the existence of these possibilities through the observation of friends and older brothers and sisters who would be engaged in new career assignments. At heart of the new career proposal is the belief that if the poor have a stake in their own destiny, if they have opportunity to utilize education for personal advantage, and if they are afforded dignity in the process, then motivation to participate in the system will logically follow. This is one goal of the new career proposal.

NOTES

1. Source: U.S. Department of Commerce, Bureau of the Census.
2. U.S. Department of Labor—*Manpower Report to the President and a Report on Manpower Requirements, Resources, Utilization and Training*. U.S. Government Printing Office, Washington, D.C., March 1963, p. 107.
3. Conant, J. B., *The Education of American Teachers*, New York, McGraw-Hill Book Co., 1963, p. 230.
4. Howard University is experimenting with development of such

training and in a pilot venture found that six weeks of training with
subsequent on-the-job follow-up produced outstanding results.

5. Sixty units of course credit could be obtained as follows: 8 units
per year supervised work experience (3 years equals 24 units); 9 units
summer school (2 years equals 18 units); one course a semester in a community college (6 semesters, 3 units each equals 18 units).

6. The Center for Youth and Community Studies at Howard University has created remedial programs for precisely this purpose.

7. If the reader is skeptical about the conversion of persons with sixth
grade skills into material for college courses, as was suggested earlier to
be the next phase in the new career sequence, there are several intermediate
factors which should be mentioned. (*a*) Curricula would be devised and
extension courses offered to give the new careerist the equivalent high
school completion in every instance; (*b*) motivation and intellectual stimulation created by new jobs and prospects should have a termendously
potent effect on motivation for increasing skills; and (*c*) concomitantly,
a highly accelerating effect on assimilation of knowledge and skill in the
case of aides with high latent potentials. Hence the need of special curricula to accommodate the rate of learning which these aides may achieve,
in their remedial and catch-up courses.

8. For example, monies secured under the Economic Opportunity
Act of 1964, or a grant from one of the foundations active in the educational field.

9. The Washington, D.C. school system and the Howard University
Center for Youth and Community Studies are engaging in a study in
which 20 disadvantaged youth are employed as teacher aides.

10. The characteristics of those in need of more intensive education
and the optimum classroom size for different categories of youth can be
determined only if these issues are rigorously investigated. It is hoped
that during the next decade educational research will be directed toward
providing answers to these basic questions.

11. There are scarcely enough fully qualified teachers to meet current
demand and asking for more is simply fanciful. Further, the intensification
of education allows for most efficient use of available professional. The
zero-sum model generated from population increases and required projection of *more* classrooms. The nonzero sum model is designed to bring
more teaching personnel into *available* classrooms.

12. For example:

R. S. Lynd and H. M. Lynd, *Middletown: A Study in American
Culture;* New York: Harcourt, Brace and World, Inc., 1929.

W. L. Warner, R. J. Havighurst and M. B. Loeb, *Who Shall Be
Educated?* New York: Harper and Row, 1944.

A. Hollingshead, *Elmtown's Youth;* New York: John Wiley and
Sons, Inc., 1949.

P. C. Sexton, *Income and Education: Inequalities in Our Public
Schools;* New York: Viking Press, 1961.

F. Riessman, *The Culturally Deprived Child;* New York: Harper
and Brothers, 1962.

13. New York: Dell Publishing Co., 1959.

14. *Ibid.,* p. 112.

15. *Ibid.,* p. 117.

CHAPTER 5

NONPROFESSIONAL AIDES IN A COMMUNITY MENTAL HEALTH PROGRAM

THE USE of the poor in human service is "catching on" in education, social service, and mental health. Schools throughout the country are employing an increasing number of "Team Mothers," and Parent Education Coordinators, "for such purposes as vision and hearing screening, escorting pupils on field trips, operating projectors and other equipment."[1] In some areas there is a Puerto Rican Community Coordinator, whose special function is to integrate the school and the Puerto Rican community, interpreting each to the other. Typically, these coordinators are not highly trained people, but rather "informal leaders" who have close ties to the neighborhood and its traditions.

Nonprofessionals have been employed as tutors or homework helpers, homemakers, directors and assistants in half-way houses (and other synthetic family-like living units), detached community workers, recreation aides, researchers in community self-study programs, etc.[2]

The Chicago Area Project has employed local residents in its antidelinquency program for over two decades.[3] Mobilization for Youth employs a number of categories of neighborhood nonprofessionals: homemakers, parent aides, homework helpers, community organizers, case aides.

George Brager, one of the directors of the project notes that in contrast to the Chicago Area Project where the indigenous workers were hired in more delineated roles, the nonprofessionals at Mobilization for Youth "were assigned a wide range of tasks, and great freedom in carrying them out. They gave advice, processed complaints, made referrals, offered support, and guided the development of community-action strategies, in addition to performing other more concrete and specific functions."[4] Brager states further:

While Visiting Homemakers, Parent Aides, and Community Development Workers were supervised by professionals, they had vast discretionary powers. If their functions had been delimited, however, or their tasks too closely defined, the differences in style which we have noted between the nonprofessional and the professional would not have emerged so clearly. Dilution of the nonprofessional's impact upon program climate might be the consequence.[5]

THE NONPROFESSIONAL AND
THE WAR ON POVERTY

The new nonprofessional jobs are related to the recent regard for the poor in at least four major ways:

1. The expanded servicing of the poor in and of itself produces a great many new jobs to be filled;

2. The traditional reluctance evidenced by many middle-class professionals to work with low-income populations, whether they be pupils or clients, produces a situation where

there is a limited personnel supply for an increasingly recognized need;

3. The nonprofessional jobs themselves function as opportunities for a large number of people from lower socioeconomic background, and thus directly serve the reduction of poverty by transforming dependent welfare cases into homemakers, delinquents into researchers, students into tutors;

4. The new nonprofessional serves as a bridge from the middle-class institution to the low-income population.[6] "Indigenous staff are conceived of as 'bridge people'; able to interpret community life and values to the professionals . . . as well as serve as interpreters of the professionals, and role models, for lower-income community persons."[7]

Anthropologists have long been aware of this bridge function. Thus in attempting to convince the population of a Peruvian town to boil their water, "hygiene visitors" are recruited "from social levels or cultural groups similar to those with which they will work. They receive instruction in such topics as hygiene, communicable diseases, environmental sanitation, nutrition, dental care, and domestic economy. . . ."

The hygiene worker was apparently able to secure more positive results with housewives whose economic level and cultural background were similar to her own. Her own background was middle class by Los Molinos standards, and she belonged to the majority group. She was apparently unable to secure equally positive results when dealing with Negroes or with families of markedly different socioeconomic levels from her own.[8]

NONPROFESSIONALS
IN MENTAL HEALTH FIELDS

Traditionally the role of psychiatric aides has been largely custodial. With the advent of the new drugs, and a community based psychiatry, these hospital based aides can take on more and more rehabilitative functions. A natural extension of community psychiatry would seem to call for the use of these aides directly in the community and home, since this is now the locus of rehabilitation. Moreover, in a mental health program in a low income community, the community based aide of low income background may play a decisive role in bridging the gap between the middle-class professional and the underprivileged patient.

The introduction of the nonprofessional aide who can help bridge the gap between the professional agency and the lower socioeconomic segments of the community may also contribute to accessibility and lessen the likelihood of remote impersonal services. The use of such personnel should also enable the professional to operate under less pressure, while others perform tasks related to his job, but not germane to his specific skill. Thus his scope in terms of the numbers he can reach can be substantially expanded and his ability to contact the client or patient may be improved. Under such conditions it is more likely that a mental health center will be better able to devote its energies to mobilizing the resources of the community to meet the needs of a citizen or family in crisis, or to anticipate situations which present unusual psychological hazards.

The use of indigenous personnel drawn from low-income communities can perhaps be a decisive factor in helping treatment agencies reorganize their approaches to low-income people. Neighborhood people functioning as nonprofessionals appear to be highly successful in developing rapport with low-income clients, including the most deprived and disadvantaged individuals in the community.[9] Their success seems to stem from the fact that they are similar to the clients in terms of background, style, language, ethnicity, and interests. For this reason, and also because they serve as excellent role models, we would recommend that a great many more nonprofessionals may be employed in halfway houses, correctional institutions, after-care programs, etc., in various capacities.

It is interesting to note that nonprofessionals have been playing a decisive role in the rapidly increasing number of lay self-help groups such as Alcoholics Anonymous and Synanon (for drug addicts). Mowrer notes that there are over 265 groups of this kind listed in a directory entitled *Their Brothers Keepers.*[10] The American Conference of Therapeutic Self-Help Clubs publishes an official magazine, *Action,* describing some of the functions of these groups.

While the lay people involved are not necessarily of low-income background, many of them have little formal education, are presently unemployed, and have become poor, if they were not poor all of their lives. We are not suggesting that these groups become the model for the nonprofessional in the mental health field, but rather that it is instructive to observe the various mental health functions, both nonspecific and specific, which the nonprofessionals in these groups appear to serve. They function as models, supporters, listeners, critics, expeditors, and so on. Perhaps, from observing these organizations we can derive valuable clues which may be of assistance in formulating the roles of mental health aides in a professional setting.

HEALING AND SERVICE

The contributions of the nonprofessional in a comprehensive community health setting can logically be divided (despite apparent overlap in practice) under two headings: healing and service.[11] The healing function is principally concerned with the various psychological and psychotherapeutic roles within the potential repertoire of the mental health aide, guided by a professionally led team: role models (ego ideals, significant others, socializers); listener role (provide cathartic outlet); supportive role (concern); intervention role (the "intervention" effect of the presence of a therapeutic agent or person connected with a therapeutic establishment such as a hospital or mental health unit—especially at crisis points); ego expansion role—provide better understanding and awareness of reality, community resources, issues.

It can be seen from this very brief and tentative listing, that the nonprofessional has the possibility of contributing both nonspecific and specific therapeutic assistance. It should not be supposed, however, that the nonprofessional can provide all kinds of even nonspecific treatment. For example, for many people the intervention effect and "expectation of cure" will only take place if the "intervenor" is a professional with authority, preferably a doctor in a white jacket. Hence, for these persons a five-minute contact with a professional, supplemented by more protracted contact with a nonprofessional may be optimal. Others may require fuller (nonspecific) professional contact while still others may have negative reactions to the "subtle intimidation of the middle-class professional's authority"[12] and consequently profit most from extensive association with the nonprofessional.

Service functions fall largely under the rubric of what Reiff[13] and Duhl[14] have independently described as the expediter role (something like the Ombudsman in Sweden and the social broker concept stressed at Mobilization of Youth). The forerunner of this role in the United States is perhaps to be found in the union counselor who has been trained by various labor unions, such as the United Automobile Workers, to utilize information regarding health and welfare laws and the structure of agencies and hospitals in aiding union members with problems. The nonprofessional expediter not only "opens doors" and provides the low-income client with information and support, but may also furnish direct aid in terms of negotiating services (e.g., filling out forms, accompanying the client to the Welfare or Housing office, etc.).[15] The nonprofessional expediter who is employed by a union or a hospital or whatever agency, carries with him the "back-up power" of this agency and thus when he functions as an expediter in aiding other people cut through red tape, obtain service, etc., he does not simply utilize the skills that he possesses or has been trained to develop, but carries with him as well the implicit and often explicit power of the agency.

As previously noted, nonprofessional aides at Mobilization for Youth were frequently involved in the expediter role through processing complaints, making referrals and the like.[16]

GROUP FUNCTIONS

Some of the work that nonprofessionals can perform in relation to groups (family, community, and therapy groups) provides an illustration of the overlap of the healing and service functions. For example, in his service capacity the non-professional can provide information regarding the existence of various groups (recreation, social action, etc.) available in the community and in some cases assist the low-income person to take part in these activities.[17]

In addition, with regard to the healing function, we believe that nonprofessionals have an important potential that has thus far been little utilized as an auxiliary in group treatment. Under the guidance of the professional therapist or group leader, the nonprofessional aide can participate in the group therapy sessions and perform the valuable function of maintaining continuity of contact with the group participants by visiting each of them on a daily basis between group sessions. Moreover, the integration of the aide's home-visiting and extra-session experiences with the patient could be integrated into the group sessions, thus enriching and enhancing their therapeutic value.

INFORMATION GATHERER: HOME OBSERVATION

One function that can be expected of the mental health nonprofessionals working with the family relates to careful observation of the home of the client and relevant behavior taking place in the home. Hence, mental health aides should be trained to observe:

1. how the apartment is furnished, how well kept and clean it is, whether the walls are marked up, whether it smells, the condition of the building as a whole;

2. the division of labor in the household—who does the cooking, who manages the children, budgeting;

3. signs of narcotics or excessive use of alcohol;

4. sleeping arrangements in the apartment;

5. how members of the family relate to each other and to the children—who talks, who leaves the room, who sits where;

6. how the family reacts to the aide, whether the aide is viewed with suspicion;

7. the leisure pattern of the family—tempo, style, how the day is spent;

8. attitudes of family toward the school, welfare, the neighborhood;

9. the family history—how recently arrived in the country, neighborhood, possibly some information regarding toilet training, feeding, sex behavior.

It is assumed that this material would be discussed and evaluated by the diagnostic team (psychologist, nurse, social worker, psychiatrist) and related to information derived from psychological testing, psychiatric interview, etc.

The aides would be trained in home visiting and over a period of time would acquire knowledge regarding the meaning of family interaction—e.g., the significance of seating arrangements, etc.

THE NONPROFESSIONALS—
GRATIFICATIONS AND ATTRIBUTES

There are possible gratifications besides remuneration in the nonprofessional assignment. The nonprofessional is able to realize personal gains from the help he gives to others, the self-respect he gains from doing a meaningful job and the sense of competence obtained from the learning of skills. In addition, as part of a mental health team, he is able to obtain a sense of belonging and an ésprit de corps.

1. Perhaps the most important characteristic the Mental Health Aide should possess is flexibility. This is far more significant than any particular personality type because it is the "trainability" of the Aide that probably will be decisive. (Moreover, we know too little about personality types that are likely to be effective with particular patients.)

The Aide may have definite personal problems but in the context of a relatively stable personality he should be able to function flexibly. Most important, he must evidence some ability to learn and develop. He should have some interest in people, be able to listen and take the point of view of the "other."

The Aide should have a degree of self-awareness and demonstrate the capacity to look at and accept differences in others and relate to various cultural and ethnic groups effectively. Some capacity to tolerate frustration and ambiguity is important.

2. It is desirable that the Aide not be too highly moralistic, judgmental, and punitive. Nor should he be easily terrified by aggression, or irrational behavior.

3. The Aide should be able to accept supervision and criticism and be able to function in a group. Hopefully, he will be receptive to learning and have a fair amount of curiosity. He should be responsible and be able to maintain confidentiality.

A brief description of some of the characteristics of one highly effective psychiatric Aide may be illuminating: This Aide appears to possess well-modulated affect, is responsive in a low key, and is able to show some detachment. He always seems to be able to find and utilize the positive aspect of the situation, often in a highly constructive manner. He is not "using" the job to fulfill his needs—his needs are met in other places; nor does he resist his role. He is secure in his masculinity in a relatively "female" setting (most of his superiors are women), and he relates easily to the professional staff. He is able to influence patients in a nondidactic, experiential fashion.

WHY ARE NONPROFESSIONALS EFFECTIVE?

In the first place the indigenous worker usually possessed a natural knowledge of the local society. Second, he was hampered by none of the barriers to communications with residents for whom the nonresident, especially those identified with "welfare" enterprise, tended to be an object of suspicion and hostility. Third, his employment was a demonstration of sincere confidence in the capacity of the area resident for work of this sort. Fourth, he was more likely than the nonresident to have access to the neighborhood's delinquent boys and, therefore, to be more effective in re-directing their conduct. Fifth, his employment represented a prime means of initiating the education of the local population in the mysteries of conducting the welfare enterprise. Hence, virtually from the first, one of the most distinctive features of (Chicago) Area Project procedure was the employment, in appropriate categories and under the tutelage of staff sociologists of the Institute, of local residents to aid in the organization of the approximately dozen community or civic "committees" which were established in Chicago over the course of two decades.[18]

Much (not all) of the literature dealing with the nonprofessional tends to see him as an extension of the arm of the professional. Thus he is viewed as someone who can help reduce some of the burden on the teacher, or social worker— he can relieve the professional or perform under supervision some of the less technical tasks of the professional.[19]

For the most part these discussions of the nonprofessional concern nonindigenous personnel. There is a marked difference in the views regarding the unique contributions of indigenous personnel. Indigenous personnel are not viewed as the handmaidens of social workers but are perceived as having a distinct role to play and unique contributions to make.

There are a number of factors that appear to account for the potential effectiveness of indigenous nonprofessionals:

1. The most obvious variable is their (peer) status attributes—they *are* poor, *are* from the neighborhood and *are* often members of minority groups. These attributes in and of themselves allow them to be perceived in certain ways and to be reacted to accordingly. Consequently, they have far less need to validate themselves and as Brager points out, this gives them "a considerable advantage over the professional from the outset."[20] Nonprofessional personnel also have potentially excellent and unique opportunities to develop relationships to "clients." Effective social workers, of course, have excellent relationship skills, but they have far less opportunity to develop a rounded, everyday type of relationship with the low-income client; and it is this very type of relationship that is desired and expected. Social workers simply cannot as easily attend weddings, family gatherings, funerals, etc. One reason for the success of the nonprofessional, then, is the fact that he is able to *do* what professionals are not in a position to do.

2. The nonprofessional is effective also because he can be an acceptable model—a "significant other"; he is not a middle-class "square"—he is one of "us"—only a little bit more effective. The model function is perhaps best seen in the homework helper role as originally designed at Mobilization for Youth. The homework helper is a high school student of low-income background with a 75 per cent average or better, who tutors an elementary school student of the same background who is doing poorly in his schoolwork.

3. Closely related to the model function is the know-how of the low-income nonprofessionals. They know how to deal with neighborhood problems from the "inside," not from above. Many of them have themselves experienced difficul-

ties similar to the ones with which they help clients. Homemakers, for example, who have been on Welfare often have
developed special skills consistent with low-income habits in
order to manage in their situation. They

> know how to stretch leftovers, use surplus foods, recognize bargains,
> plan children's schedules, as well as how to deal with merchants and
> even with public and private agencies. Their abilities and attain-
> ments, while considerable, may yet be within the grasp of other, more
> impoverished residents.[21]

Hence, there is much greater probability that their suggestions and "savvy" will "fit" their clients.

4. The "style" of the nonprofessional is significantly related to their effectiveness. As Brager notes:

> The nonprofessionals are considerably less formal. They will hug
> clients, accept—and repay—their hospitality, and share first-name
> designations. The tenants' association meeting . . . was attended by
> children with balloons and bubble gum, as well as by old women,
> middle-aged and young adults. Although they were wrestling with
> problems resulting from serious housing violations, there was laughter
> and gaiety; although much business was conducted, there was no
> formal meeting.[22] Aside from the informality, nonprofessionals tend
> more often to be "directive," "active" and "partisan." "Cursory analy-
> sis of their records further supports the conclusion that the nonpro-
> fessionals tend to provide active direction, for the reports reveal that
> they "decided," "announced" and "insisted." This differs sharply
> from professional recording, in which workers are more likely to
> "suggest" and "enable."[23] The nonprofessional "was in the center of
> activity, exhorting her "clients," training by demonstration, and pro-
> viding direction."[24] A related "style" dimension is perhaps the mili-
> tancy often found among low-income nonprofessionals. Their mili-
> tancy is expressed in various ways: they demand action, motion—
> they are less accepting of delay and "talk"; they introduce new de-
> mands—"change the Welfare Department rules," "make the Housing
> Manager listen to the people," "let's make sure that everyone gets
> a chance to talk at PTA meetings."
> The style "match" is perhaps seen in the nonprofessional's tendency
> to externalize causes rather than look for internal ones. A similar
> tendency, of course, is quite common among low-income people in
> general. "The nonprofessional tends to give stronger weight to ex-

ternal life circumstances than to internal factors. In instances where case-workers have defined clients as "neglectful," nonprofessional staff have been more likely to see the behavior as a response to depressed conditions. A Homemaker touchingly ascribes the impulsive credit buying of a woman to the fact that 'Being young,' she wants everything in life.' When the same young woman reports a conversation with her dead husband, the Homemaker acknowledges the woman's mental illness and recommends referral to a mental-hygiene clinic, although her further comment suggests that such diagnosis and referral may be the result of supervisory influence: 'My honest (sic) opinion is that she needs to remarry.' "[25]

5. The "bridge" function (bridging the gap between the agency and the low-income client) mentioned earlier, is intimately related to the nonprofessional's interclass communication and mediation skills—another important determinant in his special effectiveness.

6. Finally, the nonprofessional's effectiveness is related to the satisfaction he receives from the work he does—team satisfactions, respect gained from performing a meaningful job in cooperation with professionals, learning a skill, and most important of all, helping others. The far-reaching significance of the helping role cannot be underestimated and requires special attention.

THE HELPER THERAPY PRINCIPLE
AND THE NONPROFESSIONAL

People with a problem helping other people who have the same problem in more severe form (e.g. Alcoholics Anonymous), is a simple age old approach, well-known to all group therapists. But in using this approach—and there is a marked current increase in its use—we may be placing the emphasis on the wrong person in centering attention on the individual receiving the help. More attention might well be given the individual who has less of a need for the help: that is, the person who is providing the assistance—*the helper*—*because it is he who really improves!*

While it may be uncertain that people *receiving* help are always benefited, it seems much clearer that the people *giving* the help are profiting from their role. This appears to be the case in a wide variety of group "therapies" including Synanon (for drug addicts), Recovery Incorporated (for psychologically disturbed people), Alcoholics Anonymous (for alcoholics), SCORE (Charles Slack's program for delinquents).[26]

Cressey formulates this principle as one of his five social psychological principles for the rehabilitation of criminals:

> The most effective mechanism for exerting group pressure on members will be found in groups so organized that criminals are induced to join with noncriminals for the purpose of changing other criminals. A group in which criminal "A" joins with some noncriminals to change criminal "B" is probably most effective in changing criminal "A," not "B" . . .[27]

An interesting experimental verification of the helper principle is provided in a study by King and Janis.[28] These investigators found that subjects who had to improvise a speech supporting a particular point of view tended to change their opinions in the direction of this view more than subjects who merely read the speech for an equivalent amount of time. They describe this effect in terms of "self-persuasion through persuading others."[29]

The helper principle may have wide application. (The use of homework helpers, and tutors, for example, may not only be beneficial to the recipients of the aid, but may also encourage its dispensers to *consider a teaching career or to become apprentice teachers.*) It is probably no accident that it is often said that one of the best ways to learn, is to teach.

Perhaps then our strategy ought to be to *devise ways of creating more helpers!* Or to be more exact: how to transform receivers of help (such as ADC mothers) into dispensers of help; how to structure the situation so that receivers of help will be placed in roles requiring the giving of assistance.

The helper therapy principle has at least two important implications for the nonprofessional of lower socioeconomic background:

1. Since many of the nonprofessionals to be recruited are former delinquents, ADC mothers, former addicts and the like, it seems quite likely that placing them in a helping role can be highly therapeutic for them.

2. As the nonprofessionals benefit from their new helping roles, they may actually become more effective workers and thus provide more help to others at a new level.

Thus, what we are presenting here may be a positive onward and upward spiral in contrast to the downward, better known, vicious cycle. That is, the initial helping role may be furnishing minimal help to the recipient of help, but may be highly beneficial to the helper, who in turn because he is helped, becomes more efficient, better motivated, and reaches a new stage in helping skill.

In a sense, the principle we are advocating can be stated thus: we help others best when we ourselves are helped from trying to help.[30]

SOURCE OF THE TALENT:
ROLE OR PERSONALITY?

Sharp question has been raised by leaders of the social work profession regarding the competence of such (nonprofessional) persons, whose qualifications rested on assets of character and personal trait rather than on formal training and education. Leaders of the Area Project have always encouraged talented workers in this field to obtain as much training in the group work and social work fields as they could. However, they have regarded the talent for this work as the primary value.[31]

This quotation from the discussion of the Chicago Area Project represents one viewpoint regarding the source of the indigenous workers' skills. It sees their skill residing in "character and personal trait." But it is possible to look at the derivation of their effectiveness in a very different manner. It is possible that indigenous workers' skills emanate from the roles they play in relation to their clients, rather than (or perhaps in addition to) their personalities. In other words it may not be who they are, but rather what they do and how they do it that is decisive.[32] The reason for the success of the nonprofessional may lie in the fact that he is able to *do* what professionals don't do.

While the role is undoubtedly a decisive factor in the skill of the indigenous worker, it is equally obvious that there are a whole series of variables that he has in common with his "clients" that may contribute to his effectiveness, reduce his social distance and decrease neighborhood suspicion: residence, style, common experience, low-income know-how, ethnic similarities. In a sense, it is all of these factors that increase the probability that the behavior of the indigenous worker will be congruent with the expectations of the low-income "client." These variables allow the indigenous worker to play the role effectively.

NOTES

1. The Great Cities School Improvement Studies, Ford Foundation Project, mimeographed, 1960.

2. See *Experiment in Cultural Expansion,* National Institute of Mental Health, 1963.

3. See "The Chicago Area Project—A 25 Year Assessment," by Solomon Kobrin, *Annals of the American Academy of Political and Social Sciences,* Vol. 322, March 1959, pp. 19–29.

4. George Brager, "The Low-Income Nonprofessional," paper given at National Conference of Social Welfare, May 1964, p. 11.

5. Brager, *op. cit.,* pp. 11–12.

6. It has also been noted that the new nonprofessional contributes to the derigidification of the professions involved.

7. George Brager, "Some Assumptions and Strategies of the Mobilization for Youth Program," Unpublished, 1962.

8. Wellin, E., "Water Boiling in a Peruvian Town," *Health, Culture, and Community.* Edited by Benjamin D. Paul, New York: Russell Sage Foundation, 1955, p. 73 and p. 102.

9. Riessman, Frank, "The Revolution in Social Work: The New Non-Professional," 1963, Mobilization for Youth Report.

10. Mowrer, O. Hobart, *The New Group Therapy,* D. Van Nostrand Company, Inc., 1964, p. IV.

11. We are indebted to Robert Reiff for this specific formulation. Conference on Nonprofessionals held at Howard University, April 27, 1964.

12. Brager, *op. cit.,* p. 9.

13. Personal Communication.

14. Leonard Duhl has spoken of the nonprofessional case manager and the multi-purpose workers performing various aspects of the expediter function. Conference on the nonprofessional held at Howard University, April 27, 1964.

15. There are some similarities here to the use of nonprofessionals in the Citizens' Advice Bureaus that grew out of World War II experience in England.

16. Brager, *op. cit.,* p. 11.

17. Aside from problems which have greater social action relevance, certain personalities evidence potentialities for participating in this direction. The supervisory staff (together with the nonprofessionals) might make "social action diagnosis" and where a positive (sociotherapeutic) potential is indicated the aides might play an important facilitative role.

18. Solomon Kobrin, "The Chicago Area Project—A 25 Year Assessment," *The Annals of the American Academy of Political and Social Science,* Philadelphia, Vol. 322 (March, 1959), p. 24.

19. This position is discussed together with a more favorable attitude in "Wanted Now: Social Work Associates," remarks by Bertram M. Beck, Associate Executive Director, National Association of Social Workers at National Conference on Social Welfare, 1963. Also, Laura Epstein, "Differential Use of Staff: A Method to Expand Social Services," *Social Work,* October 1962, Vol. 7, No. 4, pp. 66–72.

20. George Brager, "The Low-Income Nonprofessional," paper presented at National Conference on Social Welfare, May 1964, p. 8.

21. Brager, *op. cit.,* p. 4.

22. Brager, *op. cit.,* p. 7.

23. Brager, *op. cit.,* p. 7.

24. Brager, *op. cit.,* p. 7.

25. Brager, *op. cit.,* p. 9.

26. We are not suggesting that there is good research evidence that these programs are effective; but various reports, many of them admittedly impressionistic, point more to improvement in the givers of help rather than the receivers. Careful research evaluating these programs is needed because there are numerous contaminating factors that may be contributing to their success: charismatic leadership of the therapist, selection of subjects, Hawthorne effects.

27. Rita Volkman & Donald R. Cressey "Differential Association and the Rehabilitation of Drug Addicts," *American Journal of Sociology,* Vol. 69, No. 2, 1963, p. 139.

28. B. T. King and I. L. Janis, "Comparison of the Effectiveness of Im-

provised Versus Non-Improvised Role Playing in Producing Opinion Changes," *Human Relations*, 1956, i, pp. 177–186.

29. We have not attempted to indicate the various mechanisms whereby the helper profits from his helper role: improved self-image from doing something worthwhile, helping someone in need; becoming committed to a position through advocating it (as is the King and Janis study); becoming part of a system through participating as homework helper, homemaker, etc.

30. Stated in a slightly different context, a teacher improves from learning through teaching.

31. Kobrin, *op cit.*, p. 24.

32. We are indebted to George Brager for the specific formulation of this issue with regard to indigenous personnel.

CHAPTER *6*

THE INDUSTRY
OF DISCOVERY:*
NEW ROLES FOR
THE NONPROFESSIONAL[1]

Joan Grant
Co-Director, New Careers Development Project,
Institute for the Study of Crime and Delinquency

RESEARCH is one of the most rapidly growing activities in the country. It is responsible for the extraordinary technological advances of recent years and it lies back of our material production activities and much of the operation of government. Business and government speak of it as "research and development," development connoting the use of research to deal with growth and to bring about change.

In the eight-year period from 1953–54 to 1961–62, research and development activities more than doubled in private industry and expended three-and-a-half times in those supported by the Federal government (13, p. 75). This

---

* ". . . the newest type of economic activity in the country, aptly named the 'industry of discovery'—the pursuit of new inventions, new techniques, new materials, and new weapons" (13, p. 22).

expansion is likely to continue, at least as rapidly as the expansion in technological change and perhaps at an even faster rate. Research and development activities are not only a response to technological change; they stimulate further change which calls in turn for further research.

In many fields, the need for research is accepted without question. This holds for the physical and biological sciences generally, and it is true for their many areas of application—engineering, medicine, agriculture, and the manufacture of new products. For the social and behavioral sciences, particularly in their applied forms, research has a less certain status. It is seen as essential in the apprenticeship served by graduate students, but once out of formal training and into real life, knowledge gained by research begins to compete with the knowledge of "experience," "common sense," and "intuition."[2] Yet even here a research approach to the problems dealt with by social and behavioral science has made substantial inroads. Advertising agencies, as well as the manufacturers that support them, have research departments. Consumer organizations rely on research in efforts to pick their way through the maze of competing advertisements. Politicians make use of research findings in the form of public opinion polls in preparing campaign strategies, and election night is now unthinkable without the research predictions of a computer.[3] Even war strategies are based to a large extent on research.[4]

This growth in the utilization of research has come about largely because developments in computers have made it possible to study problems that were earlier impractical of solution. As research has become increasingly automated it has shown a corresponding increase in the number and range of problems that may be investigated and an increase in demands for research information on which to base decisions. Automation increases both the rate of our acquisition of knowledge and our needs for further knowledge. Since research deals with ideas and with planning, it is unlikely that research activities will ever be completely automated. This is especially true in those areas that have to do with human behavior.

RESEARCH NEEDS:
THE PHYSICAL AND
BIOLOGICAL SCIENCES

A projection of needs for research personnel, per se, is difficult to make since employment figures lump together professional and technical workers of all types, some of whom are engaged in research proper, some in service roles, and some in mixtures of the two. An analysis of occupational growth over the decade of the 1950's shows a 47 per cent increase in the professional and technical group, compared to a total including all occupations of 14.5 per cent. Some professions grew more rapidly than others. The most extraordinary growth occurred in the employment of mathematicians (345 per cent). Engineers as a whole increased by 64 per cent, but aeronautical engineers by 193 per cent and industrial engineers by 142 per cent. The growth for physicists was 88 per cent, for geologists and geophysicists 75 per cent, and for biological scientists 51 per cent. There was similar growth in the technical occupations that work with these professionals. Electrical and electronic technicians increased by 679 per cent, other engineering and physical science technicians by 102 per cent, medical and dental technicians by 80 per cent (13, p. 202).

Employment projections for the next decade carry out the trends of the past. Per cent growth including all occupations for the 15 year period 1960–1975 is estimated at 31 per cent, but professional and technical employment is expected to rise by 65 per cent. The demand for engineers and scien-

tists will be even greater; it is expected to double in this
period. Yet the supply of new engineers to meet this growth
may fall below demand by as much as one-third and the
same is expected for physicists.[5] Extremely rapid growth is
also anticipated in the supporting technician occupations,
partly to meet the shortage of more trained scientists, but
also because of the increased complexity of our technology.
Requirements for technicians to work with engineers and
scientists are expected to double by 1975 (13, pp. 101–102,
125).

RESEARCH NEEDS: THE SOCIAL
AND BEHAVIORAL SCIENCES

Comparable figures for research in the social and behavioral sciences are not readily available. The Department
of Labor reports a 60 per cent growth in the social science
fields over the decade of the 1950's, with the greatest increase
occurring for economists (118 per cent) and psychologists
(150 per cent), but these figures do not necessarily cover all
work in these fields (13, p. 202). Current applications of social and behavioral science are still quite sketchy. Research
in these areas has scarcely begun to make its impact felt upon
the culture as a whole. There are at least three ways in which
social science research could immediately be greatly expanded.

1. ACCOUNTING FOR OPERATIONS

The most obvious way of expanding research can be described simply as "keeping track of." The growth in manage-
ment-science and defense-operations research since World
War II indicates the importance to industry of maintaining
an accounting system for its operations. This system is basi-
cally a matter of keeping track of input, output, and costs,

for both products and personnel, with built-in checks on the adequacy of the information obtained.

Most social agencies have some type of operations accounting. This is essential for the management of institutions in which eating and sleeping arrangements must be dealt with on a daily basis. It is also important for those agencies that rely on size of client rolls to determine the number of staff they may hire. But the kind of information necessary for rational program planning and for assessing the effectiveness of the agency's day-to-day operation is often far from adequate.

The Department of Labor, in preparing its latest manpower report, found itself hampered by the inadequacy of available information on the number and kinds of job vacancies and the nature of the labor force. Because of this, a Presidential Committee recently appointed to investigate employment and unemployment statistics recommended improvements in both the collection and the analysis of basic information in this field (13, pp. 112–114). The situation is not unique. Many correctional systems, for example, have no way of knowing what happens to the people who have passed through their programs, and it is rare for even those agencies with extensive record-keeping systems to have knowledge of their clients' contacts with other social agencies. This means that it is difficult to collect information on the relation of prison incarceration to changes in welfare rolls, to relate employment data to vocational-training experience, or to link alcoholism and delinquency. Yet, planning of new programs —especially those that represent an attack on many interrelated social problems at once—requires just this kind of basic knowledge. Information on technical problems and resources is well advanced. Information on human problems, and the resources for meeting them, is scarce and often totally unavailable. This is true, unfortunately, even in those areas in the most urgent need of social planning. The Manpower Report of the President comments:

Despite the tremendous potentialities for economic and social change inherent in automation, there is a paucity of factual information with respect to its current nature, extent, and employment effects (13, p. 113).

There is nothing inherently difficult about this kind of research. The greatest difficulty actually lies in deciding what is the relevant information to collect. The collation and summarization of information can be readily done by punched card data-processing equipment or, where these are available, by computers. One of the most striking examples of the successful use of nonprofessionals (to be discussed below) has occurred in the development of a social agency operations accounting system.

2. THE DEMONSTRATION PROGRAM

All social agencies complain of lack of funds. Social services are unprofitable and business rarely supports them, while government spending is at best a compromise between the electorate's concern for tax rates and its demands that something be done about the most visible and disturbing aspects of social problems.[6] The demonstration program is an effort to get around the problem of limited funds for social services by obtaining special funding for attacking social problems in miniature. If we show what really can be done, the argument runs, by increasing services (or upgrading staff, or changing our approach to treatment or rehabilitation), then government budget sources and the public itself will recognize the utility of expanding services on a large scale.[7]

The specially-funded demonstration program is a relatively new development in our approach to social problems. Some of these programs are funded by private foundations, but by far the larger share are financed by the Federal government. Though the argument supporting the demonstration requires that some evidence of its effectiveness be obtained, the type of evaluation and the level of sophistication required for it vary widely from one funding agency to another.

Demonstration programs in the last few years have been undertaken most often in the areas of mental health, education, delinquency, or vocational training and retraining. Of late, the broad-based program, offering an attack on several of these problems at once, has come into fashion. Thus the Mobilization for Youth program in New York City, though focused on the problem of delinquency, has set up a variety of programs in education, job training, and welfare and has worked not only with problem youth but with problem adults in the community as well.[8] Such programs may form the prototype of the demonstration programs that will be focused on poverty, and they could indeed be considered as demonstrations of ways to attack poverty. Conceptualizing programs under this larger title can broaden the base of attack and provide an overall integration of the work on social problems that is now the function of a variety of social agencies working in isolation.

As the base of demonstration programs is broadened, however, to that extent do programs tend to become diffuse? When action is taken on many fronts, the difficulties of conceptualizating a research-evaluation approach increase. It is not easy to assess the effectiveness of a total program which consists of a variety of subprograms that may not be well-integrated either theoretically or in fact.

The statement of program assumptions and goals and the framing of testable hypotheses is difficult and time consuming. Staff on demonstration programs quickly become caught up in getting the multi-faceted program underway, and planning for research evaluation is often relegated to the last (when it is too late to plan properly). Moreover, there is a good deal of impatience on the part of people involved in social action with researchers generally, particularly when research is seen as a way of delaying the implementation of a new program. Even well-intentioned staff will find that research and program goals may sometimes conflict.

In addition, it is hard to find competent social science researchers who are willing to leave tenure college and university positions (where as likely as not they have control over their own research grants) for the uncertainties of being full-time staff on temporarily funded projects.

We thus have a situation in which research evaluation of demonstration programs is often postponed in order to get the program started, turned over to part-time advisory committees, or simply not thought about at all. The approach is short-sighted in the extreme.

It is against Federal law to market a new drug without extensive clinical investigation: giving the drug to a selected number of patients and observing the results. It would be absurd to think clinical investigation needs were served by administering the drug and then failing to observe how patients responded to it, or by relying on the manufacturer's opinion that the drug, in theory, ought to be effective. Yet, this is precisely the case in many of our education, welfare, and mental health programs, our approaches to employment training, criminal rehabilitation, and delinquency prevention. Ideas are common and cheap. Implementing ideas is expensive. Implementing ideas without collecting information on how they are working, or in ways that prevent the collection of relevant information, is like giving a new drug without systematically observing its effects on patients. The demonstration is wasted.

3. SOCIAL AGENCIES AND INNOVATION

Social agencies are also engaged in running demonstration programs, though they do not always have this title. Special classes for retarded or gifted children are "demonstrations," and so are experimental parole or probation caseloads, a changed policy for administering welfare funds, or the opening of a new outpatient clinic to treat disturbed adolescents. Though these are ordinarily not conceptualized as research, they are trials of new procedures, without prior knowledge or effectiveness. Do they work? All too often, this is a matter of someone's subjective judgment, and new programs are dropped or become institutionalized as part of regular procedure without any real knowledge of whether or not they are doing what they were intended to do.[9]

Two questions must be answered if an agency is to learn anything from its innovations. (1) Did the program do what the agency convinced its budget sources it was going to do? (2) Was the program carried out reasonably similar to the program as originally planned?

Pearl has spoken of this second question as one of quality control (11). A term taken from manufacturing, it refers to the periodic inspection of a product to find out whether or not it is within acceptable limits of manufacturing standards. Social agency programs need a similar inspection. Programs on paper are one thing. Programs in practice, as is recognized by everyone involved in them, are frequently something else, a matter of compromise, expediency, loss of interest, and change in personnel. Sampling of a program to find out if it remained the same throughout a study is an important part of research evaluation, and must indeed precede that evaluation. Few agencies, however, are able to answer questions of either program effectiveness or quality control.

WHO DOES RESEARCH?

To qualify for professional research training, one must generally be a university graduate student. The present university training model is patterned after that of an apprentice in a guild. Although courses in research design and methodology have appeared on the increase since the second world war in both psychology and sociology departments, research is still taught largely by doing. The graduate student becomes qualified by conducting independent research, under supervision and conforming to accepted guild requirements.

Typically, he also gains experience by working, for low rates of pay, on faculty research projects.

The pattern has altered somewhat in recent years as basic personnel are typically drawn from the ranks of certain types of marginally employed groups: students, housewives, unemployed actors (actors have made superb interviewers). These research functions are not seen as requiring general or prolonged academic training; brief on-the-job training is the rule. The untrained person is more available to the research organization than the professional, and he is certainly cheaper. His use, however, is haphazard. Though the temporary interviewer or coder is a kind of social science technician, he does not usually see himself in this role, neither making a career out of a low-level research function nor taking training to become a more qualified research person.

RESEARCH AND THE
NONPROFESSIONAL

Considerable evidence has accumulated in the social science field to show that nonprofessionals can learn to perform complex and responsible research functions. This experience lends plausibility to the main thesis of this book: it is possible to stratify professional jobs into a hierarchy of functions, and it is possible to train nonprofessionals—persons with a high school education or less—to perform many of these functions. Moreover, there is evidence that nonprofessionals can be prepared through on-the-job training to assume professional-level positions. Our present training for research—through college and the graduate school—is not necessarily the only way to develop skilled research workers. This point is of especial importance when many young people, under our present education system, are being kept out of university-based career development, through either cultural sets or basic skill patterns that do not favor the verbal, abstract-thinking orientation of college-preparatory courses and university curricula.

CAMP ELLIOTT: THE NAVY DOES RESEARCH

In 1954, a group of psychologists set up a research program at Camp Elliott, supported by funds from the Office of Naval Research. Camp Elliott was then one of the three Naval Retraining Commands for the rehabilitation of naval and marine offenders. The research program, a study of the military nonconformist, included setting up a series of twenty-man therapeutic community-type living groups as a way of effecting changes in delinquent attitudes and behavior. The groups, incidentally, were run by nonprofessionals—marine sergeants—with consultation by professional psychologists, an early example of the use of nonprofessionals in a therapeutic role (6).

The living-group program involved some 500 confined men (retrainees), each of whom had two lengthy tape-recorded interviews and a large battery of pre- and post-experiment attitude tests. A number of other studies were also conducted, including one on delinquency prediction that was run on 20,000 naval recruits from all over the country. The amount of data collected was enormous. Computers were still in their infancy, and were not available to the five research staff members. This staff, concerned with test development, interviewing, rating interviews, consulting with treatment groups, and participating in other Retraining Command programs, had no time for data analysis.

The Armed Forces have long made a practice of using nonprofessionals to perform professional tasks within their system. Most of their medical services are performed by service-trained technicians, not by doctors, while education is largely in the hands of men without teaching credentials. This practice is the practical solution to the problem of a small professional staff and a large need for service. In the Camp Elliott study, additional staff was needed. The Command agreed that one of the next group of Chief Hospital Corpsmen sent to the Camp for duty would be assigned to research.

The Chief Corpsman chosen was selected from a group of three on the basis of his test records. Though he had not finished high school, and though he was seen as the least promising of the three by Command staff, largely because of apparently poor verbal facility, his tests showed that he was of superior intelligence and had a flair for mathematics. Beyond some limited experience in keeping medical records, he had no experience with statistics nor with research. He had no prior acquaintance with social scientists.

In keeping with Armed Forces tradition, the Retraining Command staff had previously assigned six retrainees to help give and score tests in the research program. The Chief Corpsman, faced with research program pressures, a backlog of data already collected, and his need to learn a minimum about the processing of data, was in no position to handle the workload alone. His immediate need was for more help. Retrainees were in plentiful supply, and there was little for them to do. Within a few months he had developed the research section from one using the part-time services of the retrainees engaged in testing to a semi-automated data-processing unit employing five Corpsmen and 42 retrainees.

Research was done on a production-line basis. The testing section remained, but it had doubled in size. In addition there was a section to handle population accounting for the Command as a whole (a new service taken on by research); one for data preparation and coding, which included filing and a typing pool; another for data analysis; and a fifth for computation. This last function was performed on five hand calculators which were run in two shifts, from 8:00 A.M. to midnight. This unit handled not only data from the several research studies, but was able to run an operations-accounting system for the Command as a whole and to do special studies for other Navy facilities in the area.

The data-processing unit was set up to get a job done, not to train men in research. There was thus no attempt to teach an approach to research, nor to create a hierarchy of skills which would permit the retrainee to work his way up to more responsible positions—things which would need to be done if on-the-job training were to be given to career research workers. The retrainees were concerned with return to Naval duty, not with new careers. The Chief Corpsman was, however, a different story. After five years with the data-processing unit he was ordered back to active sea duty. Two years later he retired from the Navy, and has been working since as a professional statistician. He is now nearing college graduation, with a major in mathematics and statistics, has published more than twenty technical research reports, and has given papers at two professional meetings.

What can be learned from the Camp Elliott experience?

1. Many necessary research tasks can be performed with a minimum of training. These are not limited to computational routines.

2. An apprenticeship can be served on the job as well as in graduate school. Academic experience may in fact be more meaningful and more effective if it accompanies or follows related work experience.

3. Persons who are considered relatively "nonverbal" and hence are cut off or discouraged from academic advancement may possess skills that are lost from development because of academic emphasis on verbal modes of functioning.

4. Even persons who are considered behavior problems serious enough to warrant confinement can work productively on technical white collar tasks. Though the retrainees assigned to research were usually not the pick of those available for assignment and were sometimes serving time in the brig, disciplinary problems in the research unit were minimal and morale was high. Many of the retrainees worked nights and weekends on their own initiative.

This last point is worth noting, for it has implications for training. A similar experience occurred at the California Medical Facility, where inmates perform routine laboratory work for the physicians who work in the institution. There were frequent complaints about hours and workload in the laboratory. The introduction of several outside medical research projects into the institution increased the demand for laboratory work, but the number of complaints actually decreased and there was a marked improvement in the laboratory's efficiency and output. The Research Coordinator at the Facility attributes the new esprit de corps among the inmate assistants to the role of the outside researchers who treat them as technical colleagues with a stake in the successful outcome of the research. Some have been given specialized training on new equipment and new procedures for specific projects.

This experience suggests that the use of nonprofessionals to do the "dirty work" for professional staff will not necessarily result in the effective performance of routine tasks. Routine is better performed when it is seen as a necessary part of a total team effort.

STATE PRISONS: THE INMATE RESEARCHER

Our prison system provides a captive, generally youthful, and largely idle population. Medical researchers have long taken advantage of the situation by using inmate volunteers to try out new drugs or procedures on a large scale. Social scientists have sometimes done the same, not only to study crime and delinquency problems but also as a way of finding large numbers of easily available subjects for other types of studies.

Prison administrators also make use of inmate availability. Inmates not only handle most of institution maintenance, but perform a variety of clerical tasks. In a few prisons they have also been trained to do research.

One of the most impressive examples of the potential strengths available in nonprofessionals comes from the State of Indiana.[10] Six institutions handle its adult and juvenile offenders, women as well as men. There has been little integration of program over the six and no central record-keeping system.

Three years ago a young inmate, serving a one-to-five year sentence in the Indiana Reformatory for assault and battery, discovered that some outdated Remington Rand punch card equipment, formerly used by the Motor Vehicles Department, was stored in the institution's basement. The inmate had a B.A. degree in business administration and before his arrest had worked for a year as supervisor of a medium-scale computer installation in a steel company. He saw the possibilities of using the equipment to set up a data processing system for the Reformatory and, at the same time, to provide training for other inmates.

Working with a 23-year-old fellow inmate who had taught himself something about data processing, he spent five months developing a proposal for a training program and an institution data processing system. The institution's Assistant Superintendent of Classification and Treatment was very supportive to this idea and helped in getting it accepted by other institution staff. The machines were turned over to the inmates. More important, the institution agreed that the men in the Tabulating Department, as it was named, were to be placed on an honor system, without custodial supervision. and were to be housed in a separate unit where they could work together in the evening hours.

The first inmate class opened in the fall of 1961. The course was publicized through the institution newspaper. Screening was rigorous. It was based on intelligence and achievement test records, programming aptitude tests developed by IBM, and a personal interview to assess the applicant's motivation for the course.

Eleven men passed this screening. They ranged in age from 21 to 30. Four had earned some previous college credit. Four had not finished high school. Classes were taught by the inmate who had originally conceived of the project. The eleven became the subsequent teachers for the Tabulating Department and the first to develop and run the institution's data processing system. Their first task after selection was to put the obsolete machines into operating condition.

The training program for the Tabulating Department is more rigorous than the screening required to enter it, and is constantly being revised to take account of the teaching experience and of changes in the data processing industry. The students work from 7:30 to 6:00, seven days a week. They attend classes four hours a day and work in the Department's data processing program in the afternoon.[11] There are daily quizzes and three to four hours of homework each night.

The course is divided into three parts, the total running approximately five months, and covers programming and wiring for a variety of accounting machines and computers. The only equipment available is that originally obtained from the Motor Vehicles Department so the students work chiefly from manuals donated by private organizations. A desk model educational computer is used in teaching the principles of computer operation. Students who pass all three phases successfully are awarded a Data-Processing Certificate which has been endorsed by the Central Indiana Chapter of the Data Processing Management Association.

There are course dropouts, especially in the later phases. Most of these are due to weakness in mathematics or in comprehension of the applications of the machines. As of July, 1964, 99 inmates had begun the training program; 61 were paroled or transferred out of the Department before training was completed. Of the remaining number, 26 have so far completed all three phases and been awarded the Data Processing Certificate.[12] Ten of this group have been paroled, two to data-processing jobs, and three others have since found work in the data-processing field.

The inmate who initiated the program was transferred to the State Prison early in 1963 to assume a newly created position, Director of Penal Data Processing. His job was to set up a coordinated data processing system for all six of the state's correctional institutions. He was paroled the following year and is presently in a middle management position with the Department of Correction. This man, of course, had had data-processing training and work experience before entering the prison system, but it is important to note that the program did not stand or fall with him. He had trained his successor before his transfer to the State Prison and all subsequent supervisors of the Department have received their training there.

Another model of inmate training is provided by the State Prison of Southern Michigan.[13] The State Highway Department has been running a school for computer programmers at the Prison since the fall of 1961. Students who finish the course are used to write and document computer applications of Highway engineering problems. The school was organized jointly with the Department of Corrections as a means of obtaining needed programming personnel for the Highway Department and to provide a rehabilitation program for selected inmates. Instruction was provided initially through contract with the Systems Service Company, but is currently given by staff from the Programming Unit of the Highway Department and educational personnel from computer equipment manufacturers.

The first announcement of the class drew 300 applicants. A third of these were eliminated on the basis of intelligence and education test performance. The remaining group was narrowed to 40 by tests of vocabulary and word meanings, general mathematics, and abstract and symbolic logic, most weight being given to the latter. Personal interviews to evaluate motivation for the course and ability to work with others further reduced the group to 22.

This first class had an average I.Q. of more than 130.[14] One of the group had had a year in college and another had graduated from high school. The remaining 20 had not gone beyond the tenth grade. None of the men had any notion of what computers or programming were like. They expected to be trained to run some type of machinery and were actually disappointed to find that they worked primarily with paper and pencil.

The course covers computer concepts and programming and documentation techniques. Operating manuals are provided, and a key punch has been installed in the class quarters, but other machines are not available. In addition to their formal instruction, the students, working in groups of three, are required to program sample problems. After six-and-a-half months of training, they begin programming engineering and data problems for the Highway Department. This Department, and its equipment, are 40 miles away from the Prison. To help coordinate the work of the two units, a professional programmer from the Department has been assigned to work with the inmate group.

Unlike the Indiana program, which is concerned with innovating and expanding data-processing operations, the Michigan program is designed primarily to fill an existing personnel shortage in an ongoing operation. The men do work similar to that done by civilian programmers, but the use of inmates has allowed far better program documentation than was previously possible. This record-keeping job is often slighted by programming groups because of the press of other work. The Highway Department attempts to maintain a programming staff of 12 inmates. As the number in the Prison unit falls below this, new students are recommended for screening by institution staff after the initial classification procedure at the Prison.

As of July 1964, 32 men had been given training. Eight of these have been dropped from the program and thirteen have been paroled. Seven of the paroled men obtained programming positions in private industry, but two of these failed on parole and were returned to prison. One has since returned to the programming group and the other may also be re-employed in this area.

A word is in order here on the selection procedures used at Indiana and Michigan. Although these are concerned with assessing motivational variables and with testing specific aptitudes for computer programming, heavy reliance is also placed on conventional intelligence and educational achievement tests. This may be justified when the task, as here, is to screen in a very small number of nonprofessionals with high potential for this kind of work from a very large population. There is no way of knowing, however, how many other men with equally high potential were screened out on the basis of the test requirements. Riessman and others have pointed to the dangers of using conventional intelligence test results to assess the functioning potential of children from culturally deprived backgrounds (10, 12). The selection methods used in these two prison settings do not provide a useful model for the selection of nonprofessionals for new career training, both because they may fail to screen in sufficient numbers of trainees and because they may screen out some potentially gifted people. Experimentation with new selection techniques is very much in order in developing new career opportunities. The determination of the most relevant and effective methods of selection is an important part of new career development.

The California experience provides an interesting variant on that of Indiana and Michigan. Inmates have been used to help in data processing for the past five years, but there has never been a formal training program for this work.

In 1959 an inmate clerk at the California Medical Facility, the most research-oriented of the state's prisons, was assigned to perform some routine clerical tasks for two research staff members. The problems posed by their research (the development of a personality test for classification of social maturity) involved some complicated statistical data analysis. The clerk, who had spent a good part of his life in youth and

adult correctional institutions and was then serving his fifth
term, had taken a few college courses but his formal training
and work experience had been limited to the printing and
photographic trades. He had an interest in mathematics and
time on his hands. Research staff discussed some of their
statistical problems with him, and he began to read statistics
books in his spare time.

The clerk became the first inmate member of the institution's present Data-Processing Unit. After his parole, he was
hired back by the Unit in a research position, for which he
qualified by passing a civil service examination. The State
Personnel Board, in a precedent-setting action, declared that
his research experience while confined was equivalent to
paid research experience outside of prison (which in turn
can be substituted for formal academic work). He has since
been discharged from parole, the first he has successfully
completed, and is now working in an advanced research position with the state.

The Data-Processing Unit itself has had an uneven history. Originally set up to handle the personality test project,
it expanded its functions to the processing of data for other
Department of Corrections research and for a time was handling research data from outside the Department as well. Its
equipment has grown from the original hand calculators to
include key punches, sorters, a reproducer, a collator, and
access to university computers. The machines are run by
inmates who also do statistical procedures on hand calculators as well as coding and other clerical tasks. Some of this
expansion was occasioned by the introduction of a National
Institute of Mental Health funded project into the institution.[15] The project was set up at the Medical Facility because
of the availability of inmate help; and project staff (the
director and a statistician) have hired inmates and parolees
to handle all of their data. Together the project and the
Data-Processing Unit employ some thirty inmates. The institution superintendent has been unusually supportive to this

development since its inception and has made its rapid growth possible.

Unlike both Indiana and Michigan, systematic training of inmates in data processing has not been attempted in California.[16] Inmates are recruited on the basis of their social history records and past work experience plus word of mouth recommendations from the institution counselors. Training is given for the tasks assigned. Some inmates have managed in this way to pick up a fair amount of experience in the handling of data; others have not gone beyond specific coding or calculation assignments.

It was the hope of the staff who originally developed the Unit that it would become a permanent service facility to the Department as a whole and would eventually take on some of the routine statistical accounting functions performed in the Department's central office. There has, however, been little central administrative support for this idea, while considerable concern has been expressed about the ability of inmates to be trusted with the effective handling of data. This concern has sometimes been justified. There has been frequent staff turnover and the inmates have not always received the kind of supervision necessary for persons working in an unfamiliar field. Because there is no systematic training program, there is little commitment to career development on their part, and there is often little commitment to the projects on which they are employed. The dedication and close group feeling of the original members of the Unit have been dissipated, and for many, the Unit's work has become just one more clerical job.

This difficulty has not been experienced with those inmates employed on the foundation project. Though here too there has been no systematic training program, demands for performance are higher and the inmates are in continual close touch with staff (they work in adjoining rooms and the doors are always open).

The original inmate clerk has been a clearly successful

graduate of the Data-Processing Unit experience. Others have been hired in data processing and research roles, but not all have made it. The Medical Facility project has hired back three of its former work crew as parolees. The first, a man with a severe alcoholic problem, worked effectively when he was on the job but would disappear for long periods when he got a paycheck. His personal difficulties were aggravated by the uncertainty of his job future; his assignment on the project was a temporary expedient until he could qualify for a civil service data-processing technician position. The position did not materialize and the man himself is now back in prison. The second parolee managed to last for the duration of his temporary assignment, but he too would disappear for periods of time—the problem in his case was gambling. Project staff have high hopes for the third man.

Another inmate who had had research experience in the Data Processing Unit was hired, some time after his parole, by the Youth Studies Center at the University of Southern California. His task was to collect information on community problems and resources for a study of the narcotics problem in East Los Angeles. After several months on this job, the Center released him, reluctantly, to take a research position with the State of North Carolina. He was replaced by another parolee from the Medical Facility Unit who is currently collecting interview and other data for a study of a halfway house for delinquent adolescent boys.

What can be learned from these three prison experiences in developing nonprofessionals for data processing jobs that can be applied to the use of nonprofessionals generally?

1. Administrative support is essential if new career opportunities are to be opened and maintained, at both a local and a central agency level.

2. Making an opportunity available is not enough. Nonprofessionals, as much as graduate students, need training, supervision, and guidance.

3. A great deal is still to be learned about the effective

development and use of nonprofessionals. There must be a willingness to accept failures on the part of both professional and administrative staff, especially in the early stages of these new programs.

4. A sense of commitment to a job must be fostered. This is easier when the nonprofessional is in a job that has a future, in which he has reasonable certainty of recognition and advancement. But commitment can also come about when the future itself is uncertain. What is needed—this is hardly unique to the nonprofessional—is that the nonprofessional be taken seriously as a contributing member of a work effort. Expectations for performance should be high (it is demoralizing to feel that others are making allowances for one's weakness or inadequacy) and failure to meet expectations should result in the same sanctions imposed on the professional.

5. At the same time, attention must be given to the unique problems faced by the nonprofessional. In the case of prison inmates, the problems that lead them into prison are seldom solved by the experience of incarceration and that experience in itself poses further problems. Ex-offenders are not readily acceptable as employees. They are frequently in debt before imprisonment, and often more in debt upon their release. The immediacy of financial pressures and the precariousness of employment opportunities make them wonder how much they dare commit to a new type of job that may or may not have a future for them. These problems must be dealt with in preparing people for new careers. They must be dealt with not by lowering standards for work performance, but by adjunct training and/or therapeutic experience that help them in the management of those internal problems and external realities that interfere with job performance.

Before discussing the use of nonprofessionals in research outside of institutions, some attention might be given to research experience with inmates in activities other than data processing. In California, two inmates turned to research methods, on their own, in an effort to answer questions of importance to them.

The first was confined in the women's prison. Concerned about the personal problems shown by many of her fellow inmates, she undertook a study of the attitudes of women prisoners toward group therapy. She reported on her method of sampling and its inadequacies, described her interview technique, coded responses on a scale, and related these to inmate characteristics. Though her statistical handling of the data did not go beyond the computation of percentages, research conceptions were clearly not beyond her. Staff (including research staff) learned about the study only after she had laid a report of it on the superintendent's desk. The study, she felt, called for an expansion of available therapeutic services (4).

In another institution, an inmate became upset by remarks of a visiting Parole Agent on the lack of parolees' contributions to the outside community. He was first angry, then wondered if perhaps the remarks were justified. He requested permission to study inmate attitudes in the treatment unit in which he was living and was assigned as the institution's first inmate research clerk. He began by collecting demographic data in his housing unit and relating this to social groupings within it. He developed and administered attitude questionnaires and ran some short experiments (such as implanting rumors and tracing their gossip chain, and studying the effect of rewards on interview responses). He faced the problem of dissemination of results by preparing a bimonthly research report which he distributed to both staff and inmates in the unit. He turned his attention to the study of staff behavior, and these findings also were fed back to the group. A member of the institution's research staff worked with him in studying the effect of interviewer group-membership on staff and inmate responses to questionnaires. After his parole, he reported his experience at a conference sponsored by the National Institute of Mental Health(14).

These inmates brought both a fresh viewpoint to the problems they studied and provided unique access to a population with which it is difficult to achieve frank and open communication. These are important arguments for the use of nonprofessionals from the population being studied when attitudes and feelings are the subject of research investigation, particularly when the background of the social science investigator differs widely from that of the people he is studying.

THE OUTSIDE: THE SCHOOL DROPOUT IN RESEARCH

The New York State Division for Youth recently undertook an interesting experiment. Three unemployed adolescents, all school dropouts and with delinquent histories, were hired by the Division to interview other similar adolescents. The purpose of using the boys as interviewers was to find out if they would get different kinds of information than interviewers who were professionally trained, and if the language style of the boys being interviewed would change depending on whether they were talking to their peers or to professionals. Because of changes in the Division's research staff, the experiment did not run for long, but long enough to answer several questions and to raise others.

The three did not immediately become good researchers. They did not even immediately become good workers, and could not be counted on to show up for work when they were expected. Since the object of the study was to find out how delinquents talk to each other, they were given little training beyond how to operate a tape recorder and instructions to find out what the boys being studied were doing. Professional staff largely ignored them and the group of three was too small for them to provide each other with needed social support in their new work.

However, the original questions that led to the use of the adolescents were answered. Tape-recorded interviews showed that the same subjects responded quite differently to the dropouts and to the professionals. Delinquents who appeared inarticulate and passive when interviewed by the professional researcher were far more animated and highly articulate—in the language of the streets—when talking with the adolescent interviewers. Moreover, the information obtained by the dropouts was not the same as that obtained by the professional—not truer necessarily, but different. Nonprofessionals may thus provide an entree into the lives of problem people that has not been heretofore available.

Building on the New York experience, the Center for Youth and Community Studies at Howard University has obtained a Federal grant to train ten school dropouts for new careers. Four are being trained for positions in day-care centers, four for positions in city-run recreation programs, and two for positions in research. The two are learning about research by studying the other eight.

The Howard program differs from the one in New York in three important ways. First of all, the youths have definite tasks to perform and a definite identity as new career workers, and there is consistent direction and supervision of their work. Second, they meet frequently as a total group to discuss their common problems and the group thus provides support in dealing with both their professional co-workers and their peers. Third, professional staff is supportive to the new career concept and to the young people who represent it.

The new career workers are taught on the job, with each new skill acquired as it is needed in the context of their current assignment. In their first three months of work, the two youths assigned to research have conducted interviews, administered sociometric questionnaires, done process recording (both of total group activity and of individuals within groups), and written reports. They have also had experience in coding data for key punching, in typing, using a desk calculator, and doing simple statistical analyses. The

Center expects to use these first new career workers to train subsequent ones, but as yet there is no place for them in the University job structure once funds for the demonstration project have expired.

THE NONPROFESSIONAL:
WHERE DOES HE DO RESEARCH?

Research in the social and behavioral sciences is done in four places: the university, the private research organization, the research-granting foundation, and the social agency.[17]

Universities, as they are presently structured, offer no scope for the nonprofessional. Their only use is in temporary interviewing or coding positions on projects run by university institutes or departments, and even here graduate students have first call on employment. But perhaps universities can alter the way they do research and the way they train researchers. The collaboration of university faculty and graduate students with nonprofessionals who are part of specific social problems—the delinquent, the school dropout, the mentally ill, the economically displaced, the minority group member—could revolutionize our teaching and research approach to such problems and might alter drastically the kind of social science data collected as well.[18]

This kind of collaborative research offers two things. First of all, it suggests a way of setting up training for research that bypasses the usual channels of university education. The examples cited above indicate that higher education may not be all that important, for certain types of research functions at least. An apprenticeship served outside these channels may develop a group of competent technicians who can be employed in the nation's rapidly expanding research interests. And it may build a way for persons whose school experience was too unsuccessful to make college training feasible to develop the interests and skills necessary to move back into the mainstream of academic education. The second point concerns the type of data collected. The involvement of people who represent problems in the initiation of ideas and the design of research may lead to more realistic appraisals of these problems and to new insights on ways of dealing with them.

Private research organizations, such as the national opinion polling and market research organizations, and foundation-supported projects, either private or government sponsored, may provide possible sources of jobs for the trained nonprofessional. By far the greatest area for potential employment, however, is the social agency, particularly those municipal, county, and state agencies that are concerned with aspects of the social good—public health, education, welfare, mental health, and corrections. There is no question that services in these areas are increasing, both because of a growing population and because people now demand greater amounts and variety of service.

But as services increase, so do expenditures, and as expenditures rise, so do demands for improved agency performance. The one thing of which we may be certain is that agencies charged with these responsibilities are going to make innovations at increasing rates. We may also be certain that innovation will not always be accompanied by evaluation, and that enormous amounts of money will be wasted because new ideas are tried haphazardly and experience with them is neither recorded nor communicated to other groups concerned with the same problem.

If social agencies and the governments they serve are to proceed rationally in spending money for the public good, research must be a part of their everyday operation. This means that an agency's staff should include persons whose specific job it is to sample the agency's behavior and collect information on the performance of its clients. In an education system, this may refer to methods of teaching, or organization of teaching personnel, and pupil performance. In public health, this may refer to programs of public education and incidence of disease. In vocational training programs this may refer to what a counselor does and whether or not the counselee finds an appropriate job, and how he performs on this job. This kind of evaluation is not a one time thing, but a necessary part of the agency's ongoing operation. Just as industries have built-in fiscal accounting and quality control procedures, so social agencies should have built-in operations accounting and quality control. This is all the more important when agencies begin to spend money on new kinds of programs to improve their services.

This field offers especially useful opportunities for the nonprofessional. To begin with, professionals have little interest in social agency research and would not in any case be available in large enough numbers to meet the needs that exist. Nonprofessionals may also be better able than university-trained researchers to bridge the gap that too often exists between the man who runs the system and the man who tries to evaluate it.

Not every university graduate can do research. Not every nonprofessional has the talent for it. But there is a sufficient shortage in the supply of professionally-trained researchers, and sufficient evidence that nonprofessionals can be trained to fill this gap, to suggest research as one of the most promising new careers.

NOTES

1. The bulk of the work supported by Federal funds was actually performed by private industry.

2. This is especially striking in the split between the academic training and clinical practice of many psychologists. It holds in the social work field as well.

3. Computer achievements in this area may pose real problems. The prediction of the winner of the California 1964 presidential primary 38 minutes before the polls closed in some parts of the State led Governor Sawyer of Nevada, chairman of the National Governors' Conference, to warn against the dangerous influence of early predictions on the course of voting. The Conference authorized appointment of a committee to seek

an agreement with news media to withhold computer predictions until after polls are closed in all parts of the country.

4. This extended use of research findings has led a high-ranking member of the military to complain of the dangers in the computer simulation of war games as an approach to strategy and to argue for making "volition, not statistics, the source of decisions (8)."

5. There is some disagreement with these projections. The president of a corporation engaged in defense work expects engineers to face serious competition in the near future because of the cutback in defense spending (3). On the other hand, the American Institute of Physics' Statistical Handbook 1964 predicts a shortage of one-third of the number of physicists needed by 1970, and notes serious current and future deficits in adequately trained high school physics teachers (7).

6. Contrary to the publicly expressed concern of many people about increased Federal spending (the bulk of which is actually going into defense), most spending for social services is at the State, county, or municipal level. Government employment stood at 9.9 million in May of 1964, according to the Bureau of Labor Statistics, and three-fourths of this was at the State or local level. Federal employment has grown by only 23 per cent since 1947, while State and local employment has more than doubled in the same period. The latter reflects the demand for increased social services (particularly in education), a good part of which has been made necessary by the rapid increase in our population (13, p. 21).

7. Though most demonstration programs would greatly increase social service costs if implemented on a large scale, they are expected to ultimately save money in other ways. For example, increasing the cost of rehabilitative services by reducing caseloads is expected to reduce recidivism and thus the cost of maintaining prisons or mental hospitals.

8. Other examples are the Youth Opportunities Board program in Los Angeles, the HARYOU (Harlem Youth Opportunities) program in New York, and the WAY (Washington Action for Youth) program in Washington D.C. The last named will be the first such program to build in extensive mental health concerns as well.

9. This situation does not always go unrecognized. California, for example, one of the most rapidly growing states, has had a corresponding growth in state personnel and state spending. Pressures for developing more efficient ways of operation have been on the increase and have led to state agency demands for budget support for new program innovations. In the face of such demands, the Legislative Analyst recommended in the 1957–58 budget that both the Departments of Corrections and the Youth Authority, which handle adult and youthful felony offenders, create divisions of research for the express purpose of finding out whether their new programs were any more effective than their old ones.

10. Information on the Indiana program was provided by the courtesy of the Data Processing Coordinator of the Indiana Department of Correction and the Supervisor of the Data Processing Center at Indiana Reformatory. For published reports on the work of the inmate-run Tabulating Department, see (1), and (2).

11. In addition to running a statistical reporting system for the Reformatory, the Department has helped set up and run a similar system for the State Prison. They prepare monthly reports for the Division of Proba-

tion as well as special reports for other state agencies and have helped graduate students from nearby universities with data processing on their research projects. The training program of the Department has been extended to some of the state's other correctional institutions and special classes have been given by the inmates to institution custodial staff and civilian personnel.

12. It is not necessarily the men with the most education who go the furthest. Half of the group who have completed the training program had not gone beyond high school and seven had less than a high school education.

13. Information on the Michigan program was provided by the courtesy of the Manager of Data Processing of the Michigan State Highway Department.

14. This is substantially above the average reported for the Indiana students (average grade level of 8.8 and average I.Q. of 113). However, there is no information on the tests used in Michigan and the figures may thus not be strictly comparable.

15. Social Agency Effectiveness Study. The study is sponsored by the Institute for the Study of Crime and Delinquency and is directed by Don M. Gottfredson.

16. One inmate member of the unit who had had some data processing experience prior to his confinement gave a course to a combined group of inmates and staff in "Data Processing and Systems Development," but this effort has not been repeated.

17. Training for technical occupations in the physical and biological sciences is requiring increasing amounts of formal education. It is quite possible that the new jobs opening in these fields could be filled by persons trained on the job and given opportunities to move up into more professional roles as they gained experience and skills, in much the same way as suggested here. There are already some examples of the use of nonprofessionals (prison inmates) in medical research. The Upjohn Company, which has recently acquired a complete research facility on the grounds of Southwestern Michigan State Prison, not only uses inmates as subjects in drug research but in clerical and semitechnical research roles as well. Clinical laboratory work is done by inmates under the supervision of graduate chemists or medical technicians. At the California Medical Facility inmates perform all the laboratory and related clerical tasks on medical research projects. In another of California's prisons, a private physician conducting research with prison inmates has trained a few inmates to do laboratory work on his projects. None of these programs, however, has been able to develop formal career training or technical job placement upon release.

Since the writer is unfamiliar with job needs and possibilities in the physical and biological sciences, this section is limited to a discussion of research in the social and behavioral science area.

18. ". . . this . . . points out an interesting methodological approach to the solution of any social research problem. Our inordinate desire to follow in the safe footsteps of the physical scientist is nowhere more disastrous than in the area of methodology. Had it not been for this reluctance to devise new methods, we might long ago have hit upon the incorporation of research subjects as members of the investigatory team. No doubt there have been countless times when some physicist would have welcomed the op-

portunity to ask an atom just how he might best be studied. Fantasy ceases when such a question is directed toward another communicating organism." (5, p. 12)

REFERENCES

1. A controlled training environment to challenge the EDP industry. *Data Processing Digest,* 1963, *9,* 19–23.

2. EDP behind prison walls. *Business Automation,* 1962, 34–36.

3. Engineers warned on job outlook. *Washington Post,* April 28, 1964.

4. Evans, Lois. A survey of inmate attitudes toward group therapy in a women's institution. *The Research Newsletter,* California Department of Corrections, 1961, *3,* 5–8.

5. Fowler, R. Role transactions in an integrated research unit. *The Research Newsletter,* California Department of Corrections, 1961, *3,* 11–13.

6. Grant, J. D., and Grant, Marguerite Q. A group dynamics approach to the treatment of nonconformists in the Navy. *Ann. Amer. Acad. pol. soc. sci.,* 1959, 322, 126–135.

7. Hechinger, F. M. U.S. is said to face shortage of physicists. *New York Times News Service,* July 9, 1964.

8. Howard University, Center for Youth & Community Studies—*The Community Apprentice Program* mimeo, 1964.

9. Kane, Col. F. S. Security is too important to be left to computers. *Fortune,* April, 1964.

10. Katz, I. Review of evidence relating to effects of desegregation on the intellectual performance of Negroes. *Amer. Psychol.,* 1964, *19,* 381–399.

11. Pearl, A. Quality control in research evaluation. Paper presented at National Council on Crime and Delinquency meetings, Seattle, August, 1962.

12. Riessman, F. *The culturally deprived child.* New York: Harper and Row, 1962.

13. U.S. Department of Labor. *Manpower report of the President and a report on manpower requirements, resources, utilization, and training.* March, 1963.

14. U.S. Department of Labor: Bureau of Labor Statistics. *Occupational Outlook Handbook,* 1963–64 ed., Bulletin No. 1375.

15. Werner, D. Measuring the motive. In *Experiment in Culture Expansion,* Proceedings of a conference on "The use of the products of a social problem in coping with the problem." Norco, July, 1962, pp. 91–96.

CHAPTER 7

UNTRAINED NEIGHBORHOOD WORKERS IN A SOCIAL-WORK PROGRAM

Gertrude Goldberg
Formerly supervisor, Visiting Homemaker Service,
Mobilization for Youth

HAVING SPENT ITS PROFESSIONAL INFANCY severing ties with Lady Bountiful, social work may find itself enlisting the aid of another kind of untrained person, the neighborhood or indigenous worker. For increasingly, we note that the middle-class professional worker has difficulty both in developing rapport with lower-class clients and in offering them practical help with the everyday problems of slum life. The professional is unskilled or inexperienced in budgeting or shopping on a low income, in caring for a large family, in housekeeping under substandard conditions, and in using the public-welfare agencies as a client.

Fifteen neighborhood women were employed by a social agency as visiting homemakers whose job was primarily to teach low-income families greater competence in home management.[1] Assigned to a home for several full- or half-days a week, homemakers were to help families to improve their skills in such home-management tasks as shopping, cleaning, sewing, budgeting, taking care of their children, planning their time, and cooking.

In addition to home teaching, homemakers did a variety of other tasks, several of them indirectly educational. They offered some services traditionally done by case aides such as escorting persons to clinics and helping them to establish eligibility for public assistance or public housing (which were often efforts to teach the use of community resources). Like case aides, they also provided companionship or psychological support as part of a casework plan. Homemakers maintained a baby-sitting center where mothers could leave their youngsters while they did errands or kept appointments. Finally, they performed the mother-substitute or mother's helper type of assignment usually associated with homemaker programs when it became necessary to complement existing city-wide homemaker services.[2]

The visiting homemakers appeared to be helpful to a rather large proportion of the families served, many of whom were not likely to have been receptive to casework or counseling. During the first six months of service, homemakers were assigned to approximately forty-eight cases in which there were teaching components. Of these, only six families failed to show improvement in some area of home management or to learn how to use community resources more efficiently.[3] Among the cases regarded as failures in both respects were several in which the homemaker appeared to develop a good relationship with the client but where no noticeable changes in her pattern of behavior could be detected. In escort, mother-substitute, and companionship cases, homemakers were often very helpful although it is somewhat difficult to evaluate the results of contact.[4]

The apparent ability of the visiting homemakers to decrease the self-defeating behavior of low-income clients makes it important for us to try to understand their contribution to a social-welfare program. In this article we shall attempt to describe the fifteen women who served as visiting homemakers, their selection, training, and supervision. In addition, we shall analyze the reasons for their effectiveness, discuss the ways in which the maximum potential of neighborhood staff may be realized by a social agency, and describe the types of tasks they seem best suited to perform.

RECRUITMENT AND SELECTION

MANNER OF RECRUITING

There were a large number of promising applicants for the position of visiting homemaker. Candidates were sought through various community agencies, by personal acquaintances of the supervisors who lived in the neighborhood, and by other applicants. Word was circulated that our agency was seeking neighborhood women for a position entitled, "visiting homemaker." Within a month there were many more qualified applicants than openings.

CHARACTERISTICS SOUGHT

In recruiting homemakers the agency sought persons whose social distance from our client group (the most deprived group in the community consisting mainly of low-income Puerto Ricans and Negroes) was considerably less than that of most members of the professional staff. At the same time, it was hoped that homemakers would have personality attributes considered important among candidates for social work and related professions. Among the women selected as visiting homemakers should be persons with skill in various areas of homemaking as well as some members of the same ethnic groups as our clients.*

---

* While the project described above had predetermined entrance requirements, it is the thesis of the principal authors that prejudgment of qualifications for aides prior to training may preclude both those most in need as well as those most able.

A discussion of those attributes which led us to reject applicants will emphasize the kinds of persons selected from among the sixty-odd candidates. In general, we tried to avoid both those upwardly-mobile slum dwellers who tend to shun their less-striving neighbors and persons too deprived to be helpful to others.

We felt that by setting no formal educational requirements except ability to read, write, and fill out simple forms and reports we would be more likely to attract a lower-class group. However, we did turn down persons who seemed to lack a basic intelligence or who were unable to understand the service (e.g. unaware of how the position differed from domestic employment).

We excluded persons who showed no special interest in the work and could not envision its offering more satisfaction than a factory job, for example. On the other hand, we were wary of those who emphasized the missionary aspects of the work to the exclusion of pecuniary rewards. Finally, if a candidate seemed to derive little satisfaction from managing her own home, we felt she would be unsuited to teach others.

Candidates who exhibited blatant prejudices toward minority groups, welfare recipients, or delinquents were considered unsuitable. Similarly, if they regarded themselves as utterly apart from deviant or severely deprived persons, they were excluded. For this reason, we were impressed when a candidate conceded that she could have used a homemaker at one time or that she had "gone through some bad times."

SELECTION PROCESS

Persons were seen twice, once by each supervisor, if they were at all promising. At an initial office interview we discussed the position of visiting homemaker, had them fill out a simple application, and got a general impression of their interest, availability, and ability.

Applicants were asked to give three references other than former employers. We urged them to list as references community leaders such as school principals, ministers, and social workers whose opinions we might better evaluate. They usually tended to use friends' names, but we succeeded in obtaining at least one "official" reference in most cases. However, it was probably a mistake to insist on these recommendations because we were not necessarily seeking persons with community connections. Actually, three persons who became quite satisfactory workers had no community leaders to recommend them.

We scheduled a home visit with those candidates who seemed to be good prospects. One reason for the home visit was that we hoped it would help us to assess an applicant's attitudes toward her home, homemaking, and family life. This second interview gave us a better opportunity to determine a person's proximity to the client population and to observe her in the more relaxed atmosphere of her home. In several instances, candidates who had initially seemed to be in good circumstances because they were well dressed at the interview actually lived in substandard tenements and appeared to have meager possessions.[5] More important, several of the candidates responded more spontaneously when they were interviewed at home. In the absence of trustworthy references, the home interview afforded us another chance to observe the candidate as well as an opportunity to see her in a less formal situation.

CHARACTERISTICS
OF THE HOMEMAKERS

It was our goal to hire persons who, unlike many middle-class professionals, had natural rapport with the target population or the lower class. It seems important, therefore, in describing the homemakers to determine both how close they were to the clients and concomitantly how different they were from the professional staff. The fifteen persons who joined our staff apparently were able to help a large number of very deprived persons. Thus, either they were close enough to form relationships well with members of the target group, or, if they seem to be quite different from the clients, the social distance variable may be less important than we postulated. In either case, by describing the salient characteristics of the fifteen visiting homemakers, we shall be suggesting the kinds of indigenous persons who are likely to be effective neighborhood workers.

SOCIAL PATHOLOGY

While we sought persons who were not so overburdened as to be unable to help others, homemakers were not by any means problem-free. To a much greater extent than professional staff who often have interpersonal problems, they revealed either at the onset, or in the course of employment, a wide gamut of social problems. At least five had close relatives, either sons or brothers, who exhibited serious social pathology such as drug addiction, desertion, delinquency, or school maladjustment.[6]

INCOME

The income of most homemakers was relatively low. Three of them were recipients of public assistance when they were hired. They were economically better off with their $4000 per annum incomes as homemakers, perhaps supplemented by sporadic contributions of spouses or small Social Security benefits. One of these women commented that the salary for visiting homemakers was about as good as she could expect in view of her limited skill and education. One, and probably more, of those not receiving public assistance at the time of hiring, had an income low enough to qualify for surplus foods distributed by the department of welfare. Nine homemakers resided in low-income public housing projects. Four of those who lived in tenements were in very old buildings in problem-ridden areas. One home-maker lived in a middle-income, partially-subsidized co-operative. Only three had a family car. Most of their hus-bands (twelve were married) were steadily employed but in low-status occupations such as railroad laborer and eleva-tor operator. The two most affluent women were married to a bass player in a well-known Spanish band and to a school custodian.

ATTITUDES TOWARD WORK

It is sometimes maintained that working-class and lower-class persons regard work differently than middle-class peo-ple. For the former it is said to be "just a job," a means of making money, or a necessary evil. Often low-status employment involves considerable physical activity, little cerebral effort, and highly routinized behavior. While the financial aspect of middle-class work is very important too, the middle-class employee usually has a more responsible job with a greater intellectual challenge than that of the lower-class worker. The middle-class person is sometimes a member of a profession which is associated with a way of life and a means of intrinsic as well as monetary satisfac-tion.[7] The middle-class, white-collar worker is thought to be more reliable and conscientious than the lower-class employee because his job is often more interesting and he is therefore likely to care more about it. The lower-status person is reputed to work only as hard as he has to.

Our experience with the visiting homemakers leads us to conclude either that they are not typical working- or lower-class women, or to question the assumptions regard-ing differential class attitudes toward work, or to conclude that this assignment evoked a conscientious response re-gardless of the employee's class orientation.

The homemakers responded very seriously to a demand-ing job. At times they seemed to resent being compelled to work so hard and complained of their fatigue. Actually, they drove themselves hard. With the exception of such vestiges of jobs with little responsibility as taking a two-week "vacation" with one day's notice, or failing to be circumspect in leaving messages when they called to report illnesses, they were very reliable. They were frequently more prompt than members of the professional staff and quite apologetic when they had to miss work. One voluntarily cut her vacation short to be available for shopping when a client's welfare check arrived. To miss a day's work was to fail one's personal obligation to the client rather than to be absent from a job.

Their enthusiasm and spirit were infectious. As a result, the supervisors were overburdened with work. Homemakers called us on weekends and in the evening to report "successes" that could not possibly keep until Monday and to discuss what they termed "emergencies." Curiously, women who had walked close to misery all their lives treated every problem as an emergency once they were in the helping role.

Although anxiety over failure when steady work is scarce may account for some of their elan, their enthusiasm impressed even the usually impassive institutional personnel. Teachers in the neighborhood schools frequently lauded "these dedicated women who are doing such a wonderful job," at the same time faintly concealing their disdain for the "cold" professional social worker. The administrator of the local welfare center declared to a group of new social investigators that "these women are the best thing that ever happened to the neighborhood."

The nature of this work seemed to be an important ingredient in their enthusiastic response. The job was deeply involved with the genuine needs of people, and in such a position it is hard not to take one's work seriously. One of the references we obtained from a former employer of a homemaker supports this conclusion. The respondent, who had employed the applicant as a children's nurse, described her as warm to the children but occasionally "irresponsible" (e.g. would converse for long hours with the neighbor's cook when she was supposed to be cleaning the house). However, when the employer was ill or distressed, the candidate felt that she was needed and was especially conscientious.

The homemakers' orientation to the agency may also have contributed to their dedication. They were welcomed at a tea attended by the executive director and other administrative staff. They toured every division and were given an introduction to the various services by supervisory personnel. In the middle of the first week, one of the more noncommittal homemakers remarked, "I took this job as if it were any other job, but now I see it's different: we really have a chance to do something for our people and our neighborhood." Her statement indicated that a sense of self-help rather than "pure" altruism had been generated. Another said quietly, "We're kinda' proud to be here." They began to feel both that the work was important and that they in turn would derive satisfaction and status from it.

CHILD CARE

The responses of most homemakers to caring for children in our Center differed from a middle-class approach. Most of them persisted in offering custodial care (i.e. necessary physical care of the children) despite our having stressed the importance of playing with the children or supervising their activities. They felt it essential only to feed the youngsters, take them to the bathroom, and give them an affectionate hug or pat. In fact, they would have left the children in the playroom only returning to respond to a cry or to arbitrate a quarrel were it not for the constant prodding of the supervisors.

MANNER OF RELATING

The informality of the homemakers was noted by many of the more inhibited professional staff. One sucked lemons throughout a conference with the assistant director of the agency. At the staff Christmas party they distinguished themselves by "twisting" with abandon, mostly with each other. They were disgusted with the men who stood around talking "like faggots" instead of dancing; so they were forced to choose female partners. They were probably less self-conscious about dancing with members of the same sex than middle-class women would have been. The agency psychiatrist, who danced with one of them, asked her if he was doing all right. Undaunted by his dark vest and dangling watch fob, she replied, "just fine, baby, but twist a little harder." They were quite conscious of being less constrained and remarked that the professional workers needed something to drink before they could have fun whereas they required no artificial stimulant. They asked their supervisors if they were acting inappropriately but at the same time complained that many of the social workers were stiff and unfriendly.

Some of them had a saucy manner. They exchanged wisecracks with anyone visiting the Center who responded to their informality. One of them was describing Puerto-Rican foods to a group of school teachers when a rather pedantic gentleman asked, "Is there any medical reason why you don't eat *platanos* (plantains) raw?" She retorted, "Any medical reason why you don't eat potatoes raw?"

Some of the homemakers were annoyed with a caseworker with whom they had little rapport. A somewhat phlegmatic person, the caseworker gave vague responses like "Well, what do you think?" or tepid affirmatives like, "y-e-e-s." One of the homemakers objected to her approach to a client. The homemaker described how the client, a crude, "country" person with paranoid tendencies, was upset by the caseworker's repeating or mirroring what she said—e.g. "You went to the department of welfare?" Instead of the desired psychotherapeutic effect of having the client look at herself or examine what she was saying, this person felt doubted, suspected. Possibly the homemaker reacted negatively because her own frame of reference or relationship, if not personality structure, was closer to the client's than to the worker's.

SOCIAL ATTITUDES

We felt that a certain proximity to slum life would free neighborhood staff from some of the negative attitudes toward clients which is sometimes found in middle-class professionals. However, this assumption was not necessarily valid, for we found that even those persons who have themselves lived in poverty, nonetheless have many of the prevailing middle-class attitudes toward the poor (e.g. that persons are responsible for their social circumstances, that those who do not pay for a service are getting a "favor" and have relinquished the right to make demands on the dispensers of that service). These attitudes may stem partly from negative self-images and internalization of the majority viewpoint; but they could be also the familiar reaction of persons who have bettered themselves, even if slightly, toward the group from which they have risen.

It is important to recognize that pejorative attitudes toward the deprived are not only shared by the middle classes and the more striving members of the lower-classes but by the better-functioning low-income persons as well. After all, one must shun the delinquent more when one lives on the same street or in the same housing project with him. We were, in effect, asking our indigenous staff to walk through those very doors which they had managed to slide by most of their lives. Significantly, several of our clients were considered notorious by homemakers who knew their reputations.

REAL VS. ASSUMED ATTITUDES

Some of the homemakers' attitudes toward the poor seemed middle-class. Yet, one had to distinguish between what they really thought or said among themselves, and what they believe others want to hear and, in effect, demand of them. In some layer of their personalities, unlike persons who have not experienced economic and social deprivation, they both felt and knew that social opportunities are important and middle-class norms and values do not necessarily apply to their way of life.

Early in her employment, we gave a homemaker some material on teenage behavior prepared by one of the large insurance companies. She accepted the interpretation without qualification, and when we questioned her, the only argument she supplied in its behalf was that it was "just what the teachers say." On another occasion she was upset by a school principal's extreme concern over a pornographic note written by her eleven-year-old daughter. When we helped her to separate her opinions from the judgment of the principal, she conceded that such notes are quite common and certainly not worthy of an emergency call to a parent.

The disparity between this middle-class compliance and genuine attitudes was illustrated during a training session when one of the Negro women rudely denied that color affected one's opportunities. "If you do not get a job, it's your own fault," she maintained. Later we learned that she was one of the staff who most keenly felt and expressed the sting of inequality. Once she plaintively asked a supervisor if she thought the time would come when people would judge her as a person instead of as a Negro. Such a blatant denial of her opinions as she initially attempted suggests that she was not accustomed to express her feelings candidly in a mixed group, particularly in the presence of a middle-class person who was also her supervisor.

SOCIAL CLASS

In much of this discussion we have referred to "the homemakers" as if they were a homogeneous group and have also implied that this group was lower-status, probably somewhere between lower-class and working-class.[8] They were neither the "down and out," although some have been at one time or another, nor the stable working class with skills, homes, and cars. They were, however, obviously different from middle-class professional personnel and from the clerical staff, as well. One simply could not visit the homemaking Center without tasting their salt; one could enjoy the flavor or prefer something more bland. They, in turn, felt different and thought they had a distinct contribution to make. In the ensuing section, we shall try to analyze that contribution and to account for their success.

THE HOMEMAKING
RELATIONSHIP AND ROLE

The capacity of homemakers to develop rapport with their clients is evident from a cursory reading of cases, even some where failure is noted. Above all, one is impressed by the unusual feeling of warmth between worker and client. The relationship resembled that of friends rather than of worker and client. Like friends, they were usually on a first-name basis. Significantly, some homemakers felt snubbed when they were not treated cordially by a client, e.g. offered coffee or a snack. We sometimes felt such reactions were inappropriate to the helping role partly because we failed to recognize the friendliness implicit in such responses. Clients spoke of going to a party or other social events with homemakers, and they would come to the Center to chat or visit when there was no pressing problem or official business. It is not surprising that clients revealed themselves quickly to homemakers and that a homemaker could obtain in a few visits what would have taken her supervisor quite a number of interviews. Other indications of the warm relationships are the mother who asked a homemaker to be the godmother of her child or the young woman who wanted her homemaker to be the matron of honor at her wedding.

Although the homemakers were usually better off or better able to manage than most of their clients, there was a lack of *felt* social distance. There was, of course, less actual disparity in life circumstances between indigenous staff and clients than between clients and professional workers. The position of neighborhood worker in relation to clients was illustrated when a homemaker introduced a client to some friends whom they met while shopping. This client was flattered and thanked her. Although the worker and her friends had some "status," they were within the pale of the client's set, visible enough to respect and aspire toward. Similarly, a homemaker, in speaking of one very poor house-keeper, remarked, "I wouldn't see her socially." Although the worker was being snobbish, the thought of social contact with the client occurred to her whereas it probably would not have enterd the mind of the professional worker.

The difference between our ability to form relationships and that of the homemakers was apparent when supervisors introduced a neighborhood worker to a family. We some-times felt like inhibiting influences. When we left, they could speak their own language or vernacular. We were eager for the homemaker to return to the office, for she and the client would often have conversed freely and fully. They had something to talk about instead of problems—the neighbor-hood, a mutual friend, a place on the island if they were both Puerto Ricans, or other common experiences.

One indication of the lack of condescension is the rec-iprocity between client and worker. For example, one family gave a homemaker some surplus butter they did not intend to use. Although her income was too high to get surplus foods, they felt she could use the butter and wanted to thank her for her help. When a homemaker lost a family member, two clients who had heard the news in the neigh-borhood, went to the funeral parlor or paid a condolence call at her home. Another family surprised a worker by bringing gifts to her on Mother's Day. A housewife stopped by the Center to tell a homemaker about some bargains because the worker had given her so many good tips previously. The homemakers were not perceived as belonging to the "giving class." And, in turn, clients did not see themselves as the "receiving class." Homemakers were neighbors, perhaps a little better off, but, nonetheless, persons with whom one reciprocated and exchanged.

It would be inaccurate to stress the warm feeling between homemakers and their clients without also pointing out that homemakers in some respects were less accepting than trained middle-class staff. As noted in our section on their social attitudes, they sometimes looked down on deprived people and they were contemptuous of persons who managed less well than they in what seemed to be comparable circumstances. A few homemakers were particularly offended by slovenly housekeepers. Those who had budgeted thriftily when they were penurious or had adjusted to a husband's desertion had difficulty understanding persons who handled their troubles with less pluck. They tended to be less disciplined in their responses to clients than professional workers. For example, they would fail to recognize that to berate a deprived client for inappropriate behavior was often to compound her deprivation. Similarly, they would show favoritism to one child in a family, scold a deviant youngster by saying, "If you were my child. . . ," or become offended when a client was not "grateful" enough.

Ironically, these "mistakes" and rather punitive attitudes impaired relationships between workers and clients less than might be expected. For example, a homemaker with genuine contempt for a wretched housekeeper nonetheless helped her to improve her housekeeping. Rather than reacting negatively to the worker's judgmental attitude, the family responded warmly to her. It is possible that the professional worker may also harbor prejudices toward clients but tends to express them in subtler ways that are nonetheless apparent to low-income clients. Then, too, the discipline of the professional worker may seem colder or more rejecting to the client than the homemaker's direct, candid reaction even when it is harsh. Social-class and professional barriers may be more inhibiting in the helping role than personality factors. Another reason for this seeming paradox may be the one we shall discuss below, namely the difference in the type of helping roles performed by professional and indigenous workers.

Although homemakers were in some respects less accepting than professional workers, they were more tolerant in another. They did not perceive people as problems, or at least, they disagreed with professionals about what constitutes a problem. They could understand why a client refused to discuss interpersonal problems when her welfare check had not arrived. Such behavior would not be considered "resistance." Somehow Mrs. Smith was less forbidding to the homemaker than to the caseworker. To the homemaker she was well-meaning, easily misunderstood, temperamental— "She falls out with everyone but me." To the caseworker she was, "paranoid, rejecting and abusive to her children."

The homemakers reacted to physical "emergencies" and were quite annoyed when caseworkers did not treat these conditions rapidly. On the other hand, they thought professionals made too much over "little things." "That child didn't try to commit suicide; he ran up on the roof to hide." More important, deviance did not suggest hopelessness or that people were beyond help. And indeed, homemakers sometimes may have brought about changes in persons who seemed too self-destructive to be aided. One young woman seemed determined to be killed by her common-law husband who had already stabbed her several times. With a homemaker's support, she managed to take him to court, decorate her apartment, and to obtain badly-needed medical care for herself and her children. Recently we learned that she had gained enough skill in using community resources to escort a neighbor to the clinic. It is not as though homemakers could not diagnose psychological causation, e.g. that a child did not "want" to hear, but they were less prone to assume it and, they were not trained to emphasize psychological problems.

TYPE OF HELPING ROLE

It is perhaps misleading to speak of homemakers as untrained, for it suggests that they were unskilled. Yet, as we have suggested, they had considerable ability to cope with their environment and therefore much to offer a client who was less resourceful than they. They knew how to live on a low income, to stretch leftovers, to use surplus foods (including powdered skim milk and canned meat which must have the preservative removed before it is edible), to buy inexpensive material and sew an attractive garment with it, to recognize a bargain. They had taken care of a large family and planned their schedules well enough to have some time for themselves. They were both skilled and experienced in caring for young children. They knew what detergents would best clean an icebox or a stove and which made sense on a low income. They knew their neighborhood, what stores were good, and where bargains could be found. They also had learned how to deal with the local merchants. In fact, they insisted on accompanying a supervisor to the food stores because they feared she would be cheated. They were familiar with the neighborhood clinics, the welfare center, the child health stations, and the schools, and they could show a client how to fend with these institutions—not like a professional who relies partly on the agency's power and partly on his polish, but the way a lower-class person does it for himself.

A homemaker's know-how makes it possible to get by on a little, to negotiate life in a slum. She exploits every opportunity—the barber school for free haircuts, the thrift shop, the remnant heap, free recreation, public clinics, surplus foods (if she qualifies or if her neighbors do and don't use their supply). She is not under any illusion that it is easy to get ahead. But she creates some regularity and routine, some security, and some freshness amidst the uncertainty, the squalor and chaos that surround her.[9]

The position of visiting homemaker permitted the neighborhood worker to impart her skill and know-how to clients. The following are some clients' descriptions of the homemaking service:

> The homemaker didn't talk about how to shop or bargain or sew. She showed me how, helped out, lent a hand, went along when I might have been afraid to go alone. When we went to the project office to ask them to fix the broken window, nobody hit her when she spoke up for me. She didn't do all the talking for me. I said enough to have the courage to do it alone next time. If we'd just talked about how to ask them to make a repair it wouldn't have helped.
>
> When she came, we got things done together—she ironed while I cleaned, or sewed while I cooked. When we budgeted and shopped I found it was possible to have a full icebox even when you live on welfare. I also began to believe that a cleaner house and a better way of running the house would really make a difference to the kids and me.
>
> It was awful nice to have her around. She was someone to talk to. I don't have much of a chance to get out and see grown folks. It seemed like the only people I knew were the kids. The time went fast when she worked along with me. I hardly knew we were working. Meantime she got me into the swing of things; she kept talking about having a routine or a schedule. Sometimes she made it a little easier for me to do things. Like she stayed with some of the kids while I took the others to clinic or came along to help watch a few during the long wait. Sometimes when I had to go somewhere she would come early to help me feed the kids and get them dressed. Once she even made dinner when I came back from welfare feeling too tired to do anything.

The important component in this admittedly idealized description of the service is not so much the homemaker's personality or her ability to form a relationship with the client but what she could do for and teach the client. If, for example, a child were sick, and they went to clinic, the homemaker served as interpreter, guide, and supportive companion. When this type of active and immediate service was offered, the client did not have to ask what might be called relationship questions. The service itself demonstrated the worker's concern.

The role of the visiting homemaker led to a friendly, peer relationship. If a worker shops, sews, or cleans with a client, she is perceived differently from someone who offers help from behind a desk. Homemakers performed the same kinds of physical and domestic tasks as the clients, who did not have to wonder, as did one client about the author, "Do *you* cook, Mrs. Goldberg?" In addition, a worker who spent considerable time (a half or whole day, several days a week) in a client's home was likely to develop an informal relationship with her. Under those circumstances, they may have got on each other's nerves, but the homemaker would not seem distant or aloof.

THE ISSUE OF DEPENDENCY

A homemaking service in which the worker actually did some of the client's work might be expected to conjure up severe feelings of dependency that would limit effective use of help. It was our observation, however, that while some clients did rely too heavily on a homemaker, hostile feelings engendered by excessive dependency usually did not keep them from being helped by the service nor did such feelings, if they were in fact present, need to be handled in any depth through casework intervention. Frequently the client became more restive as she became more efficient, and we felt this was an appropriate response and that the service should be gradually reduced, if not terminated quickly. Sometimes a client would resent demands made on her by a homemaker (e.g. if she had to work much harder than usual in order to move to a new apartment) and would discharge her. If we were convinced that the client could use additional help and that she would be unable to accomplish an important task without us, we attempted to prevail upon her to keep the homemaker until it had been completed.

Some clients either became overly dependent on the homemaker or tried to use her as a maid. In the former case, we slowly tapered the service; in the latter, we carefully instructed the worker to do household chores only when the client did, and if the client could not respond to this setting of limits by working along with the homemaker, we probably could not help her and would have to withdraw completely. In this approach, we were using a time-honored method of social work: doing *with*, not *for* the client.

The nature of an indigenous staff is another factor which may mitigate problems of dependency in a service for low-income clients. We have noted that there seemed to be less condescension between homemaker and client than between professional worker and client and that there was, instead, reciprocity and friendship. The relatively small social distance between homemaker and client may have made it easier for the client to accept help. The homemakers seemed like older, better-established women who traditionally help neighbors who are less capable or experienced. They also conveyed to clients that they had themselves faced similar problems. What they were doing for clients was for the neighborhood as well as for the particular individuals being helped. Their assistance to clients therefore benefited them. Homemakers may have communicated a sense of their self-help to clients who in turn did not need to feel so grateful.

TRAINING, SUPERVISION, AND ADMINISTRATION

The chief hazard in supervising, training, and administering an indigenous staff and program was that of molding workers in the professional image and thereby dissipating their ability to help the client group. Because of their tendency to comply with middle-class expectations, particularly in an employment situation, they had to be helped to feel that they had much to teach clients who lacked home-management skills. Similarly, because they could easily be induced to act as middle-class persons, we had to encourage them to be themselves rather than to behave as they felt was expected of them. A number of important aspects of training, supervision, and administration could be described. However, because our penchant to professionalize them is most crucial, we shall discuss several ways in which we tried to maintain the indigenous character of our staff.

TRAINING

The training period was really a two-week orientation in which we tried to set the tone of our service and to introduce homemakers to the agency. While we did not want to give them the false impression that treatment decisions or interpretations of client behavior were theirs to make, we did wish to convey that when it came to homemaking under the conditions faced by low-income clients, they were the experts. There were a number of specialists, a psychiatrist, day-care center director, nutritionist, home economist, and nurse who served as resource persons during the training sessions. However, these persons were not teaching homemaking or offering formulae for understanding or reacting to clients' behavior, but were evoking the homemakers' comments and stimulating their discussion. The skills sessions were to refresh them, for time had elapsed since some of them had taken care of babies, for example, or to fill in gaps in their ability since they had talents in different areas of home management.

We employed several methods to make the sessions lively and informal. Rather than a didactic format, we used the case method in nearly all sessions. That is, we described a family with budgeting, health, nutritional, or other homemaking problems. They were asked to interpret the behavior described and to say how they would handle the problems if they were assigned to the case. There was much discussion

and argument over interpretations. We continually prodded
them to state what they really thought; when a response
seemed pat or an attempt to tell us what they thought social
workers wanted to hear, we would express skepticism until
the discussion became more candid.

Role play was an excellent technique for achieving spontaneity. We often asked if one would play the homemaker
and another the client, in order to practice certain aspects of
the work. And in the dramatic situation of role-play, it was
very hard for most of them to maintain middle-class compliance.

The theme of our orientation sessions was a constant
question, "Is this how it's really done?" How does one budget
on a very low income, keep house in an overcrowded, substandard apartment in contrast to the dicta of home economists? This and other techniques succeeded in evoking
spontaneous responses. They challenged the home economist's method of budgeting as "too middle-income for us."
One worker who had monopolized several early discussions
by name-dropping and bragging about her role as a community leader became the expert when we discussed a rat-
infested apartment: "I'll be honest; I've lived in some pretty
rotten tenements, and this is how I know how to plug a rat
hole." Evidently, she had become convinced that status derived from acknowledging and then imparting one's skill in
coping with slum life.

During the session with the psychiatrist, a homemaker
offered an interesting interpretation of a client's behavior
that would not be likely to occur to someone who had not
had experiences similar to that of the client. The client, a
tenant in a public-housing project, was described as having
few friends. The implication was that she did not form relationships well. The homemaker remarked that public-
housing policies sometimes encourage a tenant to report his
neighbor's income, employment, or family composition to
management and that it was therefore unwise to be too
friendly with anyone in the project. She concluded, "It's a

lonely thing to live in a project." It was possible, then, that the client was more circumspect than alienated.

We found that individual conferences were necessary for assigning a homemaker to a family and for emergencies or special problems faced by a client but that the group was a more suitable medium for supervision. We initially chose group supervision to save time, but discovered that, unlike the one-to-one situation, it encouraged greater informality and freer participation.

An important reason why group supervision may have been effective was that it helped to mitigate authority and status problems and thus reduced the distance between professional supervisor and untrained workers. It was probably asking too much of the indigenous worker to be relaxed in the one-to-one supervisory situation with a trained person, no matter how much self-confidence she had. In a group with five homemakers and two supervisors there was more equality. Supervisors were able, for example, to argue more forcefully without the fear of overpowering. There was also the likelihood that some of the "desired conclusions," particularly regarding social attitudes, would come from a member of the group with the supervisors supporting that viewpoint rather than dictating it. If role-play were one of the activities of the group, the supervisor became a worker in that she had to demonstrate her ability to help a client by assuming a role. She thus became a member of the group.

ADMINISTRATION PROGRAM

In this program it was felt that if the indigenous character of a service was to be retained, it would have to be administered less formally and bureaucratically than many social-work programs. Not that we failed to develop forms and procedures consistent with good practice. To as great an extent as possible, however, we tried to let the homemakers set the pace in their Center which was characterized by the informal, sometimes boisterous manner of many of the neighborhood workers. The supervisors seldom sat behind desks or closed doors and were accessible to homemakers for spot conferences, success stories, and "emergencies." These attributes made clients feel more relaxed in the Center than in many social agencies. Neighborhood persons, both workers and clients, chatted and gossiped in the office. It was the professional staff rather than indigenous people who felt like outsiders.

The physical plan of the Center owed much to the homemakers' tastes. It was an apartment in a housing project rather than an office. After giving the homemakers the assignment of furnishing it as a model apartment on a low-income budget, we suggested that they visit an apartment which had been done by the housing authority's interior designer. They felt this apartment was nice but unlike their taste or that of the clients. They pointed out that while the area rugs used by the professional decorator might be stylish, to a poor person a small rug meant that one could not afford a large one. To a certain extent, the problem in furnishing the apartment was to find a solution between big and small rugs—to expose clients to economical and sound home decorating and at the same time offer something they would like, something not too remote from their life-styles.

TASKS SUITED TO AN INDIGENOUS HOMEMAKING STAFF

Teaching the newcomer, the young housewife, or the inadequate homemaker how to manage and to exploit community resources was the most significant task done by homemakers. Here they were imparting the methods they had themselves acquired in coping with slum life. Homemakers did group teaching or community education as well as individual assignments. That is, they could offer sessions to groups of clients on such homemaking subjects as budgeting, shopping, cooking with surplus food, and sewing.[10] Unlike a class taught by a professional home economist, these were informal activities. There was no basic orientation or scientific approach to cooking or meal planning. Lower-class clients are likely to be more responsive to an informal approach because they can identify more readily with the leader and because the presentation will not be academic.

Education of professional personnel was another important task of an indigenous staff. A neighborhood worker can help to bridge the gap between middle-class staff and the lower-class community. For example, homemakers introduced school teachers in the neighborhood to Puerto-Rican cuisine by cooking them a meal and talking to them informally about the various *productos tropicales.* The workers' enthusiasm and pride was intended to help teachers gain more respect for the Puerto-Rican culture. Homemakers also explained to professionals how it feels to be a newcomer, to try to talk to a teacher when you do not speak well, to live in public housing, or to receive public assistance. In addition to developing the professional's understanding of the culture of poverty and of various ethnic groups and underprivileged minorities, the indigenous worker can help the professional know how he is perceived and how certain of his methods and techniques are viewed by lower-class clients.

There is a specific community-organization task which homemakers can perform. If community resources such as a public clinic are under-used because of poor transportation, then failure to obtain medical service is not simply a matter of self-defeating patterns of behavior. In such a situation, indigenous workers could involve residents in a campaign to secure adequate transportation. Similarly, shopping and budgeting may be difficult because neighborhood stores have over-priced items as do many shops in slum areas. Also,

members of certain ethnic groups have to spend time traveling out of the neighborhood to purchase special products.
Homemakers could organize a boycott, visit a merchant, or
publicize exploitative practices in the newspaper in order to
alter those conditions which inhibit sound home management.[11]

The mother-substitute homemaker service performed by
our homemakers is not new to social work but can be offered
more effectively as a neighborhood program. There are several reasons why a neighborhood-based homemaker service
is preferable. Because of its proximity to clients, workers can
be assigned more rapidly. A smaller, neighborhood program
is also likely to involve less red tape. Further the service can
be shaped to the particular problems and needs of the neighborhood. Finally, the homemakers are thoroughly familiar
with the homemaking resources if they are assigned on a
neighborhood- rather than city-wide basis.

Child-care out of the home or a group baby-sitting service is appropriately staffed by neighborhood workers. The
homemakers were ill-suited to develop a formal program or
to cater to what might be called nonessential needs of
children. They were, however, perfectly able to give adequate physical care while parents did errands or kept appointments. They might also be used to help organize
cooperative baby-sitting groups among low-income residents, staffing them initially to encourage participation and
to demonstrate the usefulness of such a facility but eventually turning the task over to participating parents.

CONCLUSIONS

An indigenous staff can be an invaluable part of a social
agency's efforts to help low-income clients, providing the
agency appreciates and knows how to realize their poten-
tiality. Untrained neighborhood workers are sometimes

viewed as poor substitutes for professionals, hired because of a shortage of funds or trained staff. Consequently, the goal of supervision, training, and administration may be to make them as "professional" as possible. The aim is sometimes to teach them without learning from them. (Of course, they must be oriented to agency and social-work goals as well as freed, if possible, of social attitudes and actions which are clearly hostile and damaging to clients.) Because we would sometimes prefer to hire professionals if given the choice, we tend to seek upwardly mobile slum dwellers or middle-class persons who lack social-work education. We find such persons, who usually serve as case aides, easier to get along with than lower-class persons because they are more likely to share our values. Unfortunately these middle-class and middle-class oriented workers also share our difficulties in developing rapport with clients. They have neither the know-how of the lower-class worker nor the skill of the trained worker.

To a certain extent a lack of respect for the work of lower-class neighborhood staff stems from a clinical approach to the problems of the poor. We have acknowledged that our neighborhood workers were indeed unskilled when it came to psychosocial diagnosis and to psychotherapy. They were neither caseworkers nor case-aides. However, if we regard social deprivations as critical barriers for many lower-class clients, then providing them with skills for coping with difficult management problems (as well as expanding social opportunities) is an important goal of social-work practice. In this type of social treatment, an indigenous staff can make a substantial contribution. Even where there are severe psychological problems, bread-and-butter difficulties often need to be alleviated before the client can concentrate on inner or intra-psychic help. In several of our cases the homemakers' help with environmental problems was an important prelude or concomitant of psychological treatment by the casework staff.

A truly professional service is one in which diagnosis is based on social as well as psychological problems or in which the role of the total environment is recognized. Based on this comprehensive understanding, help is then offered by the staff best qualified to assist the "client-in-situation." In seeking the most suitable staff, it is important to acknowledge the limitations of trained workers, who, as we have emphasized, cannot be expected to know how to manage a low-income household or to cope with slum life. It is, however, possible to find neighborhood workers who have this competence and who can thus make it possible to offer a professional service.

NOTES

1. The homemaker service and a number of the observations and conclusions of this article owe a great deal to the imagination and skill of my colleague, Dorothy Yates. In preparing the text, I am also indebted to Florence Galkin and Phyllis Melnick for their careful reading and thoughtful suggestions.

2. Homemakers were part of the casework department of a social agency. Some families with whom they worked were receiving help from a caseworker either in that agency or another. In these instances, the supervisors of the homemaking program, both social caseworkers, participated in case planning with the referring worker but rarely saw the family except in emergencies or to introduce, interpret, or terminate service. Where the homemaking need was primary or the only one a family was willing to deal with and they were consequently not receiving casework help, homemaking supervisors handled the necessary caseworker as well as case planning and supervision of homemakers. Usually the casework role entailed referral to and intervention with social agencies, particularly the department of welfare. Homemakers sometimes reported progress informally to caseworkers or spoke to them regarding day-to-day problems that arose in a household. Case planning and evaluation of the client's use of the service, were, however, done by homemaking supervisors and caseworkers, with the homemakers participating in preliminary discussions and occasionally, in the joint conferences.

3. These figures do not pertain to changes in interpersonal relationships, nor is there any claim that a family was "cured." Rather, each of the families with whom we had some success learned to cope better with some aspect of home management.

4. To measure the effectiveness of the homemaker service a much more scientific evaluation covering a longer period is, of course, necessary. The impressionistic evidence given above is all that is currently available

and is cited only as a general indication of the value of neighborhood workers.

5. It has been observed that today's poor are misleadingly well-clad. However, they are well-dressed but nonetheless ill-housed and ill-fed. See Michael Harrington, *The Other America: Poverty in the United States,* New York: The Macmillan Co., 1962, pp. 4–7.

6. Because of the social problems of neighborhood staff, it was necessary to spend considerable supervisory time offering casework help (mainly referral) to those who requested it. We referred a daughter to a vocational guidance service, obtained casework service for a brother, discussed a marital upheaval, saw a homemaker's mother who was concerned about a delinquent son, etc. In addition to the obvious justification of this use of time, that of extending help to persons who asked for professional assistance, we felt it an important supervisory role. The homemakers would never have believed we cared about people and, in turn, would not have respected our judgment if they felt we could only respond to client's problems.

7. In a study of a group of workingmen, the authors report that the only group which deviated from the overall pattern of about eighty percent of the workers wanting to remain working if they inherited enough money to retire, is the unskilled group. Only slightly over fifty percent of them would want to continue working. The authors also observe that middle-class people see work as a chance to accomplish something or to make a contribution. Working-class people view it as synonymous with activity; the alternative to working would be to lie around. Nancy Morse and R. S. Weiss, "The Function and Meaning of Work and the Job." *American Sociological Review,* Vol. XX (March 1955), pp. 191–205.

On the other hand, some commentators have emphasized that there is little work in contemporary society that is creative and satisfying, regardless of one's social class. See, for example, Paul Goodman, "Youth in the Organized Society," *Commentary,* Vol. 26 (Feb. 1960), pp. 95–107 and C. Wright Mills, "Work Milieu and the Social Structure," *People at Work: A Symposium,* San Francisco: Mental Health Society of Northern California, 1954, pp. 20–36.

8. This discussion has omitted ethnic differences among the homemakers. (There were six American Negroes, six white Puerto Ricans, an American of Cuban descent, a second-generation Italian-American, and a first-generation German-American.) While significant differences in behavior and attitudes between the two major groups, especially, could be noted, the social-class variable seems most pertinent to a consideration of assistance to low-income clients. One observes, furthermore, that professional workers who are Negro or Puerto-Rican experience many of the difficulties and disadvantages of other middle-class workers in developing relationships with lower-class Negro or Puerto-Rican clients.

9. The homemaker service was part of a social-welfare agency that was attempting to broaden social opportunities. At the same time it was helping clients to forego self-defeating patterns of behavior so that they might use new opportunites and efficiently exploit those which existed. The homemaker service was not based on a static concept of opportunities, and there was very clear recognition that it is much more difficult to manage under adverse social conditions than with an adequate income and modern home conveniences. There is, however, abundant evidence that some lower-

class persons, largely because of the effects of social barriers, do not make maximal use of the advantages that are available. Far from lulling persons to accept their lot, a program of this sort helps them to assert their rights and to have the confidence and competence to work for their social betterment. The homemakers, themselves, were examples of lower-income persons who made the most of their opportunities but were hardly contented with their situations. Some of them were active in efforts to improve social conditions in the neighborhood, and few would allow themselves to be exploited.

10. Within a year's time the only class offered on an ongoing basis was a sewing class. There were a few scattered cooking sessions, too. We had little doubt, however, that classes in other areas of homemaking are feasible and could have been developed had time permitted.

11. Other social problems, notably substandard housing and restrictive policies of the housing authority and department of welfare bear directly on home management. However, social action in these major areas is too extensive for a homemaking staff to mount without dissipating their function in regard to self-defeating behavior. Such activities also fall out of their range of competence. Homemaking staff should certainly lend appropriate support to community action to improve these conditions.

CHAPTER 8

TRAINING THE NONPROFESSIONAL

"HISTORICALLY, THE PSYCHIATRIC AIDE had made the transition from a role of keeper-with-a-bullwhip to custodian and, sometimes, companion, and now to that of therapeutic assistant actively engaged in intervening in the illness process and in providing for rehabilitation. The training of aides to meet these increasingly complex role requirements has moved slowly, erratically, and inefficiently. Learning has been largely incidental and primarily left to the interest and initiative of the individual. Aide training began as apprenticeship with the ever-present danger of perpetuating ignorance . . ."

"Recent studies point to the inadequacy of most programs and the ineffectiveness of the most frequently employed teaching techniques. Upon questioning, aides respond that they are not being taught what they need to know. The content of planned courses covers a wide variety of subject matter extracted from the behavioral sciences, often referred to as 'watered down psychiatry and psychiatric nursing.' Many centers give classes in the management of patients, often discussing techniques as if unrelated to the interaction between two human beings. Poor attendance, low job satisfaction, unaltered functioning and high turnover document, in part, the ineffectiveness of formal training programs based on didactic lectures and other classroom exercises. Formal programs have failed to deal with problems related to the aide's low status in the hierarchy and with the consequences for his self-esteem. These programs also have not sufficiently weighed the stress of intimate and prolonged aide contact with patients, the anxiety created in aides by insufficient understanding of patient behavior, the aide's need for support in day-by-day activities, his lack of resources for guidance and his difficulty in translating knowledge into practice."

"Administrators and supervisors have become acutely aware of these training issues and share a growing conviction that informal experiential training, concrete demonstrations, and active coparticipation with professionals provide the most meaningful learning experience."[1]

OBJECTIVES OF TRAINING

Training indigenous persons to assume entry positions in human service is in many ways *the crux* of the new career concept. Training must accomplish many things: The trainee must be instructed in specific skills and taught to relate positively both to other members of the staff and to persons in his care. A feeling of belonging to the human service team must be generated in the trainee during the training process. The trainee must acquire a basic proficiency in reading and arithmetic. He must be provided with a sense of competence. In the course of training he should develop a feeling of fulfillment which comes from engaging in manifestly necessary activities.

Nothing could undermine the new career concept so much as allowing untrained persons to do meaningful work with the romantic notion that their unsullied lower-class status is sufficient qualification for helping others. The nonprofessional without training is *not* an asset; he can, in fact, be a menace to the service. Not only is he unaware of his active role, he also has no idea of what he must *not* do.

The training period is also a screening process. At the present time it is not possible to determine accurately on an *a priori* basis, the persons who will perform well in new career roles. The training provides an opportunity to assess trainees in a work situation, to introduce corrective procedures when the nonprofessional fails to measure up, and, in those cases where all else fails, to eliminate trainees who perform inadequately from consideration for assignment.

Training must be job-related rather than general. An adequate training program can be generated only if it is attuned to a precise job description. Training must provide the nonprofessional with a portfolio of specific skills. Different job roles will require varying courses of training, but for entry positions it is reasonable to assume that from six weeks to three months of intensive training will be necessary before the nonprofessional can be assigned real job responsibility, although during this training period he will be engaging in actual and simulated work activities.

After initial job assignment, the training of the nonprofessional must continue, and, in fact, it is proposed here that training should never cease. When assignment of the nonprofessional to a particular agency has taken place there should be continued contact with the training staff—which would gradually lessen and be replaced with on-the-job training sponsored by the agency and formal education under the auspices of an appropriate school system.

PROBLEMS TO BE CONSIDERED
IN THE GENERAL TRAINING OF
NONPROFESSIONALS

The training of the nonprofessional will call for the recognition and solution of many problems, however certain issues should be anticipated in the course of training. Some of these are:

1. Confidentiality;
2. Acceptance and use of authority;
3. Over-identification with the institution and under-identification with the community, or client population;
4. Over-optimism and defeatism;
5. Relationship of the nonprofessional to professionals both within and outside the organization.

Other issues to be considered in the training include: trainees becoming too involved in individual cases and being overwhelmed; destructive competition developing among nonprofessionals; anxiety over maintaining the job affecting performance; issues relating to future career and the nature of the relationship of nonprofessionals with the community (e.g. does the community feel that the agency is coopting its best leaders or are the nonprofessionals treated differently than they were before.)

The following discussion will treat of the anticipated problem areas in training with a view to advancing positive approaches for training staff and agency personnel.

1. CONFIDENTIALITY

Maintaining confidentiality with regard to information received from members of the community can often be a problem. The assumptions underlying the need for confidentiality have to be carefully discussed, not taken for granted, as they might be with middle-class personnel. An even greater problem, however, relates to the fact that some of this confidential information can be and should be revealed to various authorities in the agency. Since these authorities are often not fully trusted by the indigenous workers, the nonprofessionals tend not to want to convey certain important information received from the client. It is incumbent upon all agencies involved to maintain the strictest confidentiality with regard to such material and to have this clearly known by all indigenous personnel. What is fundamental here, of course, is the establishment of basic trust in the agency on the part of the nonprofessional. This takes time and needs to be demonstrated by the agency, not merely asserted.

2. ACCEPTANCE OF AUTHORITY

One of the leading complaints of professionals regarding nonprofessionals is directed at the reluctance of the latter to accept formal authority. Most indigenous workers have not had much experience with the dispensing of authority except in the family. On the contrary, much of their experience with formal authority is from the other side of the fence— where they are the recipients rather than the dispensers of authority, and they have frequently acquired negative feelings about this type of authority. It should be recognized, however, that low-income family and church traditions fully recognize the value of authority. It is the acceptance of bureaucratic authority, associated with the "power structure", that is resisted by indigenous personnel. To the extent that they come to feel that the agency is genuinely concerned with "their people" (ethnic-wise or class-wise) and not identified with the "power structure", to that extent will they begin to feel differently regarding the acceptance of authority. (This point is nicely illustrated in trade unions where large numbers of low-income people have accepted authority positions as shop stewards.) As a matter of fact, when nonprofessionals do accept an authority role, they often carry it out very well because of their positive traditionalistic and religious association with authority and because they do not find it inconsistent with informality and closeness to people. They do not have the ambivalence toward authority per se that characterizes many middle-class people, who find it very difficult to execute authority without being *authoritarian* and cannot easily combine authority with warmth. The low-income individual, while he resents the bureaucratic authority of the "power structure", does not resist authority or power as such. Consequently, if he gets past the initial block concerning his use of formal authority, he may employ it very rationally and smoothly.

Another deterrent, however, to his comfortable use of authority lies in his limited know-how and lack of actual practice in the use of authority. Hence, it is extremely important to provide practice in a permissive (error possible) setting (as for example role-playing such typical authority situations as leading a meeting), and to make sure that the nonprofessional acquires detailed knowledge and know-how regarding every phase of the assignment he is to carry out.

3. OVER-IDENTIFICATION WITH THE AGENCY AND ITS COROLLARY, UNDER-IDENTIFICATION WITH THE COMMUNITY

Very often the nonprofessional, being pleased with his new status, feels in debt to the institution or agency. He responds by wanting to be very obliging and adopts what he believes to be the agency's point of view regarding the "poor", etc. This is sometimes expressed in remarks such as: "Too many people around here are lazy, don't want to help themselves." Sometimes this is revealed in less dramatic form. For example, the Parent Aides at Mobilization For Youth initially tended to define their job largely in terms of influencing the parents to properly prepare and motivate their children for school. The problem was complicated here because in the early stages the Parent Education Program had, in part, a one-way communication focus, and perhaps the Aides merely reflected this. Of course, the obvious solution to this community under-identification problem is to clarify forcefully that the agency does not desire this behavior, that it does not have a negative view of the poor and the community, and that its focus is two-way communication (if this is the case)—that it is much concerned with changing the institutions of the community which are not serving the poor. Thus, in discussions with the Aides the group leader might ask: "What's wrong with the schools?" "How can the schools and Parent Associations be improved so that the people in the neighborhood will be more positive toward them?" Discussions evolving from this focus can quickly clarify the two-way influence focus of the organization and reduce the Aides' potential under-identification with the community.

4. OVER-OPTIMISM TURNING INTO DEFEATISM

Initially the indigenous worker is likely to be very hopeful about changing the community, and he often expects speedy results. The positive side of this attitude lies in his lack of complaisance and his rousing spirit. When things do not move rapidly, he sometimes becomes over-pessimistic, fatalistic, and may regress to blaming "the apathetic people" for not being more militant. Lacking a broad view or timetable for change, he may become too easily frustrated by bureaucracy or too demanding in relating to the people in the community.

Guarding against this difficulty is indeed difficult because care must be taken to preserve the noncynical, nonaloof, noncomplaisant attitudes that characterize the indigenous worker. Much of his spirit and verve may be robbed by too great an emphasis on the factors inhibiting rapid change. Moreover, some of these inhibiting factors should not be accepted. Often the professional has become accustomed to making allowances and going slow when this is not necessary.

An overall approach to the problem would seem to indicate that the initial optimism need not be dampened, but that plans (a tentative timetable) should be presented concerning the expectations for the successful achievement of objectives in the particular community. A realistic, but not ultraconservative, estimate of some of the difficulties should be made available to the nonprofessional (although not dwelt upon), and signposts of progress should be indicated at every point.

5. THE NONPROFESSIONAL AND THE PROFESSIONAL

There are many problems involved in developing and defining the relationship of the nonprofessional to the professionals both within the agency and outside of it.

Professionals frequently are not clear about the role and the ability of indigenous workers. This is particularly so in the beginning when, because of lack of training and confidence, the nonprofessional may be quite unsure of himself and his role.

Institutions employing nonprofessionals have to carefully define their roles, tasks, competencies to all professional groups with whom these nonprofessionals will be in contact —both within the agency and outside the agency. This should be done formally (through written directives, etc.) and informally.

There should be careful preparation and training of the nonprofessional before their initial contact with professionals. The nonprofessionals should know their roles, rights, and responsibilities; they should be thoroughly acquainted with the directives that have been sent to various agencies; their skill and confidence should be sufficiently developed so that they will maintain their composure. While aspects of field work can begin simultaneously with the training sessions, relationships to professionals in other agencies should be held in abeyance until more skill has been acquired. In an area such as talking informally to members of the community, much natural skill exists among the indigenous workers and therefore "on the job training" can begin almost at once; but with regard to relationships to professionals, not only is there likely to be no natural proclivity, but more often than not, there are special incapacities and lack of know-how. It might very well be a better idea for the nonprofessional to develop "practice" with professionals in his own agency first.

The use of role play practice might be quite advantageous in preparing nonprofessionals for various aspects (especially the interpersonal face-to-face and telephone encounters) of the relationship to professionals.

The indigenous nonprofessional should receive special training in how to participate in team conferences which include professionals. The tendency of nonprofessionals to refrain from speaking at these conferences should be confronted and role play training introduced to assist in overcoming the problem.

CURRICULUM DESIGN FOR TRAINING NONPROFESSIONALS

Training nonprofessionals demands planning and precision. The curriculum encompasses a wide range of different presentations and activities and must include the following areas:

1. Knowledge of the problem at hand.—If housing is to be an area of concern and the nonprofessional is to be involved in tenants' organizations then it is imperative that training include specific detailed discussion on housing. There should be constant checking to determine whether the material is understood (e.g. information on the type of housing in the neighborhood, housing laws and city agencies involved).

2. *Knowledge of the program of the agency; its goals, methods, timetable, underlying rationale and concepts.*—
These concepts and theories can be taught successfully to nonprofessional personnel provided that their relationship to experience and practice is *constantly* pointed out in detail.

3. *Knowledge of low-income culture and the organization's views regarding this stratum and its subgroups.*—
Discussion of lower socio-economic groups is particularly difficult because the indigenous nonprofessionals may feel that they know about this population through their own experience. While their experience should certainly be utilized, and they should be encouraged to look at it positively (not reject their origins), nevertheless much detailed information regarding various subgroups and ethnic groups will not be known to them, and they will have some distorted information in these areas.

The potential positive aspects, the strengths of low-income culture should be considered at length. For example, the cooperativeness and mutual aid that mark the extended family; the avoidance of the strain accompanying competitiveness and individualism; the equalitarianism, informality and humor; the freedom from self-blame and parental overprotection; the children's enjoyment of each other's company and lessened sibling rivalry; the security found in the extended family and a traditional outlook; the enjoyment of music, games, sports and cards; the ability to express anger; the freedom from being word-bound; and finally the physical style involved in learning.

4. *Knowledge regarding service-giving procedures.*—
Trainees must acquire a knowledge of community resources, programming and organized group activities. They must know how to make referrals and fill out forms. They must be

trained to disseminate such information to enable people to help themselves.

5. *Knowledge regarding the goals of a community approach to service.*—Trainees must be taught to be able to:

a. Deflect clients away from psychological self-concern and pathology.

b. Concentrate on client strength and on their efforts at coping with difficulties. Trainees must be taught to look for strengths outside the client-worker relationship in social activity.

c. Encourage latent working-class traditions and norms (e.g. cooperative baby sitting, tenants' organizations, anti-bureaucratic sentiment, the striving for personal dignity, group activity).

d. Be alert for potential generators of motion (indigenous leaders who would play an important role in the development of community health, if their external and internal difficulties were reduced).

e. Hold small group discussions aimed, not at common pathology, but rather toward common community problems —discrimination, bureaucracy, housing, employment, school improvement, reducing drug addiction, and gang behavior. These sessions would also be oriented toward developing verbal facility, know-how, and feelings of strength and power.

Imparting specific job-related skills is the underpinning of the training experience. Specific curricula will vary with the nonprofessional assignment but a core of knowledge must be obtained by all nonprofessionals. This should include:

1. *Interviewing and establishing contact.*—Making contact with the client is crucial to all human service. Nonprofessionals must be taught how to inaugurate and also terminate relationships. They must be taught to distinguish between establishing rapport and overinvolvement with the client.

2. *Reporting methods and record keeping.*—The non-professional must be trained to appreciate the significance of records and be shown how to maintain an appropriate record of his activities. Such training accomplishes two ends: not only is the worker able to do an efficient job of record-keeping, but in the process of learning that skill he also significantly increases his ability to express himself in both written and spoken language. A part of the training in record keeping might have to include training in the use of a dictionary.

3. *Meetings.*—Trainees must be instructed in how to plan and conduct informal and formal meetings. They must be taught how to elicit participation in low-income groups (preparing people for meetings, down-to-earth discussion, coffee and cake breaks, audiovisual aids). They must know how to help nonparticipants, "outsiders", take an active part in formal meetings at which they feel rejected or over-looked.[2]

TRAINING METHODOLOGY

If the nonprofessional revolution proceeds at a rapid pace, there is the strong likelihood that in the next decade the ratio of professionals to nonprofessionals will change significantly in certain areas. Perhaps the model of the future will see one professional charged with supervision and teaching of five to eight nonprofessionals, depending on the task. If this occurs, teaching and supervision method-ology appropriate for nonprofessionals becomes extremely important.

In the first stages the training should be oriented toward *learning through doing* (job simulation, role-playing[3], on-the-job learning), on the assumption that this approach fits the basic style of low income people. However progressively *more reading and writing assignments should be introduced as the training proceeds* and the trainees gain confidence and skill.

In essence, the training methodology of nonprofessionals should stress the following seven points:

1. Continuous on-the-job training and almost immediate initiation to work.

2. An activity rather than lecture approach ("do rather than write") with a heavy emphasis on role playing and role training.

3. An intensive team approach aimed at building strong group solidarity among the nonprofessional workers in any given project. This produces the kind of strong supportive base that is particularly necessary for nonprofessionals working in a professional setting.

4. Informal individual supervision at any time on request, supplemented by group discussion and group supervision.

5. A down-to-earth teaching style, emphasizing concrete tasks presented in clarity and detail, which recognizes that concepts and theory, if properly presented, are definitely within the reach of indigenous personnel.

6. Utilization of the "helper principle". Whenever possible more experienced nonprofessionals should assist and teach their less advanced colleagues in dealing with various tasks. It has been discovered that not only does the less experienced worker benefit, but the more advanced worker learns as well from playing the teacher role.

7. Freedom for the nonprofessional to develop his personal style. There should be considerable emphasis on the development of the unique style of each nonprofessional. The worker should be encouraged to explore his own possibilities for dealing with various situations, utilizing his experience, his personality, his knowledge, and his observations of other people's ways of dealing with these problems. This should be directed toward developing and extending his repertoire. In protected training exercises he should be

given the opportunity to try out various ways of meeting people, of dealing with problems, working with the professionals, etc. The group should discuss with him his strengths and weaknesses in dealing with job problems; this will provide him with a mirror of how he appears to others and will suggest ways of extending his skills and repertoire. The nonprofessional should then attempt to further experiment in this relatively unthreatening situation with new ways of coping with his tasks.

Training the nonprofessional to grow within "his own style" cannot be an excuse for foregoing training, nor are destructive or non-helpful activities of the nonprofessional to be condoned because "such is the price one pays for naturalness." The nonprofessional is to be retained and trained to perform a service; his usefulness to himself and others will be based on his ability to do the job, and on that alone.

Long preparatory training is very dangerous because considerable anxiety develops in the nonprofessional until he gets into "action". After all, he has never held a position such as the one for which he is being prepared and this generates more than the normal quota of anxiety associated with a new job. Consequently it is extremely important that he actually begin performing some tasks as soon as possible. Moreover, these tasks must be carefully phased; the initial assignments must be relatively simple and surely within the range of the trainee's skills. As on-the-job training continues, the tasks should be made progressively more difficult.

THE SPECIAL SIGNIFICANCE OF ROLE PLAYING

The principle "do rather than write" is crucial. General teaching methodology requires that people be active with material they receive via lectures or reading—e.g. writing answers to a quiz is productive, but for nonprofessionals, actually *doing* something with the material received is indispensable. This is why role-playing is such an important technique for indigenous nonprofessionals.

Experience at Mobilization For Youth[4] and various community organizations further indicates an exceptionally positive response to role-play technology by low-income people. (Particularly the low-income nonprofessional staff.) While more systematic research is needed regarding these observations, it may be useful to present a rationale for the possible special value of this technique in work with lower socioeconomic groups.

It is a technology that appears much more congenial with the low-income person's style: physical (action oriented, do vs. talk); down to earth, concrete, problem directed; externally oriented rather than introspective; group centered; game-like rather than test oriented; easy, informal tempo.

The significant factor from the point of view of style is that the low-income people appear to *work out mental problems best when they can do things physically*. This is their *habit* or style of work, and it appears when they work on academic problems, etc.[5]

Role-playing appears admirably suited to this physical, action centered, motoric style. The process itself requires a wholistic *doing* or acting out of situations, not merely talking about them. Low-income people frequently have a strong dislike for "talk"; especially talk that is isolated from experience; they want "action" and *prefer talk that is related to action*. They also like vivid (e.g. hip, slang), down-to-earth, situationally rooted talk; and this too is more likely to emerge in the role play format.

While the style of the low income person probably includes a strong emphasis on informality, humor, and warmth, he also likes a content that is structured, definite, and specific. It is often assumed that role-playing is highly unstructured, open, and free. In part, this is true, particularly in the early phase of setting the problem and mood.

But in the middle and later phases (especially the role-*training* stage), where the effort is made to teach very specific behaviors, role-playing can be highly structured, reviewing in minute detail the various operations to be learned (such as how to run a meeting, organize a conference, talk to a housing manager). Educationally disadvantaged people appear to prefer a mood or feeling tone that is informal and easy, but a *content* that is more structured and task centered. Role-playing may suit both needs.

One value of role-play is that it offers the nonprofessional a chance not only to understand the client but also to test in practice a simulated worker-client relationship. Another advantage of role-play is that it gives the supervisors a picture of what the nonprofessional is doing and the particular problems he is experiencing. Furthermore, role-playing technology easily allows, even encourages, nonprofessionals to teach each other, making use of the helper principle. The approach is particularly fruitful for less formally educated individuals, who have had scant experience with learning from books and lectures.

It is noteworthy that anthropologists and public health specialists have placed considerable emphasis on the use of role-playing techniques in teaching nonprofessional "auxiliary aides" or health workers. In Peru, for example, role-playing was one of the major methods employed in training Hygiene Workers to convince the population of a local town to boil their water.[6]

THE TEAM APPROACH

Another very important educational procedure is the use of the team approach. Tremendous esprit de corps can be built up in this manner. This is an extremely important approach in any program where there is likely to be some initial lack of confidence.[7]

It is necessary for the professional coordinator or trainer to stress at every point the need for cooperation and to strongly encourage the nonprofessionals to constantly help each other deal with problems as they arise.

It should be remembered that the nonprofessional in the new career situation is moving toward a whole new pattern of life, both on and off the job. Much of the new is ambiguous and, to varying degrees, threatening. A parent aide who relates well to people, socializes well, etc. might still find it quite threatening to organize people in a neighborhood for a parents' meeting. A group of youngsters who were formerly delinquent might find it difficult to imagine themselves as recreation aides, child-care aides, research aides, or whatever. The group that is developed in the training process can provide powerful reinforcement and encouragement in the building of the new skills, values and behavior.[8] Moreover, in the terms of the helper principle to which we have referred, each member of the group in assisting the other actually helps himself a great deal, and this contributes to the rehabilitative function involved in many of the nonprofessional new careers. Some of the new careers may not have a significant rehabilitative function but simply serve as job career patterns. But where the nonprofessional person has previously been an unemployed youngster, a delinquent, an ADC mother, a public assistance client, a mental patient—the rehabilitative function is extremely important. The importance of the group exists both in the rehabilitative area and in the job training sphere because the group provides reinforcement, encouragement and resources for the development of the new job skills and related values as well as for the rehabilitative personality dimensions; and the helper principle applies again in both cases—it applies in the rehabilitative sense, in that when one nonprofessional helps another he is himself helped in the process. It applies also in the teacher sense as one member of a group teaching or assisting another member of the group may learn through teaching.

Brager argues that the team approach plays an important

role in limiting the professionalization of the nonprofessional.

This problem can best be met by providing the nonprofessional with the safety of numbers. . . . Within the alien confines of a social agency, they need the support of one another. When they are together, on the other hand, it is the supervisor who may need help! If it is not possible, for programatic reasons, to assign the nonprofessionals as a collectivity, one solution might be a group training program.[9]

Brager notes that "If the 15 Homemakers (at Mobilization For Youth) were dispersed throughout the project, supervised by individual caseworkers rather than by the two unit supervisors to whom they are currently responsible, strain would be reduced and greater integration of individual services would be achieved." But this would have been at the expense of the "distinctive flavor" of the indigenous staff, which is maintained through the mutual reinforcements and esprit de corps of the team training structure.[10]

An interesting indication of the spirit and mutual support found among the nonprofessionals is the fact that in most of the programs in which they have worked, turnover of personnel has been practically nonexistent.[11]

EXPLICITNESS IN TRAINING

In training nonprofessionals, or anyone from a lower socioeconomic background, it is very important that the teaching be concrete. Many illustrations should be used, details should be carefully spelled out, assumptions should be explicitly stated. Ideas that are often taken for granted in other types of presentations should be enunciated almost compulsively, and material should be repeated frequently. A slow, painstaking, nonpressureful atmosphere should prevail, and active participation by each of the learners should be sought. Presentations should be well organized, few digressions permitted and frequent summary made available. Transitions should be clearly indicated and breaks in continuity should be held to a minimum or else explicitly designated.

In general, it should not be forgotten that the educational tools of individuals who have had limited formal schooling are quite deficient, and what might appear to be overly painstaking to a more educated group, will be far better appreciated in a less educated audience (provided it does not become condescending).

Concepts and theory can be successfully taught to nonprofessional personnel provided that their relationship to experience and practice is *constantly* pointed out in detail. Each time a concept is discussed the group leader must ask himself and the group: "What are the practical implications of the idea?" "How did we get the idea—on what concrete experience is it based?" No matter how indirect the relationship to practice may be, this relationship must be sought and spelled out slowly, using many illustrations. No step can be skipped, no assumptions taken for granted. Illustrations of the principle or concept should be sought from the group and/or given by the group leader in terms of the experience of these particular indigenous workers.

The discussion leader or teacher should be aware of the language he uses. Clear, basic, nonacademic English should be used at all times, and complex words should be defined or used together with synonyms.

The teacher might prepare for himself a list of the words, the meanings of which are assumed by the program. Together with this he might prepare a list of substitute phrases, and, in general, be alert to the use of these terms.

No casual lecture will suffice. Specific detailed discussion, including constant checking to determine whether the material is understood, is necessary. Information must be illustrated with many concrete examples and presented through varied media and educational devices: films, press, debates, reading short pamphlets, discussions, etc. Lecturers and group leaders must be carefully briefed on how to present material to nonprofessionals.

While much of the training is necessarily oriented toward problems directly related to the job, there will be the opportunity to impart certain broader information and in some cases to develop attitudes through the training experiences, if they are appropriately planned. Thus, broad cooperative attitudes can be stimulated by the group discussions, the role-playing group sessions, the helper therapy principle, and the overall ideology that can be breathed into the program at almost every point.

Depending upon the specific program involved, other attitudes can also be encouraged: work-discipline attitudes (in the case of unemployed youngsters, former delinquents and drug addicts); feelings of self-respect for ADC mothers, unemployed adults, and school dropouts.

This aspect of the training program might be seen as its rehabilitative, morale development focus. While this is an important dimension of new career training, care should be taken lest it become all encompassing. There is always the danger that the program might be transformed into the type of work training programs of the rehabilitative type where attitudes toward work are emphasized but no new careers emerge.

The training program also allows for the imparting of knowledge about the job market, behavior relevant to marketable skills, and the like. But perhaps most important, new attitudes toward knowledge can be conveyed and knowledge acquiring skills attuned to the action-learning style of the low-income nonprofessional can spring to life.

The rehabilitative aspect involved in the employment of nonprofessionals, can be applied in the employment as aides of certain kinds of people who have had psychological problems. Here the "helper therapy principle" is most operative, that is, through helping others, the person with the psychological difficulty improves greatly himself. Obviously, psychotic patients and patients who have been very ill would not be employed in this fashion. However, the considerable number of people who have had certain kinds of crisis problems or smaller emotional difficulties might very well profit from being employed as nonprofessionals and might function very ably in assisting others.

TRAINING THE TRAINERS

The training of the nonprofessional poses a challenging and arduous task. If millions of jobs are to be created for nonprofessionals then thousands of persons must be adequately prepared to train them. The new career proposal will be dangerously weakened unless carefully thought-through plans and programs have been devised for developing the trainers. If such care is not exercised, the training experience of the nonprofessional trainees may recapitulate the misery and defeat experienced by many of them in formal school settings.

CRITERIA FOR SELECTION OF TRAINERS

Since so little is known about training the poor, and much less about the specific problems of training for new careers, selection criteria must be considered tentative. From limited experience,[12] however, it would appear that trainers should possess the following general attributes:

1. *Nonpejorative attitude*—The trainer cannot believe that the impoverished person is a victim of his own lack of motivation or constitutional inferiority. He must believe that the trainee has a potential for growth and development.

2. *Self-security*—Only persons seemingly able to manifest an open and honest relationship with the poor should be selected as trainers. All too often the professional covers

insecurity by retreating behind the jargon and power of his position. The trainer *will* hold a position of power and anyone with the need to exploit this power at the expense of the trainee should obviously be excluded from the position regardless of other qualifications he may possess.

3. *Tolerance of tempo differences*—Many of the poor who will be attracted to new careers will be persons who failed in school because they were "slow." The trainer must be able to adjust to the pace of the trainees. To a large extent, tempo is a learned phenomenon and may stem from a variety of causes. For example, performing a job extremely slowly may be a deliberate effort to annoy the boss (or trainer), or may reflect insecurity leading to blocking or time wasting; or yet again, could be an almost obsessive concern with detail to guarantee high quality of performance. The trainer can facilitate change in tempo, but only over a period of time and only if he is able to control his annoyance with the slow learner.

4. *Nonauthoritarian posture*—The trainer will, on many occasions, find himself standing alone against organized resistance of the training group. Persons capable of dealing with group resistance without retreating to authoritarian stances should be sought as trainers. Conversely, persons unable to stand up to a group, who would surrender to resistance and thereby forfeit their responsibility, are unfit for trainer roles.

Training needs, first of all, to be defined in terms of the functions and duties which the trainee must learn. A training program for new-career trainers must accomplish at least three things. The trainer must be prepared to impart the specific skills which will be needed in a given job (e.g. research techniques of interviewing, coding and desk calculator operation for research aides; bulletin board management, lunchroom supervision and oral reading for school aides). The trainer must be provided with general skills needed for work with low-income people (e.g. role play and group discussion techniques). The trainer must be provided a basic course in understanding the life processes and problems of the poor.

At Howard University, the Center for Youth and Community Studies has established a training center which has undertaken both the direct tutelage of the poor for new career roles, as well as the preparation of the trainers. A division of function in training roles has been established at the Center. Persons who impart specific job skills to low-income trainees are styled "specialty trainers," while other persons charged with infusing and implementing the team concept for trainees are called "core trainers."

Specialty trainers can be recruited from personnel skilled in the jobs which need to be performed or they may be drawn from the ranks of graduated trainees. The core trainers require special preparation, but, at introductory levels, some graduates of the training programs may also be included.

It will be difficult to rapidly assemble a large complement of trainers, especially if only the most capable or fully qualified are to be considered. The Howard University Center recruited a training team, with each member selected for a different strength, thus seeking to overcome individual deficits by the pooling of these strengths. The training team had some members without a high school education and others with doctoral degrees.

The training function varies not only in scope but also in level. A training team could easily consist of minimally trained and experienced training aides, more advanced assistants and associates, plus qualified professionals (as discussed in the teaching model in Chapter 4).

Training must keep pace with new career development. Many possible strategies can insure this growth. The most promising seems to be the initiation of regionally-located training centers,[13] which would be responsible for providing personnel to train for all appropriate functions and levels of trainer roles. Ultimately, much of the training for new careers should be incorporated within the traditional schooling process as updated vocational and adult education courses. Universities, teachers' colleges, community and junior colleges could then become, with appropriate additions to curricula, the resources for the various levels of training personnel.

CONDITIONING SERVICE AGENCIES
FOR ACCEPTANCE OF NEW CAREERS

There is a clear training responsibility in preparing the service agencies which will employ newly-trained nonprofessionals for the changes which are implied in the new career proposal. Agencies must be provided information about new developments in manpower utilization. Dissemination of information of this nature is crucial if there is to be mutual satisfaction with the services which nonprofessional aides are able to offer. Agencies will not give up an established order unless they are provided concrete evidence that new deployments will bring new advantages. Interpretation of demonstration results is a necessary step for the institution of change in agency operation.

Human service agencies can be introduced to the potentialities and responsibilities of employing the new career forces at their disposal in institutes and short training sessions, and should be assisted in developing continuing in-service training after a strategy for utilizing nonprofessionals has been adopted. The Howard University Center has invested considerably in this aspect of training.[14]

Change will not come easy and it is important that beachheads be established by making progress where conditions are most favorable. Wherever possible, programs should be initiated with agency personnel who are receptive to the idea of utilizing nonprofessional personnel. However, it should be noted that results obtained under optimal conditions may not always have general application.

THE IMPACT OF TRAINING—
SOME ANECDOTES

The training of the poor to assume new career roles can be of real value in many areas of personal growth. The anecdotes which follow depict possible consequences of training programs, of the type described in this chapter. These accounts are taken from the Howard University Community Apprentice Program.[15] The trainees for this project were ten disadvantaged youths who ranged in age from sixteen to twenty, none of whom had progressed beyond the eleventh grade before leaving school. Four of the seven boys had delinquency records and two of the three girls had borne children out of wedlock. These young people were trained for roles in day-care, recreation and research and all ten demonstrated considerable skill in their performance on the job.

ESTABLISHING A SENSE OF STAKE
IN ONE'S OWN FUTURE

Disadvantaged youth are, in most instances, handicapped by almost complete social impotence. There is very little in their lives over which they have control. Their alternatives are few and often equally unpromising. New career training can infuse new hope into an otherwise bleak prospect. The following story illustrates that if the poor are allowed to help plan their destiny, not only will they invest more of themselves in a program, but perhaps, also, a better program may emerge.

The ten trainees were given a general orientation to the duties of day care, recreation, and research during the first two weeks of the program. At the end of the second week the group was given an opportunity to decide their own field assignments. Contrary to staff expectation, two boys with delinquency histories were chosen for the day-care center.

Concern was expressed by the day-care center administrators that these boys were inappropriate choices for the jobs. The group of trainees was then asked to justify their decision. They pointed out that during the three day orientation period the two boys in question had been the most active participants while the others had retired to observe from the sidelines. The chosen boys had played with the children, helped to mix clay and paint and otherwise become totally involved with and accepted by the nursery school children.

The boys themselves indicated that they derived satisfaction from being sought after by the children and called "daddy." They sensed that they had a unique contribution to make to a pre-school center because they were manifestly male in a field unable to attract many males.

One of the boys further elaborated his choice by saying, "Where would I go if I didn't pick day care? Into recreation? I have a 'rep' as a trouble maker on the playground. As soon as I get on the court, my friends are likely to take the basketball away. What do I do then? Drop the dime?* I can't do that. These are my friends and besides I live in the neighborhood. If I don't do anything I'll get fired. If I punch somebody I'll get fired. I'd have trouble on the playground, but I can handle those three and four year olds."

The arguments of the group prevailed, and the boys took on the day-care assignment, which they performed creditably. Most important, however, the group was given concrete evidence that this was a program in which the participants would have a real role in policy determination.

A SENSE OF COMPETENCE

It is not easy for the poor to acquire a skill that is generally accepted and respected. The lack of opportunity for competence needed within organized society may explain the development of anti-establishment norms and values. Acquiring the necessary powers to obtain a reputation as a "tough stud" is probably perceived by disadvantaged young-

* Washington, D.C. street talk for "call the police."

sters to be a better reward than to be left without any valued attributes at all. The training of youth to perform demonstrably useful tasks seems to satisfy a need for a sense of competence. Almost everything performed by the young people in the Community Apprentice Program gave them the satisfaction of helping others and being useful and appreciated.

The general theme which pervaded the youths' evaluation of the program was that its value lay in offering them an opportunity "to show what they could do." A primary objective of the training and work experience was to generate a sense of competence in the trainees. The research aides were taught to perform statistical operations on a desk calculator (Chi-square, rank order correlation(rho) and product-moment correlation). They learned the manipulations well and proceeded to become both quick and accurate in the performance of their duties. They invested sufficiently in the job to learn the rudiments of the principles underlying the operations and they were able to explain to others not only what they were doing, but the reasons for performing a particular task.

The aides were unashamedly proud of their accomplishments. When a research aide was asked to instruct a graduate student in the performance of a statistical operation, he jestingly refused, saying, "No, I'm the only one around here who knows how to do it, and I'm going to keep it that way."

A SENSE OF BELONGING

Alienation is not restricted to the poor. There is emptiness and lack of meaning in the lives of many of the affluent. But certain problems are peculiar to the poor. There is very little possibility of discovering any facet of existence to which they can make a commitment affording a sense of belonging to something which is vital and meaningful. When social scientists depict the poor as lacking in time perspective they often fail to recognize that time is not a commodity which the poor can manipulate. If planning and utilization of time were more at their command, however, the anomic characteristics of the poor might well decrease.

The four youths with assignments to recreation activities were attached to a settlement house program that had ceased to function. They asked the professional group worker how they could revive the program. He suggested that they send out postcards inviting neighborhood young-sters to attend the center. When it became apparent that no response to the postcards was forthcoming, the recreation aides, on their own initiative, conducted a door-to-door cam-paign and within two weeks had recruited 120 youngsters into a recreation program. The aides then proceeded to get their charges involved in a multitude of activities—team competition, arts and crafts, tours of the city, etc. Time now became a variable of central importance to the recreation aides. They had to plan and budget time; they not only had to be sure that they were on time for activities, but had to insure that their teams met their engagements. No longer could it be said that the aides displayed lack of time orienta-tion for short or even long-range planning.

These recreation aides became so invested in their work that they volunteered an average of almost a day a week overtime (for which they were not paid). As a clue to their feelings of affiliation, they outfitted themselves with Howard University sweatshirts, caps and whistles, at their own ex-pense, as symbols of their new sense of allegiance.

A RELATIONSHIP WITH PROFESSIONALS
BASED ON REALITY

The relationship of the poor with professionals is rarely a pleasurable experience. In the first place the poor are usually forced into the relationship, then prevailed upon to accept rules that are conditioned by agency policy and professional standards. All too often the professional projects into the relationship a promise of support and trust greater than he is prepared to deliver.

In the Community Apprentice Program, the trainees were told unequivocally that they had to develop strengths within themselves to accomplish their jobs successfully—that they couldn't place their trust in the professional staff who were likely to be absent or otherwise occupied when the aides faced crises or had to make decisions. This message must have registered with at least one aide.

At the end of the seventh week, a crisis developed in the program. Due to administrative error the stipends did not arrive in time for the aides to be paid on Friday evening. They were understandably angry.

On the same evening, by chance, two members of the staff had agreed to officiate at a radio interview. The aides had been asked to send representatives to discuss the program. The aides took the position that, angry as they were, it would not be advisable for them to appear on the program because they would say things which we would not want the public to know. The staff indicated that they should feel free to express anything they wished.

The aides continued to demur. That evening, however, three representatives did appear for the broadcast. During the interview they responded to questions with only expressions of praise for the program. When queried directly about negative features of the project they were unable (or unwilling) to offer any criticism. One of the staff reminded the youth that their checks had been delayed and that this was, at least, disconcerting. Whereupon one of the aides responded, "Oh yeah, but six weeks ago you told us we couldn't trust you. Today you proved it."

CONCLUSION

In Chapter 2 a caveat was issued against training as a cure for poverty. It was pointed out that training does not create jobs. In this chapter attention has been directed to the importance of training for newly created jobs. Job creation will not, by itself, solve the problems of the jobless. It is possible that persons most in need of jobs will be unable to perform the newly created duties adequately unless they are provided with careful training which is job specific and perceived as useful. Job development and training comprise two essential elements for a comprehensive attack on poverty. If either is lacking it is difficult to conceive of an effective result.

NOTES

1. Rachel Robinson and Melvin Roman, "New Directions for the Psychiatric Aide," presented at Howard University Conference on Use of Nonprofessionals, April, 1964.

2. The following list of down-to-earth clearly written short pamphlets is available from the Adult Education Association, 743 North Wabash Avenue, Chicago, Ill. (60¢ per copy):

P-1 —How to lead discussions
P-2 —Planning better programs
P-3 —Taking action in the community
P-4 —Understanding how groups work
P-5 —How to teach adults
P-6 —How to use role playing
P-7 —Supervision and consultation
P-8 —Training group leaders
P-9 —Conducting workshops and institutes
P-10—Working with volunteers
P-11—Conferences that work
P-12—Getting and keeping members
P-13—Effective public relations.

3. Role-playing is the flexible enacting out of various types of problems in a permissive group atmosphere, e.g., a caseworker interviewing a withdrawn client, a person being interviewed by a housing project manager in a low-income housing project. As few as two people can role-play, such as a social worker and a client in an office, but most role-playing is usually done in groups where two people can act out a situation and the group discuss it. At times, more than two people can role-play, e.g., a social worker interviewing a woman with five children present. (See F. Riessman and J. Goldfarb, "Role Playing and the Poor," Group Psychotherapy, 1964, Vol. 17, No. 1).

4. The following discussion of role-playing is taken from "Role Playing and the Poor" by Frank Riessman and Jean Goldfarb, *Group Psychotherapy* Vol. 17, No. 1, 1964.

5. Miller, Daniel, and Swanson, Guy. *Inner Conflict and Defense.* N. Y.: Henry Holt, 1960, p. 24.

6. "Water Boiling in a Peruvian Town." E. Wellin, p. 73 *Health, Culture, and Community.* Edited by Benjamin D. Paul, New York: Russell Sage Foundation, 1955.

7. It is interesting to note that the Hunter College Program for the training of teachers of deprived neighborhoods similarly utilizes a team approach. See F. Riessman, *The Culturally Deprived Child,* Harper, 1962, p. 119.

8. The Community Apprentice Program at Howard University vividly illustrates the importance of the group in providing this support and reinforcement. See Arthur Pearl, "Youth in Lower Class Settings," presented at Fifth Symposium on Social Psychology, 1964, Norman, Oklahoma.

9. George Brager, "The Low-Income Non-Professional", paper presented at National Conference of Social Welfare, Los Angeles, 1963, pp. 12–13

10. *Ibid.,* p. 13.

11. See F. Riessman, "Revolution in Social Work: The new Non-professional" for discussion of lack of turnover of Homemakers and Parent Aides at Mobilization for Youth.

12. *Community Apprentice Program.* Howard University, Center for Youth and Community Studies, 1965, mimeo.

13. Already in existence is the nucleus for such a center in Washington, D.C. (Howard University). Others include Chapel Hill (University of North Carolina); New York City (Albert Einstein Medical School, Yeshiva University); Eugene, Oregon (University of Oregon); San Francisco (San Francisco State College); Newark, N.J. (Newark State Teachers College); Los Angeles (University of Southern California).

14. MacLennon, Beryce. *Training for New Careers,* paper given at New Careers Conference, Howard University, 1964.

15. A detailed account and evaluation of the project is to be found in *Community Apprentice Program, op. cit.*

CHAPTER 9

ISSUES AND
PITFALLS

RECRUITMENT

These nonprofessionals should be people who have themselves come out of lower-class culture, and have successfully moved into a more stable way of life—either working or middle-class—but have not rejected their past. Many mobile people tend to turn their backs on the culture from which they have come, and become more hostile toward it than anyone else. Yet there are some people, who, in making the change, have developed a considerable amount of empathy toward both old and new culture. Since they know the conditions and the culture that are to be changed, and the way of life that is being sought by and for lower-class clients, they should be more successful in achieving rapport with such clients than are middle-class professionals. But while these empathic people exist in large numbers, they are hard to find. Some have been drawn into settlement houses and into group work with adolescent gangs. Most of them, however, probably earn their living in factories and offices, without ever using their talent—for it is a talent—to mediate between the classes.[1]

IMPLICIT in the bridge concept outlined by Gans is the notion that people drawn from lower socio-economic strata may have special skills for communication across class lines. But, of course, many people of lower socio-economic background will not be especially proficient in this type of communication; in fact, some may be especially inadequate (due to trained incapacities or rejection of either their class of origin or the middle class). It is also possible that some people who are effective interclass communicators may not well-represent the interests of people in the lower stratum. Thus, the problems of selection and training take on great significance.

THE INTERNAL CARETAKER'S ERROR

Gans furnishes a basic context within which to begin analyzing some of the potential limitations of the nonprofessional, and thus he indirectly provides clues as to the preparation and guidance necessary to overcome, or at least contain, these weaknesses.

Many of the new nonprofessionals will probably be recruited from a group that Gans describes as "internal caretakers."[2] These are people "such as bartenders, store owners, neighbors who informally offer various types of care to people in low-income communities."

Gans notes that most of the internal caretakers are "market oriented" and "consequently the care they provide has a number of limitations."

Whenever possible, they try to do what will please their peer group clients, even when this is not the wisest course. They do not necessarily act in this fashion to be ingratiating, but because they share the same beliefs. For example, if a person is ill and refuses to see a doctor, the internal caretaker who has similar feelings about doctors may reinforce the patient's hesitation. Also, they may cut off further care should the client refuse to follow their advice. Most important, since they often have no more knowledge than their clients, the care they give is not always what is needed. The internal caretaker functions most successfully when the client's need is for group support—be that financial or psychological—and least successfully when the need is for expertise that can be found only in the outside world. If the care cannot be supplied by internal caretakers, as is the case with medical or dental treatment, West Enders will eventually visit the external caretaker, although they may postpone it as long as possible. But if the treatment needed is psychological in nature, West Enders may feel that it can best be supplied internally by affection and advice from the peer group, in which case the visit to an external caretaker may be postponed indefinitely.[3]

This analysis suggests two important considerations with regard to the new nonprofessional: one concerns recruitment and the other training. In recruiting indigenous workers from the low-income population it may be advisable for certain purposes not to select former internal caretakers; or when employing former caretakers, care should perhaps be taken to avoid selecting those who are *excessively* market oriented (primarily concerned with pleasing their client at any cost). Moreover, in training the nonprofessional, effort must be made to reduce the narrow client centered aspect of his approach while maintaining and *maximizing the beneficial aspects of his skills in terms of communication and understanding across class lines.*

This is indeed a dilemma because, what is under certain conditions a great strength, namely the nonprofessional's ability to identify closely with the low-income individual's problems and feelings, can under other circumstances promote difficulty if the identification remains too narrow.

Brager in commenting on recruitment at Mobilization for Youth states:

In employing low-income nonprofessionals to broadly affect social climate, it is neither possible nor desirable to draw a representative sample of workers from the low-income community. The specific

goals of the program will be a major determinant of the characteristics sought. If, for example, an important objective of the service
is to enable working-class persons to strive for and reach middle-class
status, it might be desirable to employ low-income people who are
oriented to middle-class life. One consequence of such a decision,
of course, is that, if other factors are equal, less striving persons will
then be likely to avoid participation. To cite another example: if
the agency's intention in hiring non-professionals is to give the
appearance of minority-group or low-income representativeness without impinging upon the middle-class value base or organizational
prerequisites of the agency, it will choose low-income persons who
are willing to accommodate to these requirements.

These are, of course, gross characteristics, and cannot at this
stage of our knowledge be further refined. In the three Mobilization
programs we have mentioned, however, the following rough criteria
provided the framework for recruitment decisions. Persons with some
expertise in the program's area were sought. That is, reasonably good
home managers, though not compulsive cleaners, were hired as
Homemakers; Parents Aides were required to have had children in
school; and Community Development workers were expected to
have some experience in leading formal or informal groups. Persons
who seemed to be identified with other working and lower-class
people and particularly with their own culture group, but who did
not reject their less striving neighbors, were preferred. Particularly
within the Community Development program, and to a lesser extent
in the others, action-oriented residents were sought, those who believed in *group* solutions to the problems of impoverishment and
minority status and who were militantly oriented to changing social
conditions. Beyond these criteria, the intent was to recruit a cross
section of the stable working-class community as regards such demographic characteristics as ethnicity, and to select those with some
personal experience in dealing with social problems. Many workers
were, in fact, drawn from the Department of Welfare rolls. Others
had close relatives who exhibited some significant social problem,
such as school maladjustment, delinquency, or addiction. The group
reflected the minority-group composition of the low-income community.

Harry Bredemeier raises some pertinent questions regarding the recruitment of specific nonprofessionals for particular functions:[4]

If "support from a trusted source" is an essential input, are there possibilities of employing low-income persons to serve as "recruiters," "lead lambs," "community stewards" in giving other low-income persons (as well as themselves) the incentive "try"?

If "permissiveness for expression of frustration" in the learning process is an important input, are there possibilities of employing sympathetic low-income persons to commiserate with others?

If "lack of reinforcement for *deviant* performances" is an essential characteristic of the environment, is it possible to employ low-income persons to "police," "patrol," or "guard" one another to reduce the opportunities for "deviant" responses? (To provide Jane Jacobs' "eyes"?) (To multiply Highfields, Essexfields, and Provo projects?)

If "models of identification" are important, can low-income persons be employed simply to interact in certain ways with younger or more handicapped learners?

If opportunities to practice and drill are important, can low-income persons be employed to drill one another in "auditory discrimination," spelling, arithmetic, etc.? Can neighbors be employed to take turns "renting" their apartments to groups of children for supervised homework?

THE PARENT EDUCATION AIDE

Recruitment issues are perhaps best seen through examination of a particular program.

The basic charge in reference to the recruitment of Parent Education Aides at Mobilization for Youth states: "The Parent Education Aide will be a semiprofessional staff member serving at the level of the Substitute Auxiliary Teacher under the supervision of the District Community Coordinator. He (or she) should live in the area to be serviced, be familiar with the local life-styles, be identifiable with or responsive to minority groups, and be bilingual."[5]

The qualifications for the Aide were further amplified and modified by the following memorandum issued by the Mobilization for Youth World of Education Program:

Requirements:

1. Good physical health is essential.
2. Education: High School education acceptable; preferably some college training.
3. Experience: Participation in civic, social, fraternal groups desirable.
4. Residence: While it is desirable that the candidate resides in the area, evidence of ability to perform on the job is the primary factor.
5. Participation in an in-service course geared to the objective of this program with reading assignments.
6. *Maturity*
   a. Age: at least twenty-five years old.
   b. Self-awareness with the ability to look at and accept differences in others and relate to various cultural and ethnic groups effectively.
   c. Capacity to tolerate frustration.
   d. Must be warm, friendly, and sensitive to the feelings of others.
   e. Flexibility.
   f. Capacity for interdependency with acceptance of supervision.
   g. Ability to maintain confidentiality about parents.[6]

One of the basic recruitment problems, likely to arise in any program of this sort, is indicated in the following statement taken from the Progress Report of May 1963:

There was some delay in the actual hiring of the personnel due to the limited number of suitable applicants we had for the untrained positions. Part of this stems from local people's attitude about not feeling qualified to participate in a Parent Education Program.

The potential nonprofessional recruit, not realizing what special skills he possesses that are crucial for the Agency tends to underestimate his own value and is sometimes timid about applying for the position. Hence, the obvious implication is that word must spread both informally and formally. There are numerous sources that will be able to spot such people and persuade them to apply or persuade the professional agency to seek them out.[7]

An effort must be made to carefully inform all sources regarding the kinds of recruits desired, both in terms of the explicit attributes and the more subtle ones. The purposes behind the hiring of these indigenous people should be very clear to all the recruitment channels, and the ways in which they present the job opening to potential applicants whom they attempt to interest in the position, should be reviewed carefully. This is particularly important because the image of the job developed at these contact points may steer people away, may have a lingering negative effect on the individual even if he applies for the position, and may informally spread in the neighborhood, thus reducing the chances of obtaining other recruits. Moreover, the image of the position can also affect the future "clients" of the nonprofessional, drawing them to the nonprofessional or estranging them from him.

It is necessary to define the job in a way that will make it understandable and attractive in terms of low-income culture and psychology, particularly if the aim is to attract low-income people who have genuine roots in the community.

Actually it is not difficult to find low-income people who want the position, if for no other reason that the fact that the salary is much better than they are accustomed to receiving ($4,200–$6,000 per year). There were over fifty applicants for the Parent Education Aide position, from which eight were ultimately selected. The problem, however, lies in attracting a large pool of the "right" low-income people, the kind of individual desired for the position in terms of the agency's goals.

LATENT REQUIREMENTS

What qualities are desired in the nonprofessional? For the Parent Educational Aide position most of the manifest requirements have already been listed above, particularly under the heading of "maturity." But other indigenous positions may require different attributes, and there may be other qualities (latent requirements) which are more indirectly desired for the Parent Education Aide job. For example, in an interview with the Coordinator of the Program, she indicated an additional implicit "list" of attributes that guided her selection. She stated that she preferred to hire people who were "action oriented" (doers) not just "listener types." She did not want "over emotional" people or gossipers; she preferred applicants who felt the need for change in the neighborhood—who experienced some discontent. The Coordinator also indicated that she portrayed this position as a difficult one in talking to the applicants, in order to screen out the less motivated, less work-centered candidates. Finally, she was especially interested in finding candidates who were "curious" and "receptive to training."

In a sense, a crucial latent attribute might be defined as "militancy." Is the nonprofessional to be a protest person, critical, socially aware, or is he to be more pleasant, efficient at communication across class lines? Myrdal's old contrast between Negro "protest leaders" and "accommodation leaders" springs to mind here, although this traditional classification might have less bearing in the present Negro Revolt period.

Obviously, for different types of nonprofessional positions, the attribute of militancy will have varying relevance. It may be that for the development of indigenous community leaders, militancy may have a high priority, but it may be less important (although not necessarily unimportant) in the selection of homemakers. In the original formulation of the Parent Education Aide position, militancy seemed quite irrelevant if not downright inconvenient. But with time, this latent attribute became far more decisive and perhaps indirectly played a role in a major shift in the focus of the Program from a predominantly service orientation to more of an action centered, community organization bias.

THE MIDDLE-CLASS
ASPIRATION ISSUE

An interesting problem arises in connection with the attributes desired of indigenous personnel. In retreating from "middle-classness" in the helping professionals, the demand is often made of nonprofessionals that they be exceptional or ideal "lower-class" types in identification, style, goals, language. For many purposes this kind of low-income person may indeed be preferable, albeit difficult to recruit. But for various positions a *wide range of low-income* types may be suitable and these individuals should not be rebuffed. For example, a highly bilingual Puerto Rican may reside in a low-income community, but still have definite (although not necessarily strong or overpowering) middle class aspirations and skills (e.g. fluency in formal verbal situations). This individual might do exceptionally well in many nonprofessional jobs—better in some important respects than the "typical" low-income person. Moreover, there is no reason to automatically assume that he will not identify with his low-income constituents (his "own people"), or that he will not represent them well or that he will "sell them out"[8] It is instructive to note that Franklin Frazier's old thesis regarding the Negro bourgeoisie separating itself from and exploiting the Negro masses is not too applicable in the present historical situation, where we see the Negro middle classes (recently of low-income origin) closely allied with and representing the interests of the Negro population as a whole—at least on some very crucial issues.

A related error in this connection is the tendency to idealize the better functioning "typical" working class individual who is recruited. The homemakers at Mobilization for Youth who clearly represented stable low-income types, evidenced many weaknesses in their attitudes even though they did an excellent job.

It may well be then, that each different "type" of low-income person has different potential strengths and weaknesses with regard to various nonprofessional tasks. The important question is how these individuals are to be trained and directed.

CALCULATED RISKS:
DIVERTED MILITANCY AND
PROFESSIONAL "CONTAMINATION"

The operation of a technology depends fundamentally on the ideology, goals, and strategy that lie behind the technology. To some extent, however, various technologies in and of themselves constrain in certain directions. Until now we have been arguing the case for the use of indigenous workers on the implicit grounds that their use, almost inevitably, functions for greater involvement of the low-income community and indirectly leads to the development of increased influence from "below." In other words, that this approach reflects a "progressive" technology. But while various technologies may constrain per se in one direction or the other, it would be a mistake to assume that they operate independently of the social structure, power forces, and trends, (e.g. the shifts in power produced by the labor and Negro "revolutions"), or more specifically the goals of the institutions employing the indigenous personnel.

The main danger here is that indigenous low-income workers may be utilized to forestall, reduce, or deflect the militancy of the community they represent. In other words, because of their skills in interclass communication and their contacts and closeness to the low-income community, they can be employed with a one-way communication focus to subtly and effectively convey the wishes of their employer —whether in the school, the social agency, the City administration, or the Welfare Department. To put it crudely, they can become a new kind of indigenous stool-pigeon.

Moreover, the positive value of the indigenous worker can be diverted in an even more direct manner through the hiring of the more militant representatives of the community and transforming or modifying their role. This might be termed the coopting of militancy.[9]

A danger toward professionalization may arise as the indigenous worker is trained and "socialized" by professionals. (What Goldberg describes as the "pitfalls of assimilation"). Of course, this possibility may not be perceived as a danger, if the goal is to develop a professional career-line for the indigenous worker or if it is assumed that the more professional norms and attitudes he obtains, the better. But most views regarding the special value of the indigenous worker see his talent actually deriving from his nonprofessionalized status. This is not to imply that professionals are bad and that it would be better if all our personnel were nonprofessionals, but rather that because professionals can do certain things, they are limited in doing others, and conversely some of the tasks of the nonprofessional preclude a professional relationship.

This view does not prevent us from teaching various professional skills to indigenous personnel; nor does it prevent us from "disciplining their practice," codifying their skills. We may want to professionalize their tasks, but not to professionalize *them*.

Professionalization includes, but implies much more than, task rationalization. It implies a variety of norms and attitudes and a perspective that covers a broad spectrum. It connotes, or should connote, looking at the broader implications of behavior and practice; seeing the relationships to some degree, of a broad range of phenomena. The indigenous nonprofessional is very much task centered and "now" centered and this is his strength and his weakness. Moreover, professional socialization constrains toward much more role-segmentation in relation to the client. Indigenous personnel, on the contrary, have the capacity for a much more wholistic client relationship and again this is their strength and their potential limitation.

With these professional-nonprofessional distinctions in mind, we can now examine at least four sources of potential professional "contamination" of the indigenous workers; that is, ways in which they may acquire professional attitudes that interfere with their indigenous strength:

1. Through being trained by professionals;
2. Through increased general association with professionals in the agency;
3. Through being given status and recognition by the agency and thereby acquiring some identification with professional models (or competing with professionals for this recognition);
4. Through searching for a career line, and acquiring related education.

It can actually be argued that the typical strains in the relationship of the professional and the nonprofessional may actually be functional for maintaining the integrity and skill of the indigenous worker. Perhaps more to the point "lower class" traditions and norms should characterize their training. The team training and esprit de corps mentioned in our discussion of training methodology is relevant to this point. Being housed or "officed" together may also be important.

The more crucial question, however, relates to the training and supervision itself, most of which will probably have to be administered by professionals. It may be asked: "What can professionals teach other than their professional skills?" Fortunately the picture is not so simple. Trainers can be recruited, in part, from among the experienced nonprofessionals who evidence some ability to teach; certain professionals have great affinity for and similarity to indigenous personnel either because of similar cultural background, style or attitude (also some professionals have less of a professional style); and finally, professionals have much to teach nonprofessionals other than professional attitudes.

Nevertheless, there is no doubt that a strain exists whereby unanticipated professional "contamination" can take place coordinately with the training for various tasks. One suggestion that has emerged to curtail this possibility, is to keep the training of nonprofessionals to a minimum and to simply turn loose their talents, their feeling for the neighborhood, their down-to-earthness, their militancy. The idea here is to give them an assignment (e.g. change the character of the Parents Association or involve more people in the Tenant's Council) and then simply to provide broad direction.

In contrast to this view is the "new careers" concept which has been developed throughout this book. In this view, professional careers are seen as a distinct possibility for many nonprofessionals and special avenues for achieving subprofessional and professional positions are envisioned. Most important here is the development of various combinations of on-the-job training and continued schooling. In this context, professional association may actually be highly useful in providing models, information and contacts.

A SURVEY OF ISSUES

At various points throughout this book a variety of issues have been suggested which we should like to briefly review here in the form of questions to be considered by developers of new career programs:

1. Should nonprofessionals be assigned to a wide range of tasks with great freedom in carrying them out or should they rather have more circumscribed assignments? Or, perhaps this apparent difference between the Chicago Area Project and the Mobilization for Youth orientation can be resolved by phasing—with the more circumscribed assign-

ments operating in the early on-the-job training phase and the more advanced flexible assignments requiring considerable initiative coming at a later period.

2. Will the increasing role of employed nonprofessionals limit the use of volunteers in the social services? Is it possible to delineate different functions for volunteers and nonprofessionals?

3. While it seems likely that a fair number of low-income people can be trained to perform efficiently in new career positions, is it really possible to train millions of the poor to do these jobs? In other words, is the initial success we have been witnessing a function of selecting the most motivated and best equipped low-income candidates?

4. Is interest in nonprofessional human service positions likely to be limited more to the female sex? Will it be increasingly difficult to recruit unemployed males after the "cream of the crop" has been removed? Will it be necessary to masculinize the social services in operation and in appeal in order to draw large numbers of males into these occupations?

5. Is the initial success reported for indigenous nonprofessionals a function of the "Hawthorne effect" and thus temporary and not long lasting?

6. Is it necessary to always employ indigenous nonprofessionals or is it wise in some cases to hire nonindigenous low-income people?

7. Is it wise to "tinker with" important service functions by employing untrained nonprofessional people? Haven't there been sufficient difficulties in the service areas where trained professionals have been used to warrant considerable caution regarding the use of untrained personnel?

8. The potential skills of the indigenous nonprofessional for community organization have dovetailed with an increasing emphasis on social action in social work and in government supported community programs such as HARYOU (Harlem Youth Opportunities Unlimited) and Mobilization

For Youth. The question arises as to whether the government (and most private foundations) will long continue to support organizations that "bite the hand that feeds them." Isn't it perhaps more logical that community organization of a militant social action type takes place outside the realm of public support, and that when low-income people function in such organizations that they not be paid and therefore, not be under the potential control of governmental and private agencies? Perhaps these individuals can function more adequately as social action organizers in their capacities as citizens rather than as employees of governmental and private social agencies.

9. Can the employment of nonprofessionals really play a decisive role in the structure, programs, character and style of work in the social service field? Or is their role likely to be that of handmaidens or "aides" to professionals, performing minor tasks that expand the job market for the poor but leave the character of the professions essentially untouched?

10. Is the development of millions of new jobs and careers an unfeasible, utopian goal which will be resisted by the professions, professionals, the taxpayers, the social agencies, educational accrediting institutions and civil service traditions? What are the forces and groups that can propel the new careers movement and do they have sufficient strength? Will the Civil Rights movement, the leaders of the War on Poverty, the farseeing professionals, and the poor themselves exert sufficient pressure for the creation of large numbers of new jobs and careers? Or will public works and the leisure dole dominate the automation age?

11. Can professionals who manifest all manner of difficulties in working with the poor, really select, train, and supervise nonprofessionals in relating to the disadvantaged and deprived? Perhaps professionals can function best in a broad consultative capacity (with nonprofessionals having

much bearing in accepting the consultation and advice offered), rather than as direct trainers and supervisors?

12. Is there likely to emerge considerable misplaced enthusiasm on the part of some professionals who will attempt to assign nonprofessionals to tasks not uniquely suited to their special skills, but rather requiring specific professional skills?

13. Are the new positions and the associated training to serve mainly for rehabilitation and attitude change or are they to have as their primary function the development of skills and careers? Perhaps the emphasis will vary depending upon the population involved, with the rehabilitative focus being greatest among unemployed youths, ADC mothers, former delinquents and drug addicts who are hired as nonprofessional workers. The skill and career emphasis might be greater among mental health aides, school aides, research aides, vocational aides, etc.

14. Will it be necessary to "middle classicize" the low-income nonprofessional in order that he be able to negotiate his new career in a middle-class world? Or is it possible that he can adapt to *selective* middle class requirements and develop appropriate know-how regarding the system, without deeply internalizing many or all middle class values and without surrendering important working class traditions?

All these questions add up to one basic question: whether new careers are going to develop into a movement of the poor for the poor, serve as a basic approach to poverty and to the reorganization and derigidification of the professions, or simply be an expansion of the nonprofessional job market.

PITFALLS TO AVOID

There are a number of potential dangers or pitfalls to be guarded against in the utilization of nonprofessionals:[10]

1. ANTIPROFESSIONALISM

Sometimes in accenting the value of the nonprofessional, there arises a tendency to devalue the professional. Invidious comparisons are made, and arguments are developed purporting to show the lack of need for professionals because of their alleged failures in working with the poor. Our thesis throughout has been that both professionals and nonprofessionals have separate contributions to make and that the employment of nonprofessionals produces new roles for professionals as consultants, supervisors, teachers and coordinators. Moreover, the nonprofessional revolution will require all the allies it can get, and professionals can be among these allies and should not be alienated.

2. LOCKED OUT

There is the ever-present danger that the new nonprofessional positions will provide jobs but not careers, that there will be no provision for advancement, or that whatever advancement takes place will be essentially rather narrow. The new career concept calls for the possibility of promotion to various levels of subprofessional and professional positions. For this to occur, both public and private sector requirements will have to accept combinations of work experience plus education which can be acquired concomitantly with employment or intermittently with temporary leaves of absence. New employment, civil service and educational practices will be needed to insure the mass formation of nonprofessional jobs into new careers.

3. REJECTION OF THE POOR

We have indicated in Chapter V and Goldberg has noted similarly in Chapter VII the tendency on the part of some indigenous nonprofessionals to feel superior toward their less fortunate compatriots among the poor.[11] Aside from our ideological rejection of this tendency, it should be obvious

that this type of reaction strongly militates against the effectiveness of the nonprofessional particularly in his two-way
communication bridge role. Great care must be taken in
both selection and training that this tendency is removed or
is severely limited. Both the ideological and pragmatic weaknesses in this attitude should be explicitly exposed and
clearly opposed. Nevertheless, as careers develop, it is likely
that some distance from the poor may eventuate and thus
the problem or pressure will probably have to be dealt with
continually.

4. OUT-PROFESSIONALIZING THE PROFESSIONAL

HARYOU (Harlem Youth Opportunities Unlimited, Incorporated) warns that "there is evidence that indigenous
persons who become involved in social welfare and civic
activities often see such activities as a way of enhancing
their own power and prestige. In short order, many of them
are out-professionalizing the professional."[12] This is frequently a corollary of their rejection of the poor and perhaps
should be dealt with in the same way.

5. SCHISMS WITH PROFESSIONALS

One of the special problems that is frequently encountered in work with nonprofessionals relates to the schisms
and conflicts, very often petty, that develop in relation to
professional staff. Complaints are made about the professionals having better offices, being treated better, having
secretaries, and a variety of status symbols. This is an
important issue, because it very often works against a cooperative relationship between the nonprofessional and the
professional and is often contaminated by the professional's
lack of respect for the nonprofessional and/or an inability
to work in genuine team fashion with the nonprofessional.
In other words, there are some attitudes of professionals
towards nonprofessionals which require genuine criticism
by the nonprofessionals. But these legitimate causes for

strain are often added to by attitudes of nonprofessionals
which are irrational, self-defeating and prevent the harmonious functioning of a team in which the professionals are the
leaders and justifiably receive more status. This fact should
be made very clear to the nonprofessional staff in the early
training phases, just as the professional has to be educated
to respect and cooperate with the nonprofessional. The nonprofessional should understand that there are status differences related to function and that the professionals are
the leaders and supervisors in the team, which of course
does not entitle them to be disrespectful toward the nonprofessionals, to refrain from listening to them, or to be non-
egalitarian in a whole variety of areas, but that there are
functional status differences related to the roles and requirements of these roles. Thus, the nonprofessional might
share a room or office with four or five other nonprofessionals, while the professional has an office to himself.

6. WATERED-DOWN TRAINING

Since a protracted orientation training period is contra-
indicated for nonprofessionals, and on-the-job training is
strongly recommended, there is always the danger that the
training will be watered-down. In other words, the possibility arises that the job placement will be assumed to be
furnishing the necessary training, rather than providing the
experience base for systematic, directed-training. It is therefore extremely important that on-the-job training be carefully planned and periodically evaluated.

7. SUBSTITUTION OF MIDDLE-CLASS NONPROFESSIONALS

Sometimes, because it appears easier, nonprofessionals
who have more education and/or a middle-class background
are substituted for indigenous low-income personnel. The
rationale offered is that these middle-class nonprofessionals
will provide a temporary phasing in of other indigenous low-
income nonprofessionals. We suspect, however, that the real
reason is that most professionals find it easier to work with

the better educated nonprofessionals who are more like themselves. But, unfortunately these nonprofessionals do not typically possess the relationship to the low-income community so necessary for effective interclass communication. Thus, in the long run, what seems easier may produce new difficulties. And what was supposedly to be "phased in" may never come about as the entire operation becomes distorted to fit the skills and limitations of the middle-class nonprofessional.

8. UNDER-PROFESSIONALISM

The proper utilization of the nonprofessional requires a reorientation on the part of the professional in terms of delegation of tasks and responsibility. The danger exists, however, that professionals will not fully and appropriately utilize nonprofessionals, but will instead continue to be occupied with tasks that could be appropriately taken over by nonprofessional assistants. This tendency toward under-professionalism represents something of a lag and will probably have to be combatted particularly in the transitional period in which new career patterns are being developed and institutionalized.

9. PATRONAGE

There is the possibility that the employment of non-professionals in the public sector will be exploited by politicians as a source of patronage. While recognizing that this possibility provides another potential ally for the new career movement, we think that its dangers outweigh its benefits; consequently we strongly recommend a well-articulated merit system with carefully defined requirements for each position on the new career ladder.

10. DIRTY WORK

Care must be taken lest the nonprofessional be given only menial tasks which professionals shun. There is no question that such tasks will be performed by nonprofessionals, but nonprofessionals must also be assigned more meaningful tasks, increasing in proportion as they advance in position. Actually, they can do some meaningful work from the very beginning, commensurate with the human relations, "people" skills they possess which we have described in discussing their unique effectiveness.

11. RAPID TURNOVER AND "BURNING OUT"

Rachel Robinson[13] notes that turnover is very high among psychiatric aides working in hospitals and Reiff[14] observes that nonprofessional Child Care Workers in Europe "burn out" and leave the positions in five to ten years. On the other hand, there has been practically no turnover among the Parent Education Aides, Visiting Homemakers and Community Organizers employed at Mobilization for Youth, and Saltzman reports a similar phenomenon among the Team Mothers and School-Community Coordinators employed in the Great Cities projects in Philadelphia and Pittsburgh. Of course, these nonprofessionals have only been employed for about one year as of the present writing and it is therefore premature to make comparisons with the Child Care Workers, although some comparisons can perhaps be made with the psychiatric aides whose turnover appears to be not only frequent but rapid. One of the hazards in the psychiatric aide position is the strain of over-identification with the disturbed patient and this is perhaps a contributing factor to the turnover rate. Robinson also notes the inadequate training of the aides and poor relationship to the professional as significant contributing causes.[15] Unquestionably, also the assignment of much unpleasant menial work plays a role in the turnover problem.

It would seem, then, that a number of suggestions that we have already outlined would be essential for developing high morale and limiting turnover: appropriate training oriented, among other things, toward controlling over-identification with the client where this was a problem;

insuring that the nonprofessional is genuinely listened to as part of the professional-nonprofessional team; providing group satisfactions both in the training period and on the job; providing career lines (and horizontal job shift opportunities) to counteract boredom and "burning out." As a matter of fact it is most interesting to observe that the Child Care Workers referred to above moved toward administrative positions when they "burned out"!

These potential pitfalls have been presented as guideline warnings for institutions that become involved in the development of new careers for the poor. We believe that these dangers are by no means insurmountable obstacles, nor that they need necessarily arise. Awareness of possible difficulties, however, may represent an important deterrent to their emergence and spread. Enthusiasm without this awareness could easily turn to cynicism and defeat of the new career movement; on the other hand an overemphasis on problems to be encountered, independent of a context of spirited enthusiasm, can lead to inaction.

NOTES

1. Herbert Gans, *The Urban Villagers*, Free Press, 1962, p. 277.
2. Gans defines internal caretakers as "agencies and individuals who not only give patient care, but other kinds of aid that they think will benefit the client, and who offer aid as an end in itself, rather than as a means to a more important end," *op. cit.*, p. 142.
3. Gans, *op. cit.*, p. 161–162.
4. Harry Bredemeier, comments, April 22, 1964 on subprofessional conference held by President's Committee on Juvenile Delinquency, April 14, 1963.
5. Mobilization for Youth Proposal, 1962, p. 303.
6. Progress Report on Parent Education Program, May 1963.
7. The recruitment of Parent Education Aides came from two main sources:
   1. Formal
      a. Personnel Department of MFY
      b. New York State Employment Division
      c. Newspaper Ad
      d. Principals at local schools.

2. Informal
   a. Community Organizers at MFY and Lower East Side Neighborhood Association
   b. Homemaking Services at MFY
   c. Local Settlement Houses
   d. Parent Association Presidents
   e. Housing Managers
   f. Churches
   g. Indigenous leaders in the neighborhood
      (Progress Report on Parent Education Program, May 1963)

8. The leaders who emerge in the communities organized by Saul Alinsky and the Industrial Areas Foundation appear to reflect a wide range of low-income types—some are quite articulate—and they generally do not "sell out" their constituents.

9. Some agencies quite unwittingly become involved in this pattern and thus forewarning and consciousness may help to restrict this danger. With regard to those institutions that are intentionally oriented toward this use of indigenous people, it is extremely important tha the public at large be aware of this potential manipulation.

10. Many of these pitfalls have been noted throughout the book in various contexts.

11. See also *Bright Shadows in Bronzetown*, Chicago, Southside Committee, Inc., 1949.

12. HARYOU, *Youth in the Ghetto*, New York, 1964.

13. Rachel Robinson, *op. cit.*, p. 3.

14. Robert Reiff, *op. cit.*

15. *Ibid.*, pp. 1–2.

CHAPTER *10*

A STRATEGY FOR
NEW CAREERS
DEVELOPMENT

J. Douglas Grant
Director, New Careers Development Project,
Institute for the Study of Crime and Delinquency

THE RECENT EMPHASIS on poverty as a national problem is linked to a growing awareness of the implications of automation and the importance of the population explosion. To cope adequately with poverty, we must face the problems presented by more people and fewer jobs. New vocational career opportunities must be opened for people whose jobs have been taken over by machines, for those for whom jobs have not been available, and for the increasing number who will enter the labor market and find no work. The alternative is a society in which large numbers of people are supported on a dole.

The problem is not simply one of developing new lines of work. The new jobs of today may be obsolete by tomorrow. Planning for new careers must take account of continuing technological and social change. A strategy for the development of new careers must include a strategy for meeting change. While reducing material production-type jobs, automation allows a new kind of society to develop. For the first time in the history of man, most men can now be freed to develop their nonmachine interpersonal and creative capacities. How do we change from a society in which most of us are occupied in producing material things to a total culture commitment to educating, planning, creating, researching, developing, traveling, understanding, and recreating? How do we expand for mankind in general the pursuits which until now have been reserved for leisure classes and for those most intellectually competent? We are in the early stages of a kind of culture none of us can fully comprehend and many can not even imagine. Hence, we must think in terms of careers and jobs as components of change and development, rather than as roles in a fixed society.

THE PROBLEM OF NEW JOBS

Jobs will not be created through programs of remedial education and vocational training alone. We must radically alter the job structure of our society and even our concept of work. We must look for new job opportunities within the person-to-person and person-to-idea spheres. Both private industry and public agencies are engaged in such activities. Industries are concerned with planning, inservice training, public education, research, and recreation. They should be examining, possibly with Federal assistance, appropriate expansion of these activities and ways to utilize the less professionally qualified by redefining roles and using apprentice-type training. As the activities in which private industry are engaged become more and more automated, it is a question as to just how far they can and should expand the use of personnel in staff functions. It is plausible that many of their people can be used profitably in part-time planning and part-time production activities. However, it appears that the major expansion of person-to-person and person-to-idea activities will be found in the public sector of our economy. This requires public funding. There are at least three approaches to making funds available for the creation of new career opportunities.

UTILIZATION OF EXISTING BUDGETS

In earlier chapters of this book it was proposed that new careers could be developed by redefining professional activities so that many functions now handled by highly trained and skilled persons could be performed by specially trained nonprofessionals. Pearl suggested, for example, that only 30 per cent of the projected budgets for new teachers through 1970 be used to hire certified teachers and the remaining 70 per cent be used to create new jobs, the forerunner of new careers in the education field. Nonprofessionals hired for these jobs would handle the technical, but less complicated aspects of classroom work, such as running visual aids, assisting with programmed learning, taking attendance, grading tests, and doing supportive tutoring. This would free the trained teacher for teaching and for other directly professional activities, including consulting and supervision of the nonprofessional. This modification of the employment structure in the field of education could create a half million new jobs with no additional cost to the taxpayer.

BUDGET CONVERSION

A second approach to changing patterns of employment involves the use of present budgets to finance new types of activities that offer more scope for career expansion than is presently available. The State of North Carolina, for example, has had a work-release program within its prison system for the last three years. Under the terms of this program, a man serving a felony sentence of five years or less may be released to work in the community, spending his nonworking time in a nearby correctional facility. Men in the work-release program not only support their dependents while they are serving time, but also reimburse the state for their room and board. A thousand men are presently on work-release. Because of this program, North Carolina has been able to close one of its prisons, and $100,000 of the savings has been channeled to the support of a Youth Development and Research Center (15).

The Center is a small living-unit, housed in buildings made available by the University of North Carolina, for twenty young first-term offenders. It is staffed by new career positions and its purpose is to develop new careers for the inmates assigned to it.* The task of the staff, with the help of University and state government consultants, is to work with the inmates in developing demonstration programs for the state's attack on delinquency, crime, and poverty and to train the inmates for jobs in these demonstration programs.

Present budgets might well be utilized for new functions in the field of national defense. Think of the jobs which would be available if half or more of the defense budget were converted to massive exchange and acculturation programs for all seventeen and eighteen year olds. Each young man and woman, on reaching seventeen, could be sent for two years to work and study in another country, and his or her counterpart in these countries might be brought here for a similar purpose. The foreign youth might be housed in small living-units which in turn could bring together young people with a variety of national backgrounds. The precedent of education abroad established by the leisure classes in the past could be converted into a cross-cultural approach to defense through increasing understanding and shared

---

* Staff consists of six parolees transferred from the State of California. Five of these men had extensive experience in therapeutic community living units while they were confined; they were selected for their demonstrated leadership in these programs. The sixth had some training in research through his assignment to an institution data processing unit and through employment on a University project after his parole. None of the six had prior professional training.

values. Besides the jobs involved in planning and carrying out the logistics of such an enterprise, there would be many jobs to be filled as interpreters and language tutors. Orientation programs would be needed to help prepare the visiting youth for living in this country. Suitable education and work experiences would need to be arranged which would require new types of teachers and work supervisors. Specially-trained group workers could be used as counselors in the living units. Theatrical talents could be employed in "spontaneity theater" and for other uses of the stage to interpret problems of cross-cultural communication. Many of these new jobs might well utilize experience gained by young people who have returned from a foreign country.

NEW BUDGET SOURCES

The third way of changing the job structure of our economy calls for expanding the money available for educating, welfare, healing, research, planning, creating, and re-creating activities. An example of developing new careers in this manner would be the establishment of pre-school development centers throughout the country. Current pilot work with four and five year-old children (2, 17, 19) suggests what can be done when the so-called culturally deprived pre-school child is exposed to an environment which offers him the sensory, verbal, emotional, and ideational stimulation lacking in his own home. Such children, who frequently appear apathetic and retarded, are likely to drift through their school experience and to drop out of school early, becoming unemployable adolescents. Those participating in special preschool programs have been found to be well ahead of children with similar backgrounds when they enter kindergarten and first grade. By creating preschool development centers on a large scale throughout the country, we could expand the potential of our people by widening their horizons of understanding in their early, most formative years. Further, new careers could be created by training nonprofessionals to work with the preschool children in such centers. There would also be an increased need for professional workers who would serve as consultants and trainers for these new career positions.

THE PROBLEM OF CHANGE

New functions have always been instituted as new knowledge arises, but it is the deliberate, conscious development of such functions on a more extensive basis than heretofore with which we must be concerned. Implementing a strategy implies that structural changes need to be brought about more systematically and more rapidly than has been done in the past. We need to make the process of change explicit. It is not only a matter of developing a number of new careers to take care of the people displaced by automation. Rather, we need to establish a *system* which fosters the continual changing and expanding of career opportunities. New jobs which could be created today as aides to teachers are almost certain to be replaced tomorrow as the function of education and methods of teaching change. Our changing society and changing technical knowledge will demand continual innovation and reorganization.

The establishing of change and expansion systems will in itself lead to the development of new types of work. As society makes explicit the examination of what it is doing— the improvement of ways to perform its present functions, the proposing of new functions, and the systematic evaluation of the effectiveness of its proposals—new career opportunities inevitably will be created. These new careers will build vital roles into our society. As automation takes over the routine, machine-like activities of man, he will have the opportunity to turn to the uniquely man-like activities which in the past have been reserved for only the selected few.

A CASE HISTORY OF NEW CAREERS DEVELOPMENT

In our efforts to formulate a systematic plan for the development of new careers, we might examine the case history of one program which did not have the benefit of an explicit implementing strategy. Although this new career does not immediately increase available jobs, it offers an example of the creation of a new job function which opens a new career line in the professional field for persons without formal professional training.

The California Department of Corrections is in the process of creating a new career, the Correctional Program Supervisor series. How did this come about? More than a decade ago, Norman Fenton (5, 10,) started lay-group counseling in California's prisons to bring staff and inmates together in the task of rehabilitating offenders. Correctional officers (prison guards) were encouraged to work with groups of inmates. Instruction consisted of observing demonstration groups which Fenton initially conducted himself. A small textbook (6) and a manual (4) were written setting forth the principals of group counseling.

There was some support for this development, particularly in top administration—for example, limited overtime funds were provided to pay for the officers' participation—but it was an uphill fight to obtain financial, administrative, and professional backing for this innovation. Nevertheless, the program continued to grow. At present more than 900 of the Department of Corrections' staff are conducting groups, and 17,000 inmates, more than half of the prison population, are participating in them. Five institutions have mandatory counseling: each inmate is automatically assigned a group upon his arrival at the institution. In addition, many groups are being developed among parolees.

Evaluation of the group-counseling innovation in the Department of Corrections has been exceedingly hard to come by. There was none for many years. Finally, the first

National Institute of Mental Health grant in the correctional field was assigned to the University of California at Los Angeles in 1959 to conduct an evaluation study. Paralleling this, evaluation efforts were made within the Department itself. No research staff was budgeted for this evaluation, however, and the records kept were extremely inadequate. It has been a decade in which a new function, the forerunner of a new career, has grown with little budget, administrative power, or rational evaluation to support its development.

These group-counseling achievements were a necessary prerequisite for the current milieu therapy efforts within the Department. New institutions are being designed and old institutions reorganized for closer staff-inmate participation in and analysis of daily living and working concerns. Current research tends to support the value of a therapeutic milieu in increasing the effectiveness of correctional institution programming. Vinter and Janowitz (23) have shown that milieu therapy-oriented institutions tend to have much greater shared staff-inmate understanding than more custody-oriented institutions. In the latter, there is greater diversity of attitudes and goals between staff and inmates, with the inmate leaders differing more from the staff than the average inmate. In the more milieu therapy-oriented institutions, staff and inmates are more alike in their attitudes and goals, and the inmate leaders are even closer to the staff than the average inmate.

The U.C.L.A. studies (16) show that staff participating in group counseling have more positive attitudes toward rehabilitation than those who do not. Harrison and Mueller (9) have presented data showing that inmates who continue in counseling with the same group leader for a year or more do better following release on parole than comparable groups of inmates who have less consistent counseling or none at all.

A lay-group-counseling function is now firmly established within the Department of Corrections. Formalization of career development opportunities for performing this function are now being established. Advanced counselors are officially recognized and considered qualified to train beginning counselors. Further, specifications for a Correctional Program Supervisor series have been worked out with the State Personnel Board. The series is in a demonstration phase and eventually will be incorporated as a new career series with the state. Three levels of Correctional Program Supervisor have been established, allowing personnel, with or without professional training, to qualify and advance in the performance not only of counseling functions, but also in new roles emerging out of milieu therapy developments in corrections. These developments call for the staff to work much more closely with the inmates—to be more a part of the program *with* the inmates—than was the case in past correctional efforts. In milieu therapy, the traditional staff functions of controlling, counseling, and administering are blended and shared with the inmates themselves.

The Program Supervisor series is available, with appropriate special training, to custodial and counselor (social work equivalent) personnel alike. Both the professional counselor and the correctional officer can move into the series at a pay level slightly above their current salaries, the counselor entering at a higher level than the custodian. Custodial personnel, who can enter the Department without benefit of a high school education, but who seldom do, can now move into a career development system that allows them to perform functions that were previously reserved for the professional, and that enables them eventually to compete for jobs on an equal basis with college-trained persons. Through the Correctional Program Supervisor series, a non-high school graduate could advance from a correctional officer position through three levels of Program Supervisor to become a Program Administrator. From Program Administrator it would be possible for him to qualify for any of the top administrative positions within the Department.

Impressive as this new career development has been, its greatest value should be in providing leads for establishing a process specifically designed to develop new functions and new careers within professional fields. What can we learn from the Program Supervisor development to apply to a general strategy for new careers development? What could have been performed better, if more resources and a more conscientious strategy could have been applied?

In the case of the group-counseling example, an implementing strategy should have been able more systematically to foster a climate favorable to the introduction of the new function. This could have been done by supplementing Fenton's demonstrations of group counseling with organized study-groups to bring together conflicting interests—inmates, custodians, and clinicians—to formulate the development of the group counseling function.

There could have been a much better conceptualized model for training the nonprofessionals in the new function. How do we develop the nonprofessional? What training, education, and experience should be provided, and in what ways? It seems apparent that textbooks and lectures will not be enough. We need further explorations in learning through doing and through teaching others. Ideas for new ways to learn should be obtainable from re-examination of apprentice training programs and role-playing techniques. We need to think not only of teaching specific job skills, but of ways of developing appropriate attitudes, values, and the interpersonal coping skills needed for these new functions.

Few of the professional staff gave any support to lay-group-counseling. The movement developed outside of and, in many ways, in spite of the clinical services personnel. How do we build the professional into emerging new functions? How do we get the professional's involvement for consulting, training, and supervising roles? What kinds of models do we need to retrain effectively the professional so that he will be supportive to new functions and new careers?

Besides providing an effective climate within the agency concerned—in this case the Department of Corrections—how could we have enhanced development of the new function through public education? How could we have used the developing nonprofessional in community education? What would have been gained by having lay-group counselors themselves take part in community lectures, panel discussions, and television appearances? Could the community be reached through plays and documentary films which used both lay-group counselors and counselees?

Built-in evaluation and process studies would have provided much more of the concrete information needed in the development of the new function. How can we establish a procedure to study systematically new functions and new career development efforts? How far can we go in utilizing the developing nonprofessional and the clients themselves in a self-study approach to the emerging new function?

PROBLEMS TO BE MET

This case history example offers suggestions for the generalized strategy of new career development. Before discussing some principles and a specific strategy, let us examine the problems to be met in attempting to implement a new careers attack on poverty. It can be safely assumed that a change in our country's job structure and social agency organization will not come about easily. What are the specific problems to be met in such an attempt?

1. *How do we get available funds to the poor through employment in new careers and new career development?*— One of the things we have learned so far in our efforts to help the underprivileged is that there are powerful forces operating to keep whatever money is available for new programs in the hands of professionals. In the last few years, several large projects have been initiated as demonstrations of ways to increase the opportunity structure for the underprivileged, particularly for underprivileged youth. Examina-

tion of the budgets of these projects shows that most of the money goes to social workers and researchers. Though they may have done little to increase the opportunity structure for the underprivileged, these projects have greatly expanded the opportunity structure for already scarce professionals. A major concern in initiating a strategy for new careers is how to get the jobs and salaries past the bureaucracies and the professionals to the underprivileged and those in economic need.

2. *How do we handle professional resistance?*—How can professionals be made to feel and to be a part of the change process? Our present training of the professional does not make him sympathetic to nonprofessional colleagues and often does not equip him to play the supervising and training roles required in the development of new careers. Retraining for the professional will be needed. Moreover, the professional worker must be convinced that working with nonprofessionals does not threaten his own hard-won status. The present shortage of professional workers, which has resulted in the hiring of people who are less than fully qualified to do professional jobs, is in fact leading to the downgrading of many professions. The increased responsibility for consulting, supervision, and training in new careers programs will actually serve to improve the status of the professional and upgrade standards for the profession as a whole. The professional will be free to devote himself to the level of work for which he has studied and trained. The professional truly can be the leader in the development of knowledge, the innovation of programs, and the establishment of appropriate training in his field.

Retraining of professional workers will be costly and difficult. The cycle of training and retraining could be short-circuited by having the future professional work with nonprofessionals at both the undergraduate and graduate levels. These nonprofessionals should include not only those in new career programs, with whom the professional will later be working, but those who will later be his clients as well. The future correctional worker, for example, might well benefit by participating in seminars or working on study projects with delinquents; the future mental health worker might benefit by working collaboratively with emotionally disturbed persons.

3. *How do we overcome the disadvantaged person's defense of indifference?*—Consciously or unconsciously, our society has put a great deal of effort into screening people out of intellectual and professional pursuits. We have seen the need for professional people as limited, and we have set up guilds which have spent much of their energies in controlling the number of people allowed into the professions. Our educational examinations primarily test one's ability to remember information which is largely forgotten within three years (7). The major function of such examinations has been to screen-in those who have had the background to allow rapid short-term memory of specific course content, while screening out those whose cultural experiences as well as specific abilities limited their performance in this short-term memory feat.

Those who have not been let into educational and professional systems can be expected to have attitudes, values, and feelings which defend against their being too upset by their exclusion from these systems. People whose educational experience has marked them as failures cannot be expected to take advantage of new educational opportunities. Young people growing up without hope of a job or future cannot be expected to have developed the kinds of attitudes toward work that make a commitment to a long-term career possible. Making new career opportunities available may not be enough. We must also find ways to bridge the gap between those who have been allowed in our higher education systems and those who have been kept out.

The disadvantaged must be given a role in planning and developing new careers. In addition, appropriate learning and training models must be developed which emphasize learning through doing, teaching, and making short-term expected achievements explicit.

4. *How do we get agency participation?*—Any social agency tends to have a vested interest in the status quo. At present, empires and budgets are built around functions that have been able to establish themselves as necessary routines. It is almost inevitable that there will be strong resistance—both conscious and unconscious—to the development of new functions and new careers in performing these functions. This principle holds for routine activities, such as changes in record and filing systems, as well as for such major policy innovations as the substitution of community programs for institutionalization. Such institutions as hospitals, prisons, and homes for unwanted children and the elderly, become accepted budget and personnel empires irrespective of their ability to cope with the treatment and adjustment functions for which they were originally designed.

Implementing a new careers strategy calls for a *system* of change. We must realign the pressures that now foster empire building and maintenance of the status quo so that they will become just as powerful implementers of a change system as they now are resisters to change. How do we shift the emphasis in budgeting from increased workload justifications for more of the same programs to budget incentives for innovation? In other words, how do we mobilize political and public pressures for change?*

5. *How do we arouse public concern?*—The expanding of our society's professional functions will take more than the acceptance of the task by agency heads, professionals, and legislators. Certainly agency administrators and legislators are to some extent servants of the people, but the people themselves will also have to be a part of the new careers at-

---

* Developments in community mental health offer many leads for ways of formulating a total system for change (3).

tack on poverty. How are they to be reached? How do we get them to feel that what they do or say can affect agency policy and play a part in social change? How do we get them involved in the developing of a new careers strategy? How do we work with public stereotypes and the public's own resistance to change? Can we use their paid participation in community planning and development as a motivating force for task-oriented concern with education about their community in particular and social development in general?

6. *How do we establish a system for change?*—A strategy of change requires a continuous cycle of innovation, evaluation, feedback, and reinnovation. Until now, even our most progressive efforts have been centered around selling and implementing the latest answer to a social problem. Today it is the new way of improving mental health or fighting delinquency. Tomorrow, it will be *the* new way to combat poverty.

Two assumptions, which must be overcome, are inherent in these efforts. First, each problem is viewed primarily as a single problem, unrelated to other problems and activities of our society. Educational programs have been seen as unrelated to the problem of delinquency, and delinquency even has been defined—in the not too distant past—as not a problem of mental health.* Such thinking would say that when we are planning attacks on poverty we are concerned only with those unemployed now rather than working with the ongoing forces of automation, population explosion, demilitarization, and integration.

A second assumption is that each problem has a single solution which will be right for all time. If the solution of today will not eliminate the problem, it will certainly provide a way to handle the problem tomorrow.

The pace of technical and social change is becoming so

---

* It is only in the last eight years that the National Institute of Mental Health has accepted research proposals dealing with the problem of delinquency.

rapid that it should be obvious that our task is not to discover the appropriate solution for each of a number of isolated problems, but rather to build a rational approach to meet the change we are bound to witness and which we hope to influence.

An effective strategy should be based on plausible assumptions and a logical rationale which follows from them. Several assumptions have been made in developing the strategy outlined below for dealing with the problems of developing new careers.

1. *The nonmaterial production functions of our society must be markedly expanded to make room for those displaced by automation.*—If man is not going to occupy his time with material production or by tilling the soil, he will by definition be involved in other functions.* Since man must have some way to procure the products of automation, he must be provided with purchasing power. The question becomes: to what extent is obtaining purchasing power (pay) to be related to man's achievements when he is no longer involved in material production activities?

There are two basic approaches to this question. Michael (18), for example, envisages a world in which a handful of men will do the thinking necessary to determine what the machines will do while the rest of mankind will have to develop a leisure time society.

There will be a small, almost separate, society of people in rapport with the advanced computers. These cyberneticians will have established a relationship with their machines that cannot be shared with the average man any more than the average man today can

---

* A number of proposals for handling the problems of automation and unemployment are based on the premise that man can continue to be occupied in material production jobs. These include tax cuts and other means of stimulating the economy and a variety of spread-the-work proposals. It is assumed here that such proposals will provide at best only temporary relief and components of a total strategy. Any long-range view must take account of a decreasing number of jobs in material production.

understand the problems of molecular biology, nuclear physics, or neuro-psychiatry. Indeed, many scholars will not have the capacity to share their knowledge or feeling about this new man-machine relationship. Those with the talent for the work probably will have to develop it from childhood and will be trained as intensively as the classical ballerina.

Some of the remaining population will be productively engaged in human-to-human or human-to-machine activities requiring judgment and a high level of intelligence and training. But the rest, whose innate intelligence or training is not of the highest, what will they do? We can foresee a nation with a large portion of its people doing, directly or indirectly, the endless public tasks that the welfare state needs and that the government will not allow to be cybernated because of the serious unemployment that would result. These people will work short hours, with much time for the pursuit of leisure activities. (pp. 44–45).

In effect, this means paying people even though they do not work or do not do the kind of work we recognize today. A committee of economists and other scientists (1) recently outlined a plan which includes incomes guaranteed by the Federal government whenever unemployment rises over 3 per cent of the nation's work force.

A second approach would combine the earning of income with a man's achievements in nonautomated functions. One way of viewing automation's taking over of jobs in agriculture and material production is to see our society as having a heretofore undreamed of potential to expand education, health, welfare, and recreation functions, as well as creative efforts including planning and research. These functions will never be competely automated. It is difficult to imagine a society that could exhaust its capacities in these areas. Advances in communication techniques make it possible to expand the numbers of people taking part, particularly in planning and research.

The basic assumption of the strategy proposed in this chapter is that much can be gained by combining the earn-

ing of purchasing power with these kinds of contributions to
our society.

2. *Any function which has existed less than five years
needs developing; any function which has existed more than
five years needs changing.*—Social development has probably not yet reached the pace where "if it works, it's obsolete." While we are perhaps not quite ready to make that
statement, our efforts to cope with the problems of our
society's development are, or should be, in a constant state of
change. The effects of automation, in particular, and the
increased knowledge obtained from research, in general,
presents us for the first time with a situation in which parents are no longer raising children to meet approximately
the same world they knew. It is problematical as to just what
the adult world of our children will be like. The only certainty is that it will be different from the world we are facing
today.

Programs to handle social problems or to meet social
needs should be viewed as experiments, the findings from
which are used as leads for further program modification.
Program effectiveness should be continually questioned in
the light of new knowledge, new resources, and new developments in social organization. Our entire culture should
be enjoying the increased morale that comes from being
a part of experimentation. We should institutionalize the
"Hawthorne effect (20)."

3. *Bureaucracies conform to administrative and political
pressures, the most powerful of which are the requirements
for their budget approval.*—If we are going to put teeth into
a change-inducing system, the system must be part of the
budget preparing and approving procedure. An example of
effective budget pressure would be limiting the availability
of funds for new programs to those proposals that meet speci-
fied conditions for encouraging change, including systematic
evaluation.

4. *There is a rational approach: evaluation data will in-*

fluence budgeting sources.—Although irrational forces partially determine which programs get budgeted and for how much money, it is assumed that a reasonable proportion of the variance in budget decisions is rational. Already there is evidence (8) from operations research in public agencies that as sound evaluation information becomes available, it will be used to settle points of conflicting interests over which programs to advance and which to curtail. As budget sources become aware of the utility of such information, agencies will be forced to provide evaluation data on their programs and to modify their budget requests in accordance with the data. This increased use of evaluation data will provide a built-in system for expanding new functions and new careers in programs that are shown to be effective.

5. *Ideas for innovation grow out of appropriate climates and frames of reference, not out of isolated ivory towers.*— Innovations, plans, and ideas—very much including new career ideas—will be urgently needed in the changing society of the future. Reliance on a few idea specialists will not be enough.

Hutchins (14) has said that "the problem of all creative work is how to get outside your culture so that you can see it." New ideas come from transcending the sets of the present culture's values and routines. As people become involved in the development of ideas and rational approaches to change, rather than the suspicious recipients of the mysticism of science, the more favorable the climate will be for ambiguity tolerance, freedom from culture sets, and the use of the scientific method. Feelings of trust, purpose, and responsibility are maintained by becoming a participant in the system.

There are other advantages in involving increasing numbers of people in the development of ideas. Even though the number of creative ideas per individual would probably decrease as more and more people were included in planning innovations, the overall probability of obtaining creative ideas would be greatly enhanced as larger numbers of people were involved. Moreover, as people with many different experiences and points of view become concerned with a given idea, the greater the likelihood of covering all necessary issues for the idea's implementation.

6. *Man needs to be needed.*—It would be a tragedy not to be able to develop a meaningful purpose in life as machines replace man in soil tilling and material production. To live on a dole is demoralizing. To educate people in the effective use of leisure may require generations of change, if it can be done at all. Pay for work performed is important not only as a means of obtaining purchasing power but as a recognition that a man is valued and needed by the society of which he is a part. With automation there is a tremendous opportunity to involve man in general in what Piel (13) has described as the jobs that "relate people to people, not people to things," while improved technical communication devices make it possible for many people, previously kept out of the planning done by industries, social agencies, and communities, to become active participants in the development of new ideas.

Suppose, for example, that a state correctional agency wished to plan a way to implement research findings which demonstrate that new types of parole supervision can be substituted for time served in institutions, giving the taxpayer more protection for less money (11, 12). Stratified study groups, composed of twenty offenders, correctional officers, correctional counselors, parole officers, and administrators could be set up throughout the entire state. Using closed-circuit television, the research findings and a preliminary plan for implementing them could be presented simultaneously to all the groups through a 15-minute panel discussion by the agency's central planners. The field groups could review, comment, and suggest. Such things as the mechanics and effects of early release from institutions could be discussed by those actually doing the releasing and those being released. Recent advances in communication devices would make possible almost instantaneous feedback from these groups to the central planners. The new ideas, questions, and concerns of the study groups could be collated electronically, providing in outline form the unique ideas which were developed. The central planners could modify their thinking as a result of the feedback and be prepared, the next day, to present their new formulations to the field groups for further suggestion and modification.

With the technological and sociological changes inherent in the future, the ways in which man in general could be used in planning and innovation are almost infinite. Some immediate examples are the problems posed by unemployment, racial discrimination, and urban development. The ways in which social agencies and industries conduct their operations will need continual review. Problems of community planning, particularly in such areas as education, care of the young and the aged, and the development of adequate housing, transportation, and recreational facilities, will also need continual study. We may want to consider the possibility, for example, of setting up paid local community study and planning roles as we now have paid representatives of the public in city, county, state, and Federal legislative bodies and paid citizen participants in our judicial system.

A PROPOSED STRATEGY

At least four pressures will force Federal support for a new careers strategy in the attack on poverty.

1. Increasing automation will increase the problems of unemployment and the need to provide purchasing power to consume the products of automation.

2. The integration movement will be forced to change the emphasis of its efforts as it recognizes that minority groups cannot progress until more jobs (preferably careers) and purchasing power are made available to all. The integration force will become one of the most powerful lobbies for new careers.

3. Reduced Federal spending for armaments will further increase the unemployment problem.

4. Although there should be a growing political awareness throughout the country, the increasing industrialization and urbanization of the South, in particular, will lead to the election of Congressmen who will have mandates for social action. Reapportionment and increased Negro voting are steps already taken in this direction. These mandates will bring a break in the irrational equilibrium which is allowing our society to stall in facing the demands and opportunities inherent in automation.

When these pressures become expressed in Federal action other alternatives should be available than promoting specific programs as solutions to the problems of poverty, unemployment, and urbanization. What is needed are not new large bureaucracies which become committed to maintaining or expanding given programs, but a strategy which supports local community involvement in study, innovation, and change.

It will not be enough to create some new career positions to provide jobs for those people currently employed. We must be concerned, as well, with developing rational ways of meeting change as it arises in the future. The strategy proposed here is a strategy for change. As outlined below, it is neither complete nor sufficient to deal with even the problems in this chapter. Rather it should be considered as a framework within which planning for a new-careers approach to poverty might proceed.

There are three basic components in this strategy: (1) the fund, (2) local community self-study units, and (3) new career development centers.

THE FUND

It is assumed that money will increasingly be made available by both Federal and state governments to finance a coordinated attack on the problems of poverty and social change. The allocation and administration of these funds— to whom they are to go, and under what conditions—can in itself be a source of conflict and cause difficulty in getting new programs started.

Although it has many administrative and bureaucratic complications within itself, the "project proposal" system* provides a way of cutting through bureaucratic vested interests in maintaining the status quo. This system requires that a detailed plan of action for a new program (including its purpose, goals, and a rationale for the methods used in reaching these goals) be put into written form by the persons or agencies requesting funds and the proposal then submitted for review to a panel of experts appointed by the funding agency. This system not only requires agencies to justify the programs for which they seek budget support; it would also allow conditions to be imposed by the funding group that would require agencies to take account of problems of change in order to have proposals for new programs considered.

In order to keep a proposal system from becoming enmeshed in the complexities of large organization concerns, proposal reviewing and funding should be decentralized. Each state, according to its population and the nature of its problems, should be allocated Federal funds to finance new career development proposals. Establishing such a funding activity at the state level would in itself force some re-integration of state functions which are often now organized to meet social problems as these were viewed fifteen to fifty

---

* This is the method presently used by most funding agencies to allocate monies for research and demonstration projects in the biological and social sciences.

years ago, so that separate agencies deal with the interrelated problems of employment, education, delinquency,
housing, and welfare. The state would in effect be a sub-
contractor for the Federal government's rational approach
to the problems of change.

To meet the demands for change and expansion, a few,
but powerful stipulations should be written into the legislation providing funds for the attack on poverty.

1. Funds can be utilized only to support new career
development proposals from local community self-study
units.

2. At least 60 per cent of the funds for each project must
go directly to salaries for nonprofessional people who are
being trained or used in potentially new careers.

3. A specific rationale and the feasibility of operating
the project must be spelled out.

4. Provisions must be made not only for providing outcome evaluation of the project, but also for providing meaningful information and quality control checks on the actual
operation of the program.

A special section of the legislation would encourage the
development of new careers in the arts and in communication media. For example, new careers projects might utilize
nonprofessionals in films, television, and writing, especially
as a means of public education in new career development.
Nonprofessionals could be used as resource persons, as
planners, and as actors and technical aides in such activities.

This proposed utilization of newly budgeted state and
Federal funds to develop new careers in no way precludes
the utilization of existing budgets, as outlined earlier, to
finance new career positions. The impetus of new funding
will be needed, however, as well as the results of several
successful demonstrations before agencies can be expected
to convert some of their present budgets to new careers on
a large scale.

LOCAL COMMUNITY SELF-STUDY UNITS

Many communities have set up formal or informal organizations in efforts to handle local community problems, but the people who constitute the problem under study have rarely been involved. An exception is a project (21) recently conducted by the Youth Studies' Center at the University of Southern California which brought together agency personnel, community leaders, and both delinquent and nondelinquent youth in an effort to plan programs to combat delinquency in the community.

The self-study units proposed here would be permanent state-sponsored groups set up for the purpose of getting people involved in community study, innovation, evaluation, feedback, restudy, and reinnovation. Each group would include members representing four local community interests: people representing the problem under study (e.g., school dropouts, delinquents, recipients of welfare aid), professionals from the agencies that serve them (including agency administrators and researchers), community leaders, and citizens at large. To avoid the development of bureaucratic entities, membership in the study groups would be held on a rotating basis and would be determined for each such group through selecting by random numbers from a large pool of nominees.

Funds for administration of the units and for technical consultation would be provided by the Federal or state government. Study group members would be reimbursed for their participation just as people are now reimbursed for serving as jurors in our judicial system.

The task of the units would be to prepare formal proposals for programs to develop new careers which would then be submitted for review to a panel set up by the state fund. Guides and procedure manuals would be made available to help the study units in the preparation of proposals. These guides would include examples of new career de-

velopment that are now taking place in different parts of the
country and research findings that have relevance for the
development of new careers.

Many illustrations of such proposals come to mind. A
number of communities, for example, are becoming increasingly concerned with the problem of minority-majority
group relations. Special race relations consultants have been
proposed for agencies, industries, and local governments. It
may well be that the most valuable resource for such new
roles can be found in those nonprofessionals who have had
to work through problems of intergroup relations in small
closed communities. The administrator of a California prison
which houses young and difficult offenders has reported that
a recent potentially dangerous situation of intergroup conflict in his institution was averted through the discussions
held by the milieu therapy groups to which all inmates are
assigned, and that the men who showed the most leadership
in this situation and were most sensitive to the interpersonal
problems involved were members of minority groups. Correctional institutions, where minority groups are still over-
represented and where feelings about integration and discrimination are intensified by the confinement experience,
might well serve as a training ground for men who could be
used to work with similar problems in the community upon
their release.

Another example is suggested by research in the correctional field. Findings from pilot projects (22) indicate that
young delinquents may be better handled in small community living-units than in institutions. These units (a kind
of synthetic family) are staffed by nonprofessionals, some
of whom have themselves been delinquent, and counseling
is provided to the units by professional workers. The development of such a new function on a large scale would
open career opportunities for many people. It would also
increase the community's ability to deal with its delinquency

problems and eliminate some of its needs for expensive correctional institutions.

A third example of a community-study proposal occurs in the field of higher education. Suppose that the products of the community's problems—its unemployed, aged, delinquents, and mentally ill—were trained as aides for university courses on community organization and planning. Such courses would be concerned with expanding the students' awareness of the problems of social change and with preparing them to assume professional roles in programs to meet change. The nonprofessionals could be used as resource persons and group leaders in seminar discussions and as co-workers with the students in fieldwork projects. Fieldwork assignments might be made, for example, in public child care centers, in tutoring and recreation programs for disadvantaged youth, or in halfway houses for men released from prison. These assignments would enable the student to get firsthand experience in working with community problems and with problem people.

A final example to illustrate the kind of thinking which needs to be stimulated. Spanish-speaking residents in many of our communities find the use of their native language a detriment to formal education. Why not develop Spanish-speaking youth as paid part-time tutors for English-speaking youth who are now being taught Spanish by English-speaking teachers in the schools' effort to improve their understanding of other cultures. At the same time English-speaking youth could be paid to serve as part-time tutors for the Spanish-speakers. This would not only make new jobs available but the relationship between the two groups, now often strained, might be improved.

As new approaches to community development could be demonstrated to be more effective than currently budgeted programs, existing agencies would be pressured by legislators, administrators, and the public to revise their programs and budgets in accordance with findings from these demonstrations. New careers would thus be made available in agency programs as these were modified as a result of demonstration projects.

NEW CAREER DEVELOPMENT CENTERS

To round out this proposed strategy for building new careers into our employment structure, special centers would be established by the state, in cooperation with universities and social agencies, as vehicles for providing consultation to the local community self-study units, the demonstration projects developed by them, and the agencies that will make use of the demonstration findings.

Center staff would include both professional and nonprofessional workers. They would be concerned with the development of appropriate training models for nonprofessionals who will fill new career roles and retraining models for the professionals who will work with them. Their primary functions would be to systematize the ideas, hypotheses, rationales, and findings of the projects developed by the community self-study units, to relate these findings to basic social science knowledge, and to build this knowledge into models for new career development. This last means that center staff would also be engaged in conducting research of their own. This could include studies on such questions as the effectiveness of different kinds of learning media for different kinds of learners and ways of combining individual and group therapy procedures with content and technique learning in new career training.

We must not expect new career roles to emerge nor the nonprofessional to fill them successfully without a great deal of systematic study and hard work. New career development centers could become the core professional entities dedicated to finding ways of screening people into professional pursuits rather than devoting energies to screening them out.

THE STRATEGY: IN SUMMARY

The new careers strategy proposed here as an approach to the problem of poverty would (1) apply the pressures of budget procurement and proposal requisition to systematize social change, (2) involve man-in-general in new career planning through local community self-study units, and (3) create necessary basic knowledge through new career development centers.

REFERENCES

1. Ad Hoc Committee. The triple revolution. Report submitted to the President, Reprinted in *Liberation*, 1964, vol. 9, pp. 9–15.

2. Blake, Patricia. A big break for poverty's children. *Life* magazine, April 3, 1964.

3. Boucher, Stanley W. The planning process. In Roma K. McNickle and Marion H. Higman (Ed.), *Planning mental health programs*. Boulder: Western Commission for Higher Education, 1964. Pp. 13–23.

4. Dunbar, Walter. *Group counseling manual*. Sacramento: California Department of Corrections, 1962.

5. Eaton, Joseph W. *Stone walls do not a prison make.* Springfield: Charles C. Thomas, 1962.

6. Fenton, Norman. *Group counseling in state correctional service.* New York: American Correctional Association, 1957.

7. Freedman, Mervin B. Studies of college alumni. In Nevitt Sanford (Ed.), *The American college.* New York: John Wiley & Sons, 1962.

8. Grant, J. Douglas. It's time to start counting. *Crime and Delinquency*, 1962, vol. 8, pp. 259–264.

9. Harrison, Robert M., and Mueller, Paul F. C. Clue hunting about counseling and parole outcome, *Research Report No. 11.* Sacramento: California Department of Corrections, In press.

10. Harrison, Robert M. Mental health applications in the California correctional system. In *Chatham conference on mental health applications in correctional practice.* Boston: Boston University, 1960.

11. Havel, Joan. Special Intensive Parole Unit Phase IV: The high base expectancy study, *Research report No. 8.* Sacramento: California Department of Corrections, 1963.

12. Havel, Joan, and Sulka, Elaine. Special Intensive Parole Unit Phase III, *Research Report No. 3.* Sacramento: California Department of Corrections. 1962.

13. Helstein, Ralph, Piel, Gerard, and Theobald, Robert. *Jobs, machines, and people.* Santa Barbara: Center for Study of Democratic Institutions, 1964.

14. Hutchins, Robert M. *On education.* Santa Barbara: Center for the Study of Democratic Institutions, 1963. P. 6.

15. Institute of Government, University of North Carolina. *A progress report of the Training Center on Delinquency and Youth Crime.* 1964, pp. 38–40.

16. Kassebaum, Gene G., Ward, David A., and Wilner, Daniel M. Group treatment by correctional personnel, *Monograph No. 3.* Sacramento: California Board of Corrections, 1964.

17. Long, Eugene R. Efland Project: The effect of programmed instruction in special skills during the pre-school period on later ability patterns and academic achievement, Quarterly Progress Report, Project No. 1521, Contract SAE OE 3–10–002. Chapel Hill: University of North Carolina, Jan.– June 1964.

18. Michael, Donald N. *Cybernation: the silent conquest.* Santa Barbara: Center for the Study of Democratic Institutions, 1962. Pp. 44–45.

19. Moore, Omar K. Orthographic symbols and the pre-school child—a new approach. In *Proceedings of the Third Minnesota Conference on gifted children.* Minneapolis: University of Minnesota, 1960.

20. Roethilsberger, Fritz Jules. *Management and Morale.* Cambridge: Harvard University Press, 1941.

21. Sigurdson, Herbert R., Dodge, Donald, Gramfin, Annette, and Sanfilippo, Rudy. Community education for delinquency prevention. In *Monograph No. 4.* Sacramento: California Board of Corrections, In press.

22. Slack, Charles W. *Project SCOPE,* Report to the Ford Foundation, Part III, April 1964, Mimeo.

23. Vinter, Robert D., and Janowitz, Morris. *Comparative study of juvenile correctional institutions: a research project.* Ann Arbor: University of Michigan School of Social Work, December 1961, Mimeo.

CHAPTER 11

NEW CAREERS—ITS ALLIES

THE NEW CAREERS CONCEPT is an antipoverty measure. If new careers are to be embedded into permanent social agencies and organizations, then considerable system change must occur. Change does not come easily. There will always be resistance to overcome even if the resistance reflects no more than inertia. Resistance is overcome only when there is pressure for change. In our society the pressure for change must be consistent and organized.

THE CIVIL RIGHTS MOVEMENT
AND NEW CAREERS

Most logically the poor would provide the force for the necessary changes. But the poor are disorganized and scattered without either platform or power. One segment of the poor—the impoverished Negro—has organization, the organization which has spurred the civil rights activities of the nation. The civil rights movement has had a concern with poverty and unemployment. Civil rights campaigns for fair employment have been primarily directed to private employers but for most of the unskilled Negro laborers, the progress has been compromised because of the decreasing number of unskilled jobs.

The inability of the civil rights movement to create job opportunities has, to some extent, disengaged the poor from the movement. For the impoverished Negro the last decade has been a nightmare. While being told that he has made gradual, but consistent progress, he has seen himself slowly slipping backwards. He has not made economic progress. He is more economically disadvantaged today than he was ten years ago. Every year for the last 25 years the dollar gap in median income between the Negro and white is getting larger. In 1939 the median family income for Negroes was $652 less than the median white family income. In 1949 this had increased to $1,368. By 1954 this was further increased; the difference was $1,623. In 1962 the difference in median family income between Negro and white families was $2,439![1]

The differences in Negro-white income are obscured by class status, and for the poor the differences are even more startling than are represented in the figures. The relatively affluent, well-educated Negro has been able to secure considerable progress during the past decade. These gains have been made not only in employment, but also in education and in social access to areas that were once forbidden. Employment opportunities for Negroes with college educations have never been as good as today. Employment opportunities for Negro youth with less than high school education are dwindling daily and the unemployment rate for poor Negro youth is rising.

The impoverished Negro youth is in an anomalous situation. The life he leads is becoming increasingly disfunctional. He is caught up in what has been labelled the revolution for civil rights, which really does not directly affect him. He cannot afford to live in the areas where there is action for desegregation. He is financially unable to patronize the restaurants and resorts that are now forced by law to accommodate him. He is denied meaningful education in integrated as well as segregated schools.

The battle for equality for the relatively affluent Negro is not yet won. To win full equality, he needs the support of the disadvantaged Negro. To obtain that support he must represent the needs of the poor, and the primary need of the poor is for jobs.

Civil rights advocates must fully appreciate that "freedom now" is feasible only if the currently unneeded are allowed to make a contribution. Demands for representation at administrative levels should be accompanied by demands for restructuring for jobs at entry levels, and the furnishing of programs to insure that the gifted can advance. Acceptance of dead-end, menial jobs as even the temporary solution to the problems of the poor would be a tragic error.

The new career proposal is directed toward offering hope to those now rejected by society. It is argued that potential for significant contribution is dormant in the current crop of drop outs, delinquents, and dependents. Doctors, lawyers, teachers, social workers and other desperately needed trained personnel can be recruited from the population, if only the machinery is established to allow entrance and advancement.

The civil rights movement is essentially a struggle for dignity. The one connecting link between all strata of mankind is the desire for full and equal participation in society. Whereas for those who do relatively well financially, the issues are social, for the poor, the issues are economic. Request for dignity is request for self-respect. Our society, through its traditional approaches of providing services to the poor, resolutely divests them of dignity.

In hospitals, the poor are subjected to inconveniences,

lack of privacy, and the dislike of the physician.² The welfare recipient suffers the contempt, or sometimes something even worse, the over-solicitousness of the welfare worker, and in addition is subjected to constant investigation, interrogation, and stigma.

In employment centers, job seekers encounter bureaucratic routine and indifference. Persons return daily to inquire about openings at which times they are made to feel the worthlessness of their existence, while offered little solace in the form of meaningful employment. In the school, as has been described in Chapter 4 the attack on dignity and self-worth is consistent and insidious.

The support of civil rights groups for the new careers concept could change the total complexion of the helping services. The essence of the philosophy of "obtaining service from" in place of "giving service to" is the difference between self-respect and self-abnegation.

CIVIL RIGHTS AND THE BACKLASH

The civil rights movement has been confronted by organized resistance. The organized resistance comes mostly from persons perceiving threat in the movement of Negroes to obtain equality in our society. The perception of threat is not entirely delusionary. As long as there are insufficient jobs to go around and the threat of any organized group is to rearrange *unemployment*, there will be resistance to change. Equal rights to employment for Negroes, when jobs are scarce, is translated into equal rights for unemployment for non-Negroes. It is unrealistic to expect altruism in any section of our society. It is particularly unrealistic for that section of the society which is being victimized by the inroads of automation. The unskilled white worker has seen himself attacked simultaneously at two levels—by the machine which is eating up available jobs and by the organized Negro who wants equal opportunity to be hired for the fast disappearing job. The backlash can only be rationally countered if there are sufficient jobs for all. In the new careers concept the stress is upon the creation of jobs in sufficient numbers to eliminate unemployment, thereby establishing a base for securing greater cooperation and coordination between all low-income persons, be they Negro or white.

The civil rights movement is directed toward elimination of inequity. There is a residual of past prejudice and lack of equal opportunity which intrudes into the present. Often programs designed to change the situation only reinforce relative inequity. We are quickly moving into a caste society which does not permit mobility or change. New careers provide an opportunity for opening up the system. Those relatively unequal at one point in history will be given the opportunity to enter the emerging industries (health, education, and welfare) which will be principal employers of tomorrow. Thus, in the next decade the new nonprofessionals will become the supervisors or the advanced workers in these industries. Those disadvantaged in the next decade, if given the opportunity to come in on the ground floor of new employment opportunities, can similarly attain relative advantages a decade later. Unless there is continuity and long-range perspective in programs designed to eliminate inequality, and, unless the programs are extensive enough to include all the disadvantaged, there will be destructive opposition from those threatened by the change.

PREJUDICE AND THE NONPROFESSIONAL MIDDLE-MAN

The problems confronting the poor are not solely structural. Changing employment opportunities which enable the poor to improve their economic position will have positive influence on the current scene, but there is something more that can be contributed by new careers, namely the introduction into sensitive decision-making posts of persons with a direct understanding of the problems of the underprivileged Negro. Prejudice in some instances is blatant, but more often it is subtle, practiced by persons who understand partially the problems of the impoverished Negro, but not completely; who sympathize with the strivings for advancement, but who lack the understanding of cause; who have never felt the sting of insult, never have experienced the indignity or the humiliation of discrimination; who can understand indignation, but not desperate action; and who, because they comprehend only in part, are unable to prevent the occurence of destructive strife. Prejudice, more often than not, is a word left unsaid or a deed not done.

Prejudice occurs in all settings—on the job, in the neighborhood, and in the school. While it must be first appreciated that prejudice has no part to play in a modern society, it should also be understood that prejudice will only be irradicated when change is rational and communication unclouded. The new careers offer an opportunity for rational change and a means to facilitate the communication process. The new careerist in the school, hospital, and park can play an important role in reducing the impact of prejudice. He can be the person to whom the alien and disadvantaged can bring their grievances. He can also explain to the professional the impact of the unintended insult.

Consider an incident, unfortunately one too frequent today, reported by the *Chicago Daily News*.[3] The incident had to do with violence in the schools, with the teacher the victim of a student attack. The report told only the teacher's story.

The setting was the fifth grade of a "ghetto school" in Chicago during the late spring of 1964. The incident occurred in the midst of a controversy about "de facto segregation." Two extensive boycotts had taken place during the controversy. The teacher found obscene words scribbled on her attendance record. She asked the class why it was rude to her. One boy responded, after prolonged silence, "Because you are white." The teacher reported that "everyone else giggled" and that she was "dumbfounded and unable to speak and managed only to keep order until the noon break."

At the noon break, the boy who responded to the question came up to her and "stomped on her foot as hard as he could."

There is much to be gleaned from this story. The teacher was (as reported in the article) well-regarded and with better than average skills. But consider what happened. The teacher asked a question. It was not an easy question to answer, and apparently she was willing to entertain silence for a while in order to get an answer. One child responded. The answer probably came close to the truth. The response could have been acclaimed as being in the finest tradition of our culture. It could have been acknowledged as help to the teacher (since she was dumbfounded by the answer). It could have been used to establish rapport with the youth. The boy, however, was not rewarded for candor or courage. He was not informed why the response was improper. He was met by hostility from the establishment. He, at the same time, acquired status among his fellows for being effectively anti-establishment. Denied an opportunity for a place on the side of the school, he was encouraged to join the opposition.

Violence in a school can never be condoned, but it can be understood and prevented. One course of action for youth who are repelled and frustrated in the school may be violence. Violence will not be prevented by more frustration or more oppressive authority. Only dealing with the source of frustration will prevent violence.

Introduction of new careers in teaching posts could, in two ways, act against the occurrence of such an incident. The indigenous teacher, by his existence a social stimulus, might reduce to subthreshold levels the classroom tension which leads to student disorder. Secondly, were there to be an individual outbreak, the indigenous teacher could prevent it from erupting into a major problem.

New careers and civil rights are fitting allies. However, the new career concept should have wider appeal than only to those actively engaged in the civil rights fight. The new careers concept is likely to appeal to certain segments of organized labor where jobs are declining and also to some national and fraternal organizatons whose membership is being affected by automation. But the group whose support is most needed, and one which should be most vociferous in support, is the professional (e.g. the teacher, the medical doctor, the social worker, and the psychologist). However, this group has rarely made its presence known as an organized force for social reform.

NEW CAREERS—AN APPEAL
TO THE PROFESSIONAL

The fastest-growing subdivision of the labor force is that of the professional and highly-skilled technician. The escalation in numbers of this occupational group is due to precisely the same influences which have almost obviated the need for unskilled labor. The professional has limited his lobbying activity, for the most part, to issues which are specifically relevant to his practice. Professional societies have been concerned with licensing and certification. They have not been sufficiently or consistently concerned with broader social issues. The new careers proposal needs the active and organized support of professional societies.

Most functions projected for new careers fall into the province of the professional. The specific activities recommended for nonprofessionals have, in many instances, been performed by professionals, and only by organized action can the professionals relinquish these activities. But the issue of professionals' interest should transcend the concern of encroachment. There should be a more candid commitment to determination of social policy.

A complex democratic society can function only if the electorate is able to make its interests known. The communication of interests and programs require organization. In part, organization is needed for fact finding and partially for pressuring executive and legislative bodies. If any segment of the society defaults in its social obligation, the process is skewed and fails to function to maximum efficiency. If the group that is unorganized is both large and growing larger, and consists of persons who in their daily course of activities handle complex concepts and have access to most of the relevant information, the lack of participation is most sorely felt.

The professional has a stake in the new career concept. It is only by restructuring of service that the needs of our nation and the world can be met. It appears that a much greater investment in education, health, welfare, and recreation is projected for the next decade than was indicated three or four years ago. And further investment in these areas must strain already overdrawn resources. The solution can only come through changing the nature of the service (health, education, and welfare) through more efficient use of highly-trained personnel supplemented by cadres of less highly-trained staff.

There is still another cogent reason for professional support of new careers. The human service professions are the strongholds of "liberality". Here are to be found the persons with social consciences, and yet to a very large extent they perpetuate the conditions in their fields which presently exclude the poor. The necessary credentials for employment are determined almost exclusively by the professional. But the "liberal" does not seem to recognize that by insisting upon "professionalization" without creating subordinate subprofessional roles and nonprofessional entry roles, he is contributing to the forced exclusion of the poor from functioning society. Through such ignorance or inaction, the white liberal becomes, as James Baldwin argues, an "affliction" to the Negro in his struggle for equality.[4]

NOTES

1. Source: United States Labor Department; *Manpower Report of the President*, U.S. Government Printing Office, March 1964, p. 275.
2. See for example: A. B. Hollingshead and F. C. Redlich, *Social Class and Mental Health*, New York: John Wiley & Sons, Inc., 1958, p. 344.
3. *Chicago Daily News*, March 7, 1964.
4. Stated in *"Liberalism and the Negro—A Round Table Discussion,"* *Commentary*, March 1964, p. 37.

CONCLUSION:

THE WAR ON POVERTY
AND NEW CAREERS

THE ECONOMIC OPPORTUNITY ACT of 1964 calls for the development of community action programs for the poor, with the poor, and by the poor. If appropriately implemented, this requires involvement and self-determination by the poor and can provide the basis for millions of nonprofessional and subprofessional jobs and new careers. The main danger lies in the possibility that the jobs created by the local communities receiving grants under the Act, will not be integrated into the system but will remain as appendages. In other words, the local groups may gladly accept funds to hire the poor in nonprofessional positions that will last as long as the funds are forthcoming. But these local groups will probably be unwilling to change their tables of organization to fully incorporate nonprofessional career lines, unless the administrators of the Act make this an indispensable prerequisite for receiving federal support. Thus the antipoverty warriors can be among the most crucial allies of the new careers movement, if the Act is utilized as an impetus for changing the employment system.*

* See Chapter 2, for a discussion of some of the issues involved in the Economic opportunity law.

This book is predicated on the assumption that there will be a continuing increase in the need for human services in the health, welfare, and education fields, and that the jobs created will not easily be automated out of existence. We envision millions of new nonprofessional jobs and careers in the helping professions, largely in the public sector.

Any proposal has minimum and maximum possibilities. The new careers concept has three major objectives, the achievement of which should be possible, to varying degrees, depending upon whether the new jobs are simply appended to the system on a temporary basis, or whether they are incorporated and become an integral part of the system. The three aims are:

1. Development of large numbers of new nonprofessional careers for the poor including the opportunity for advancement into subprofessional and professional positions. In order to achieve this objective it is necessary to reject the irrational job definitions that have characterized our credential-centered society. Moreover, the relationship of work and education has to be recast so that the two become more concomitant and overlapping, thus enabling disadvantaged youths and adults to enter rapidly into the mainstream of American work life. The first objective, then, is offered as one very important dimension in the war on poverty; but, of course, it is recognized that it is only one dimension, and that various aspects of the alternative anti-poverty strategies (critically evaluated in Chapter 2) must be integrated in a total approach to the problem.

2. Greatly improved service for the poor by taking service from the poor—hiring the nonprofessional. This objective derives from a highly expanded version of the helper-therapy principle outlined in Chapter 5. The helper principle holds that one very important way in which people are helped is through helping others. The entire book suggests that the poor be employed as nonprofessionals in the helping professions, and that in the process of serving others they will be helping to rehabilitate themselves. This can be done on a grand scale because of the great need for services as well as the need for improving the quality of services.

3. A major change in the helping professions themselves through a reorganization of the professional's role in the direction of increased supervision, consultation, teaching, programing, and planning. The achievement of this objective would allow the professional much greater flexibility and range. He could be more fully a professional, less engaged in nonprofessional tasks, and could be far more creative as his energies are released in the new role functions. Finally, his new connections with the poor, resulting from the increased service for the poor and from the poor, can reduce the tremendous interclass distance which has hampered the development of both the disadvantaged and the professional. The new careers movement can begin to provide the basis for the much needed unity of the professional and the poor.

APPENDIX:

NEW CAREER
JOB DESCRIPTIONS

HEALTH SERVICES

There is a need to improve health services provided to
the neighborhood as there is a need to bridge the gap between hospital professional staff and low-income patients,
particularly with regard to ambulatory and preventive services. Residents of the communities to be served, both men
and women, can be utilized in a number of nonprofessional
and subprofessional roles to achieve these purposes. Some
of these are as follows:

Health Visitor—to assess simple obvious problems of family health
and recognize family members' need for health service. Examples
might include: encouraging pregnant women needing prenatal care
to obtain it; checking on immunizations; answering simple questions
about care of a new baby; arranging for medical care for someone
obviously sick in bed.

Baby Sitting and Child-Care Services—particularly to enable patients
to keep clinic appointments.

Neighborhood Health Aide—to be used in a program directed at
delivering existing medical knowledge and health services to low-
income families. These aides, who are indigenous to the community,
will speak the same language, be conversant with the folklore and
wives' tales, and develop better communication with their low-income

neighbors. Careful supervision by medical personnel will be provided so that the aides will have the benefit of accurate information and referral resources. In this way they can serve as a bridge between professional and lay patterns of language, health attitudes and practices.

Health Service Aides—to use elderly residents to meet some of the many health needs of their elderly neighbors. All are from low socioeconomic groups.

Health Assistance Aides—to provide help to the home-bound with light housekeeping, shopping, meal planning and "following the doctor's orders." Escort service and reassuring companionship will be provided with out-patient treatment. Check-in home visits will be paid to convalescents and to the incapacitated. Referrals for service will come from nearby clinics and hospitals, public housing management, Department of Welfare, private agencies and individuals.

Floor Manager—to assist doctors in greeting patients, directing them, setting them at ease, translating instructions, arranging appointments, etc., in order to achieve better and smoother clinic relationships with ambulatory patients.

HOUSING PROGRAMS

Housing-related service has considerable potential as a source of nonprofessional and subprofessional jobs in terms of both present activities and particularly expanded activities. In this field if *new* programs were devised, thousands of workers could be used each year. Activities in this field are concerned more directly with *human* renewal rather than with physical renewal, and include child care services, homemaking services, supplementary education and tutoring services, home medical and nursing services. This phase of Urban Renewal closely ties in with the neighborhood conservation activities.

Neighborhood Conservation involves a mutually contrived, integrated program of conserving present physical structures, improving landscape and grounds, and enriching the life style of the urban neighborhood. This means not only the physical tasks of painting, repairing, and improving residential structures, the beautifying of boulevards and yards, the cleaning of alleyways, streets, and vacant lots, and the social problems of neighborhood life, but also in the latter phase would include such activities as stepped-up supervision of playgrounds and parks, an opening of neighborhood centers, the launching of surveys on land use, the provision of services such as libraries, homemaker, and housekeeper activities, relocation assistance for families dislocated by Urban Renewal projects, and other home services.

The kinds of tasks and jobs potentially available in this field would include at least the following:

Home Visitor—This person would be most needed working in low-rent housing, orienting new residents, counseling and educating with regard to housekeeping standards and identifying special needs of individual families.

Duties and responsibilities:

Making regularly scheduled apartment visit to counsel resident regarding ways of improving conditions as needed. Orient new tenant families with regard to responsibilities and methods of taking care of their apartments and premises. Refer serious family problems to the appropriate Authority or agency staff person. Make home visits to applicants for public housing. Acquaint families with health and welfare services available within the development and the wider community and encourage them to participate in activities in and around the area. Keep records and prepare reports of activities as required.

Monitor—This person would be most needed in low-rent housing. He would live in an apartment within the housing development and there should be a sufficient number of these persons so that, in high rise developments at least, there would be one person for every one or two buildings. He would not be a policeman or assistant custodian but rather would focus on the general conditions within "his" building(s).

Duties and responsibilities:

He shall live within a housing development apartment and, although not an assistant custodian or policeman, will be "responsible" for his building. He shall become acquainted with as many as possible of the families in his building(s), establishing a positive relationship to the greatest degree. He shall be aware at all times of the general conditions within his building(s). He shall observe and pinpoint difficulties and attempt to correct or resolve problems through education and interpretation, in general attempting to enlist the cooperation of the people in his building(s). He shall work to establish and maintain a feeling of pride and esprit de corps among the residents in his building(s) in order that this might manifest itself in building cleanliness, lack of vandalism, acceptable behavior, etc. He shall be of whatever assistance may be possible to other Authority personnel such as the Neighborhood Coordinator, Family Counselor, Home Visitor, Project Manager, etc.

Family Counselor—This position would be equally applicable to both housing and renewal areas. He would, upon referral by other personnel, work directly with families who are having problems, assisting them in such areas as family relationships, care of children, financial and employment difficulties, health problems, etc. In the case of a renewal program he would also help to expedite the relocation or rehabilitation process, including helping the family "adjust" and become a part of their new environment. In all instances he would involve and work closely with all relevant community agencies.

Duties and responsibilities:

In a housing development: Explore family and individual problems of residents which are of serious concern to the family. Wherever possible, based on this exploration, draw upon such services of community social agencies as may be indicated by the specific circumstances. In the absence of other agency services, work directly with the families to alleviate to the greatest degree possible the problems involved. Be alert to any "trouble spots" developing within his area, investigating and pinpointing the nature and source of the difficulties and working with other Authority personnel, social agencies and residents to remedy the situation.

In an urban renewal area: Upon referral from the relocation staff, work with those families and individuals who have special problems which are hampering efforts to rehouse them. Upon referral from other Authority personnel, work with those families and individuals who, because of special physical or socioeconomic problems, are not able to participate fully in the renewal program. Wherever possible, draw upon the services of other community agencies and organizations to assist in meeting the needs of the families involved.

Regardless of the setting: Maintain records and prepare reports on various phases of his work as required. Perform such other duties as are commensurate with his role as a specialist in the area of human relations and individual physical, emotional, social and economic problems.

Neighborhood Coordinator—Applicable to both housing and renewal areas. This person would be responsible for stimulating and guiding resident organizations, aiding them in the development of a wide variety of social, educational and "self-help" programs. He would emphasize the discovering of local indigenous leadership, working with them and others toward their gradual assumption of more civic responsibility and participation.

Duties and responsibilities:

Develop services and educational programs based on the needs of his area as seen by the residents, the worker, other Authority personnel and community leaders, making full use of the appropriate community resources. Expedite the establishment of resident organizations, assisting in their continued growth and effectiveness. Make continuous efforts to discover new potential leaders from among the residents, working with them to develop their skills as well as their impact on the life of the community. Establish and maintain a good working relationship with residents, keeping abreast of their opinions and attitudes, as well as their ideas concerning current problems and interests within the area. Work in close collaboration with other Authority personnel, including project staff in low rent housing and physical planners in renewal areas. Participate in related neighborhood organizations through which better community relations and conditions might be achieved. Maintain records and prepare reports on various phases of his work as required.

Home Economist—Needed in both housing and renewal—this person would focus on providing services in the areas of money management and budgeting, nutrition, clothes maintenance, etc. In general, work with individuals and through classes would help residents get the most value out of their limited resources.

Duties and responsibilities:

In collaboration with other Authority personnel she shall conduct classes in money management and budgeting, nutrition, clothes maintenance, etc. If determined advisable, she may conduct classes in home decoration, simple home maintenance, etc. Where requested, she shall work with tenant organizations or block branches to give instruction in one or more areas of home economics. Upon referral from other Authority personnel will work directly with individual persons and/or families on specific problems of money management, food preparation, sewing, and so forth. Provide on-the-job training sessions in simple home economics for other personnel such as the

Home Visitors and Family Counselors. Keep records and prepare reports of her activities as requested.

LEGAL SERVICES

There is an acute need, felt by that portion of the legal profession concerned with legal services to the poor for competent persons to carry out duties which lawyers now perform but which do not require legal expertise or which require only readily acquirable skills. This need will increase quantitatively as legal services are extended to the poor as a result of constitutional mandates concerning the right to counsel of the indigent person accused of a crime.

Job assignments in a progression of roles (such as contact or referral agent, receptionist, interviewer, and post-trial process) professionals.

YOUTH PROGRAMS

As nonprofessionals, youth and young adults can function in all areas of the typical youth serving agency:

Recruit membership (may be done as a door to door campaign)
Assist or take over receptionist duties
Supervise locker room and game room
Organize groups to participate in programs outside the agency
Work with community groups
Work out in the neighborhood (local playgrounds) to encourage youth to participate in agency programs
Work in canteens in organizing activities
Maintain the grounds and building of the agency
Supervise visits to zoos, public beaches, museums, etc.
Conduct story hours for the younger children
Assist in day care programs
Visit shut-ins, to play cards, do shopping, read to the blind
Aid in conducting health programs by distributing literature and enrolling people

Prepare and serve meals
Help out in the teenage lounge

SUBPROFESSIONAL FUNCTIONS

Some examples of subprofessional jobs are:

Group Work Aide—to assist in the development of group programs. Typical duties would include maintenance of equipment and supplies, preparation of materials for group activities, keeping records of group processes, future plans, and group problems. Also provide direct leadership for group activities.

Arts Specialist Aide—under guidance of the arts specialist, assist in teaching such skills as ceramics, painting, woodworking to beginners, helps prepare materials and seek out persons in the community who could benefit from the program.

Recreation Aide—develops small group recreation programs with boys and girls who find it hard to maintain themselves in formally organized settlement house recreation groups.

Athletic Aide—under supervision of a professional, helps with the care and maintenance of equipment, the teaching of games and sports, the refereeing of games, helps the lifeguards with the maintenance of the pools, organizes special sports clubs and takes boys and girls to athletic events.

Nurses' Aides and Orderlies—to assist regular nursing staff by performing less skilled and routine tasks. Bathes and dresses patients, answers call bells, makes beds, serves food and nourishment, arranges flowers, performs personal services for the patients, could be extended to cover preparation for licensing for Practical Nurse.

Psychiatric Aides—will provide personal services, recreational services, and occpational therapy for the patients under professional supervision.

Occupational Therapist Aide—under supervision of the therapist, helps prepare occupation therapy materials, assists and trains the patients to use hands and performs simple tasks, bring patients to therapy room and returns them to their rooms, and maintains occupational therapy equipment.

Laboratory Assistants—performs simple laboratory tests such as urinalysis, blood tests, biological skin tests, takes responsibility for the care of the laboratory animals and for the maintenance of the laboratory equipment. Performs other tasks as directed under the supervision of the laboratory technician.

X-Ray Technician Aides—prepares patients for X-Ray, affixes protective lead plates, assists in the keeping of X-Ray room records, develops plates, manipulates switches.

Clerical and Stenographic Aides—to perform a variety of clerical, stenographic and bookeeper helper tasks, including typing, filing, mimeographing and collating and operating simple computing machines.

Pharmacy Aide—to assist pharmacists in maintaining stock of drugs, chemicals, and other pharmaceutical supplies, may also assist in performing routine tests and maintaining equipment, performs other duties as directed.

Diet Aides—to assist the professional dietitian in planning, preparing and serving regular and therapeutic diets to patients and instructing them and their families relative to purpose and content of prescribed diets, also, assists in requisitioning supplies and equipment and preparing records and reports concerning technical and administrative operations. Performs related duties.

BIBLIOGRAPHY*

1. Beck, Bertram S., "Wanted Now: Social Work Associates." National Conference on Social Welfare, 1963.
2. Brager, George, "The Low-Income Nonprofessional." Paper presented at National Conference of Social Welfare, May 1964. (Mobilization for Youth, New York), pp. 4, 7, 9.
3. ——, "Some Assumptions and Strategies of the Mobilization For Youth Program," chapter in *The Mental Health of the Poor* (edited by Frank Riessman, Jerome Cohen and Arthur Pearl). The Free Press of Glencoe, 1964.
4. Bredemeier, Harry C., "Suggestions to Communities for Participation in the War on Poverty," Urban Studies Center, Rutgers—The State University, New Brunswick, New Jersey, August 1964.
5. Burgess, Ernest W. *et al.* "The Chicago Area Project," *Yearbook of the National Probation Association*, 1937.
6. Clinard, Marshall B., "Perspectives on Urban Community Development and Community Organization." *Social Welfare Forum, 1962* (Proceedings of the National Conference on Social Welfare, 1962). New York: Columbia University Press.

* This bibliography was prepared by Robert Reiff and Frank Riessman for *The Indigenous Nonprofessional*, Nile Mental Health Program, Dec. 1964, N.Y.

7. "Community Apprentice Program," Center for Youth and Community Studies—Howard University, 1964.

8. Cooper, Charles N., "The Chicago YMCA Detached Workers: Current Status of an Action Program." Paper presented at *Symposium on Alternative Approaches to Gang Research and Action*, Conventions of the Society for the Study of Social Problems and the American Sociological Association. Los Angeles, August 1963.

9. Cytryn, Leon and Audrey Uihlein, "Training of Volunteers in the Field of Mental Retardation—An Experiment." Presented at 1964 American Orthopsychiatric Conference, Chicago, Illinois.

10. Day, Max and Alice M. Robinson, "Training Aides Through Group Techniques," *Nursing Outlook*, Vol. 2, June 1954, pp. 308–310.

11. Duhl, Leonard J. (ed.), *The Urban Condition*, Basic Books, 1963.

12. Epstein, Laura, "Differential Use of Staff: A Method to Expand Social Services," *Social Work*, Vol. 7, October 1962, pp. 66–72.

13. "European Mental Health Programs as Viewed by Mental Health Specialists and Legislators," a study conducted by the Southern Regional Education Board, pp. 74–80.

14. "Experiment in Culture Expansion." Proceedings of a Conference on *The Use of Products of a Social Problem in Coping with the Problem*. California, July 1963. Sponsored by National Institute of Mental Health in cooperation with Youth Studies Center, University of Southern California.

15. Fort Logan (Colorado) Mental Health Center, "The Psychiatric Technician Training Program." 1963.

16. Gans, Herbert, *The Urban Villagers*, Free Press: 1962.

17. Goldberg, Gertrude, "Untrained Neighborhood Workers in a Social Work Program." Mobilization for Youth, 1964.

18. "The Great Cities School Improvement Studies." Ford Foundation Project (Mimeographed, 1960).

19. Harlem Youth Opportunities Unlimited, Inc. *Youth in the Ghetto: A Study of the Consequences of Powerlessness.* HARYOU, New York, 1964, pp. 380, 607–609.

20. "Highlights from Survey of Psychiatric Aides," Manpower Studies Unit, Training and Manpower Resources Branch, NIMH, 1964.

21. Hobbs, Nicholas, "Mental Health's Third Revolution," *American Journal of Orthopsychiatry*, Vol. 34, October 1964, pp. 822–833.

22. Holzberg, Jules D. and Robert H. Knapp, "The Social Interaction of College Students and Chronically Ill Mental Patients." Paper presented at 1964 American Orthopsychiatric Conference, Chicago.

23. Holzberg, Jules D., "The Companion Program: Implementing the Manpower Recommendations of the Joint Commission on Mental Illness and Health," *American Psychologist,* Vol. 18, 1963, pp. 224–226.

24. Isales, Carmen and Fred G. Wale, "The Field Program," *The Journal of Social Issues,* Vol. 9(2), 1953.

25. Jackson, Maurice P., "Their Brothers' Keepers: A Directory of Therapeutic Self-Help Groups, Intentional Communities and Lay Training Centers," June 1962.

26. Kelly, James G., "The Mental Health Agent in the Urban Community." Paper presented at the *Symposium on Urban America and the Planning of Mental Health Services,* Committee on Prevention Psychiatry, Group for the Advancement of Psychiatry, November 1963. (Philadelphia.)

27. Kobrin, Solomon, "The Chicago Area Project—A 25-Year Assessment," *Annals of the American Academy of Political and Social Science,* Vol. 322, March 1959, pp. 19–29.

28. Lee, Ann N., "The Training of Nonprofessional Personnel," *Nursing Outlook,* Vol. 6, April 1958, pp. 222–25.

29. Miller, S. M. and Martin Rein, *Change, Ferment and Ideology in the Social Services.* Address given at Council of Social Work Education, Toronto, January 1964, pp. 26–27.

30. Mitchell, William E., "Fictive Siblings and the 'Unworthy' Child in Changing Rural Vermont." Presented at 1964 American Orthopsychiatric Conference, Chicago.

31. "The Neighborhood Service Center in a Mental Health Program: A Proposal to Implement a Community Mental Health Network." Lincoln Hospital Mental Health Services. New York, 1964.

32. New Careers for Disadvantaged Youth, Conference Proceedings; Center for Youth and Community Studies, Howard University, April 1964 (in press).

33. *Nontraditionally Trained Counselors/Psychotherapists—Their Training, Employment Progress and Perceived Employability.* A Symposium presented at the American Psychological Association Convention, Philadelphia, August 31, 1963. (Counseling Center, Mental Health Project Studies, University of Maryland; College Park, Maryland.)

34. Pearl, Arthur, "Guidance and Education for the Disadvantaged Child—The Need for Structural Change." Paper given at American Personnel and Guidance Association Conference, March 1964.

35. ———, "Youth in Lower Class Settings." Paper presented at Fifth Symposium on Social Psychology, 1964, Norman, Okla-

homa. (The Community Apprentice Program; Center for Youth and Community Studies, Howard University.)

36. Peck, Harris B., "Extending and Developing Manpower for Urban Community Mental Health Centers." Lincoln Hospital Mental Health Services, 1964.

37. "The Psychiatric Aide: Exit the Key Keeper," *Mental Health in Illinois,* Vol. 1, March–April 1964. (Illinois Dept. of Mental Health.)

38. Reiff, Robert, "The Use of Nonprofessionals in Community Mental Health." Conference on New Careers for Disadvantaged Youth, Howard University, 1964. (Conference Proceedings to be published.)

39. ―――― and Frank Riessman, *The Indigenous Nonprofessional.* New York, NILE Mental Health Program, Dec. 1964.

40. Reinherz, Helen, "College Student Volunteers as Case Aides in State Hospitals for Children," *American Journal of Orthopsychiatry,* Vol. 33, April 1963, pp. 544–46.

41. Richan, W. C., "A Theoretical Scheme for Determining Roles of Professional and Nonprofessional Personnel," *Social Work,* Vol. 6, October 1961.

42. ――――, "Utilization of Personnel in Social Work: Those with Full Professional Education and Those Without." Final Report of the Subcommittee on Utilization of Personnel, National Association of Social Work, 1962.

43. Riessman, Frank, "The Coming Revolution in Social Service," *Transaction,* November–December 1964.

44. ――――, *New Approaches to Mental Health Treatment for Labor and Low Income Groups.* New York: NILE Mental Health Program, February 1964.

45. ――――, "The Nonprofessional and the Poor." Keynote address given at 1964 Joint Conference on Children and Youth, Washington, D.C., April 1964. Sponsored by the National Committee for Children and Youth.

46. ――――, "The Revolution in Social Work: The New Nonprofessional." Mobilization for Youth Report, October 1963.

47. Rioch, Margaret J. *et al.,* "NIMH Study in Training Mental Health Counselors," *American Journal of Orthopsychiatry,* Vol. 33, July 1963, pp. 678–689.

48. Robinson, Rachel and Melvin Roman, "New Directions for the Psychiatric Aide." Conference on New Careers for Disadvantaged Youth, Howard University, April 1964. (Conference Proceedings to be published.)

49. Taran, Freida B., "The Utilization of Nonprofessional Personnel in Social Work Services." Paper presented at Conference on New Careers for Disadvantaged Youth, Howard University, April 1964. (Conference Proceedings to be published.)
50. *The Use of Case Aides in Casework Agencies.* National Social Welfare Assembly, New York, 1959.
51. Wale, Fred G., "The Division of Community Education—an Overview," *The Journal of Social Issues,* Vol. 9, 1953.
52. Weed, Verne and William H. Denham, "Toward More Effective Use of the Nonprofessional Worker: A Recent Experiment," *Social Work,* Vol. 6(4), pp. 29–36.

NAME INDEX

* Reference appears in a footnote.

SUBJECT INDEX

* Reference appears in a footnote.